Youth

Volume One

True Fantasy

Curt Pires Writer/Co-creator
Alex Diotto Artist/Co-creator
Dee Cunniffe Colorist/Co-creator
Micah Myers Letterer
Ryan Ferrier Design

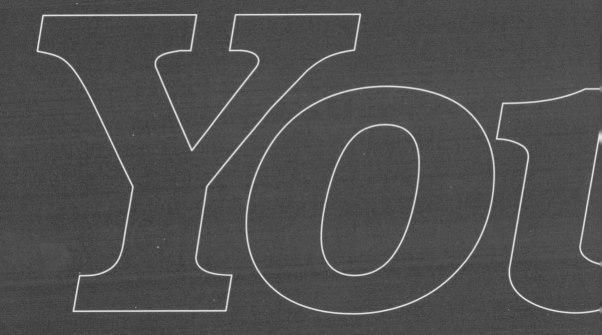

uth

DARK HORSE BOOKS

TECC

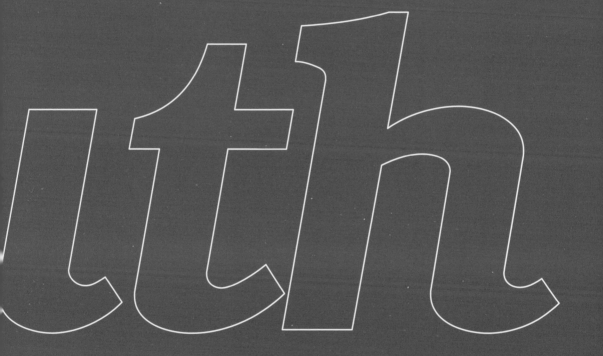

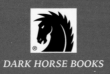

Dark Horse Team

President and Publisher	Mike Richardson
Editor	Daniel Chabon
Assistant Editor	Chuck Howitt
Designer	Brennan Thome
Digital Art Technician	Jason Rickerd

Neil Hankerson Executive Vice President • Tom Weddle Chief Financial Officer • Randy Stradley Vice President of Publishing • Nick McWhorter Chief Business Development Officer • Dale LaFountain Chief Information Officer • Matt Parkinson Vice President of Marketing • Vanessa Todd-Holmes Vice President of Production and Scheduling • Mark Bernardi Vice President of Book Trade and Digital Sales • Ken Lizzi General Counsel • Dave Marshall Editor in Chief • Davey Estrada Editorial Director • Chris Warner Senior Books Editor • Cary Grazzini Director of Specialty Projects • Lia Ribacchi Art Director • Matt Dryer Director of Digital Art and Prepress • Michael Gombos Senior Director of Licensed Publications • Kari Yadro Director of Custom Programs • Kari Torson Director of International Licensing • Sean Brice Director of Trade Sales

Published by Dark Horse Books
A division of Dark Horse Comics LLC
10956 SE Main Street
Milwaukie, OR 97222

First edition: April 2021
Trade paperback ISBN: 978-1-50672-461-4

10 9 8 7 6 5 4 3 2 1
Printed in China

Comic Shop Locator Service: comicshoplocator.com

Library of Congress Cataloging-in-Publication Data

Names: Pires, Curt, writer. | Diotto, artist. | Cunniffe, Dee, colourst. |
   Myers, Micah, letterer. | Ferrier, Ryan, book designer.
Title: Youth / Curt Pires, writer/cocreator ; Alex Diotto, artist/cocreator
   ; Dee Cunniffe, colorist/cocreator ; Micah Myers, letterer ; Ryan
   Ferrier, design.
Description: First edition. | Milwaukie, OR : Dark Horse Books, 2021- | v.
   1: "This volume collects Youth #1-#4." | Summary: "YOUTH is a coming of
   age story that tells the story of two queer teenagers as they run away
   from their lives in a bigoted small town, and attempt to make their way
   to California. Along the way their car breaks down and they join up with
   a group of fellow misfits on the road. Embarking together in a van
   travelling the country they party and attempt to find themselves. And
   then something happens . "-- Provided by publisher.
Identifiers: LCCN 2020045071 | ISBN 9781506724614 (v. 1 ; trade paperback)
Subjects: LCSH: Comic books, strips, etc.
Classification: LCC PN6728.Y84 P57 2021 | DDC 741.5/973--dc23
LC record available at https://lccn.loc.gov/2020045071

This volume collects *Youth* #1–#4.

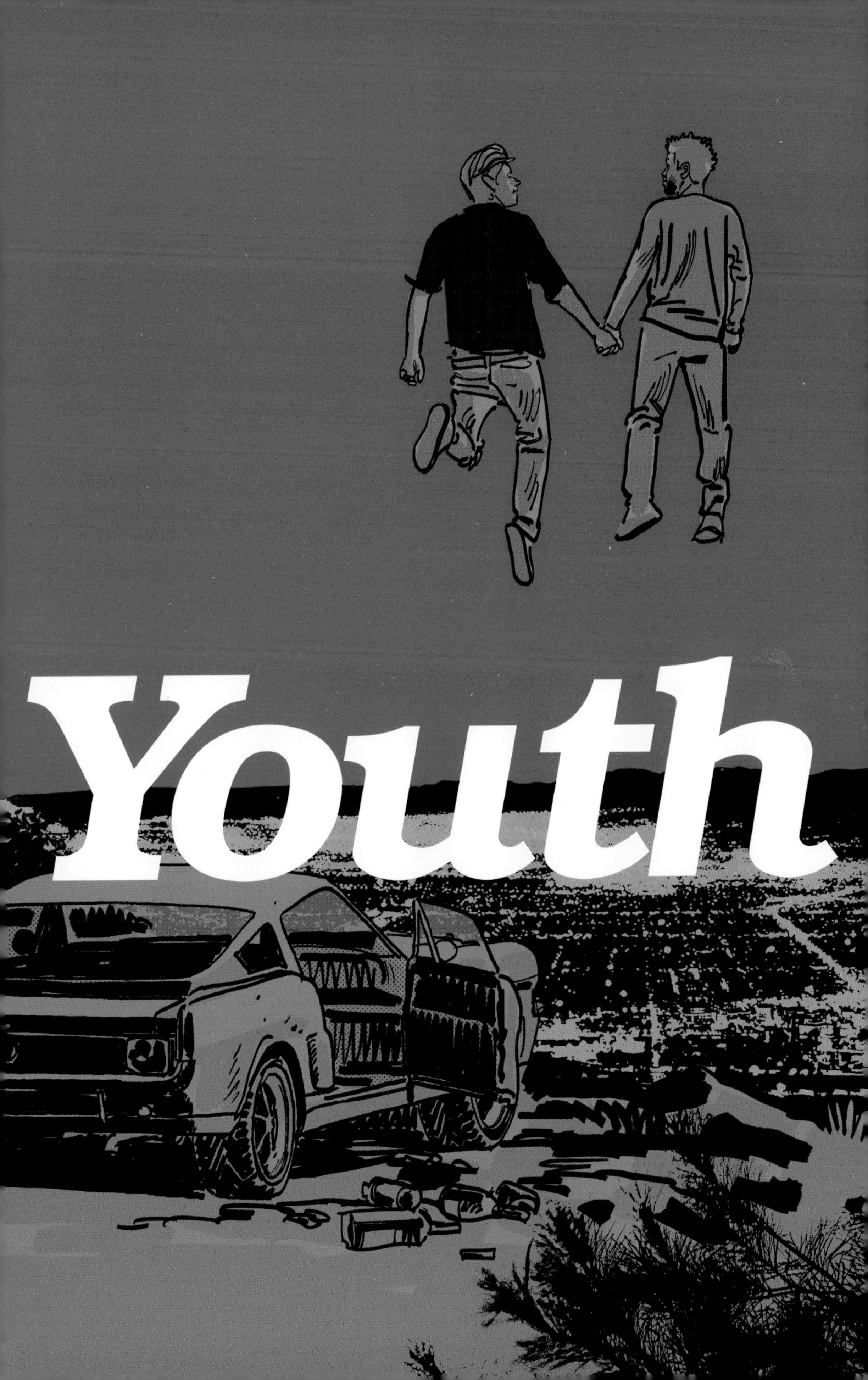
Youth

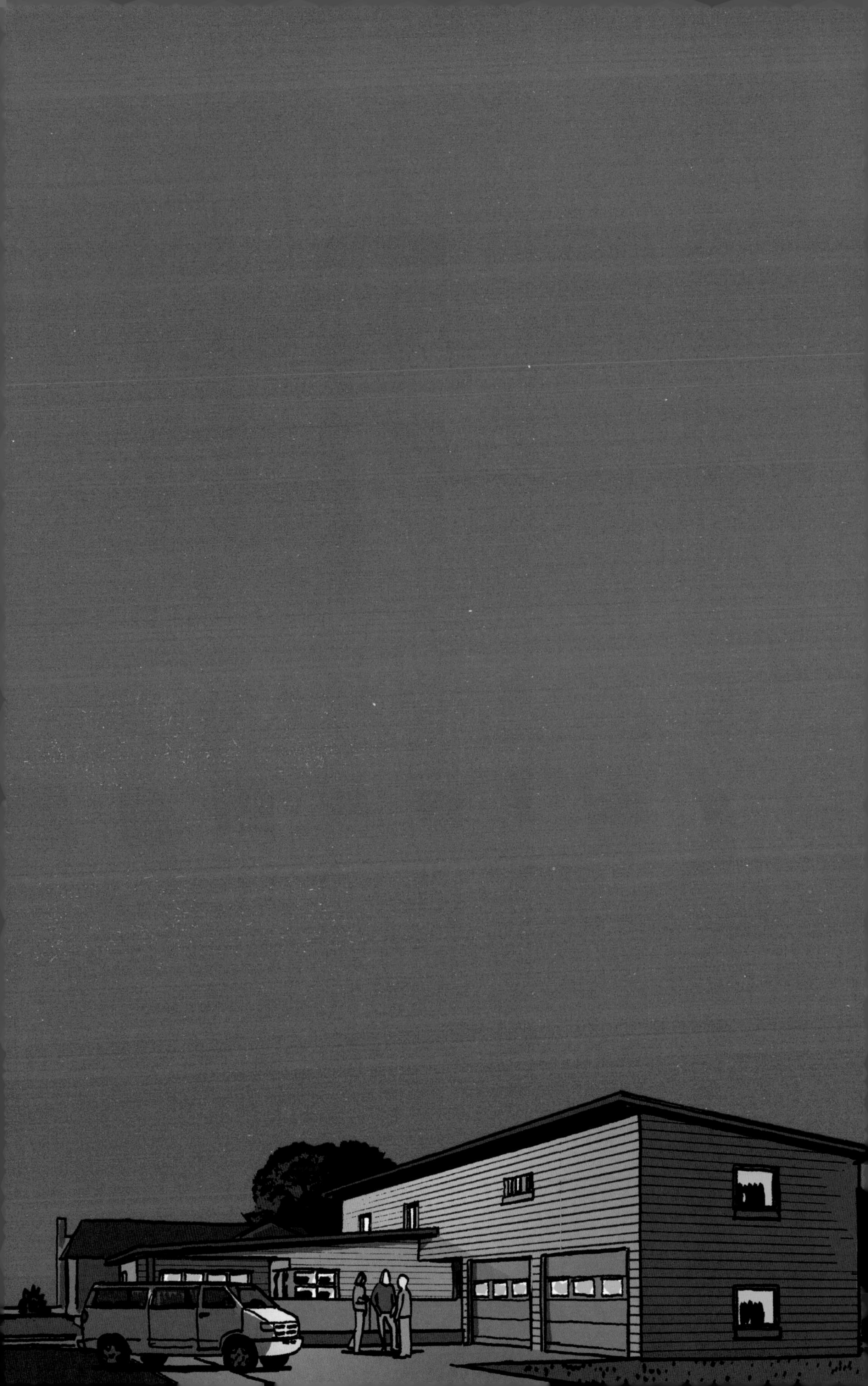

SOMETIMES I STILL THINK ABOUT THAT SUMMER. THE WAY THE HEAT FELT. LIKE WE WERE ALL DISINTEGRATING INTO NOTHING. RIGHT IN FRONT OF EACH OTHER. THAT HEAT SO HOT THAT YOUR T-SHIRT STICKS TO YOUR BACK IN THAT WAY THAT TELLS YOU IT'S REAL, THAT THE SUMMERTIME'S HERE.

OTHER TIMES I THINK ABOUT THE WAY THE SUN BEAT DOWN ON US. SATURATING THE WORLD WITH ITS COLORS. LIGHT IN YOUR EYES--THE AMBER OF YOUR HAIR.

LISTEN TO ME NOW. I'M DOING THAT THING I ALWAYS HATED. WHEN A MOTHERFUCKER GETS TO SOUNDING PROFOUND--LIKING THE SOUND OF THEIR OWN VOICE--SO THEY JUST KEEP ON TALKING.

I'LL SHUT UP NOW AND TELL THE STORY. OUR STORY.

THIS IS WHAT HAPPENED TO US.

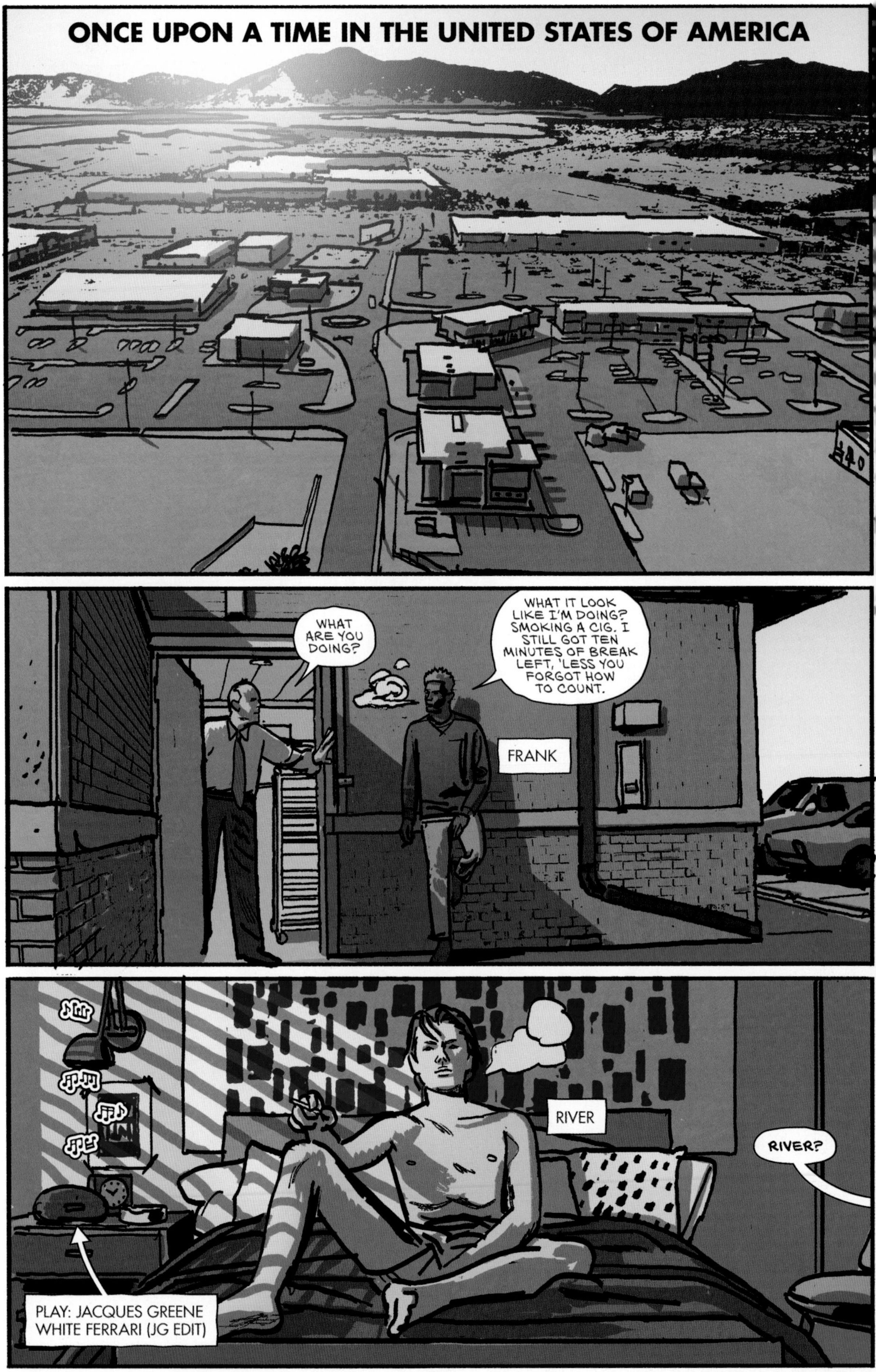
ONCE UPON A TIME IN THE UNITED STATES OF AMERICA
WHAT ARE YOU DOING?
WHAT IT LOOK LIKE I'M DOING? SMOKING A CIG. I STILL GOT TEN MINUTES OF BREAK LEFT, 'LESS YOU FORGOT HOW TO COUNT.
FRANK
RIVER
RIVER?
PLAY: JACQUES GREENE
WHITE FERRARI (JG EDIT)

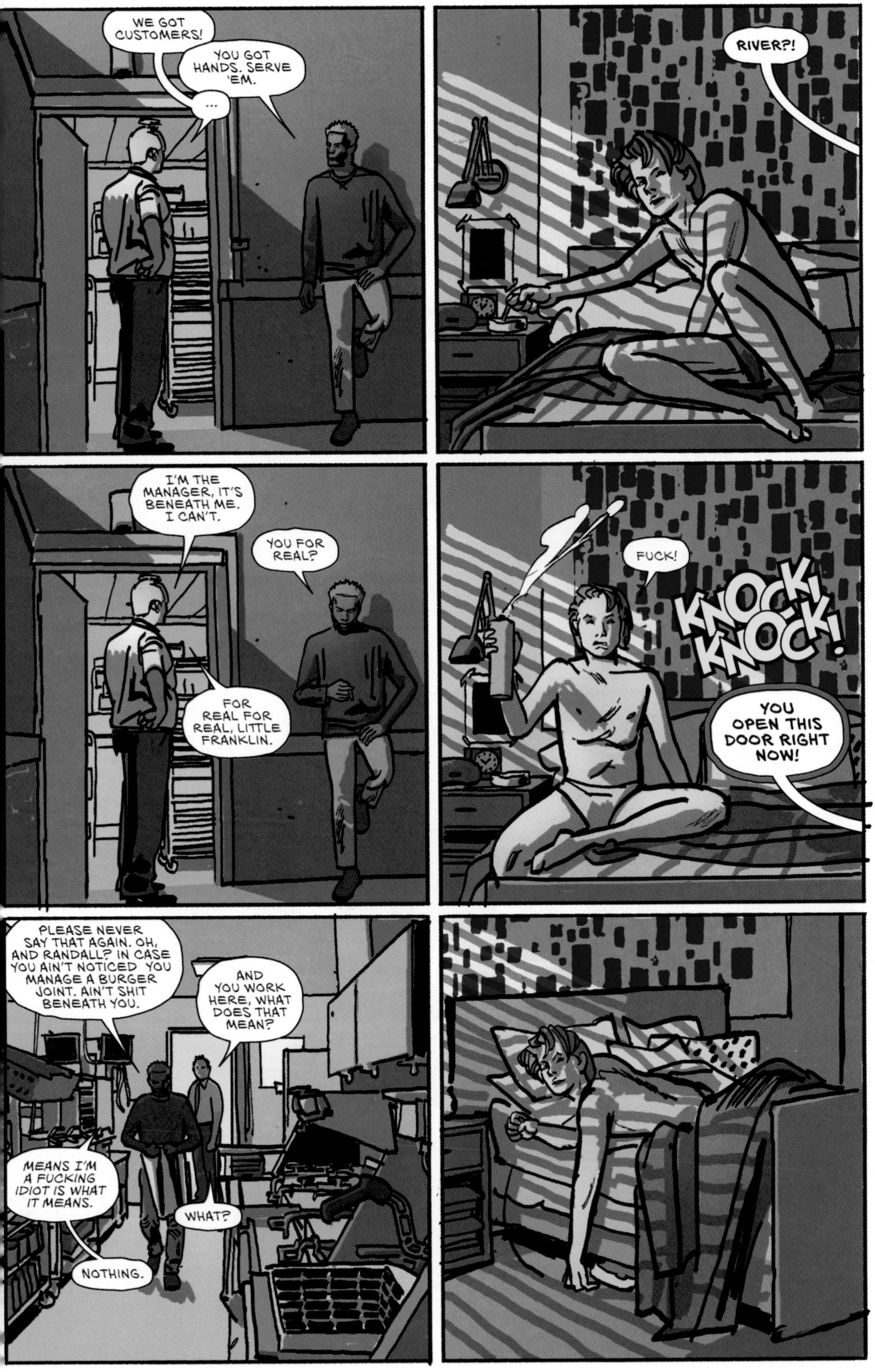
WE GOT CUSTOMERS!
YOU GOT HANDS. SERVE 'EM.
...
RIVER?!
I'M THE MANAGER, IT'S BENEATH ME. I CAN'T.
YOU FOR REAL?
FOR REAL FOR REAL, LITTLE FRANKLIN.
FUCK!
KNOCK! KNOCK!
YOU OPEN THIS DOOR RIGHT NOW!
PLEASE NEVER SAY THAT AGAIN. OH, AND RANDALL? IN CASE YOU AIN'T NOTICED YOU MANAGE A BURGER JOINT. AIN'T SHIT BENEATH YOU.
AND YOU WORK HERE, WHAT DOES THAT MEAN?
MEANS I'M A FUCKING IDIOT IS WHAT IT MEANS.
WHAT?
NOTHING.

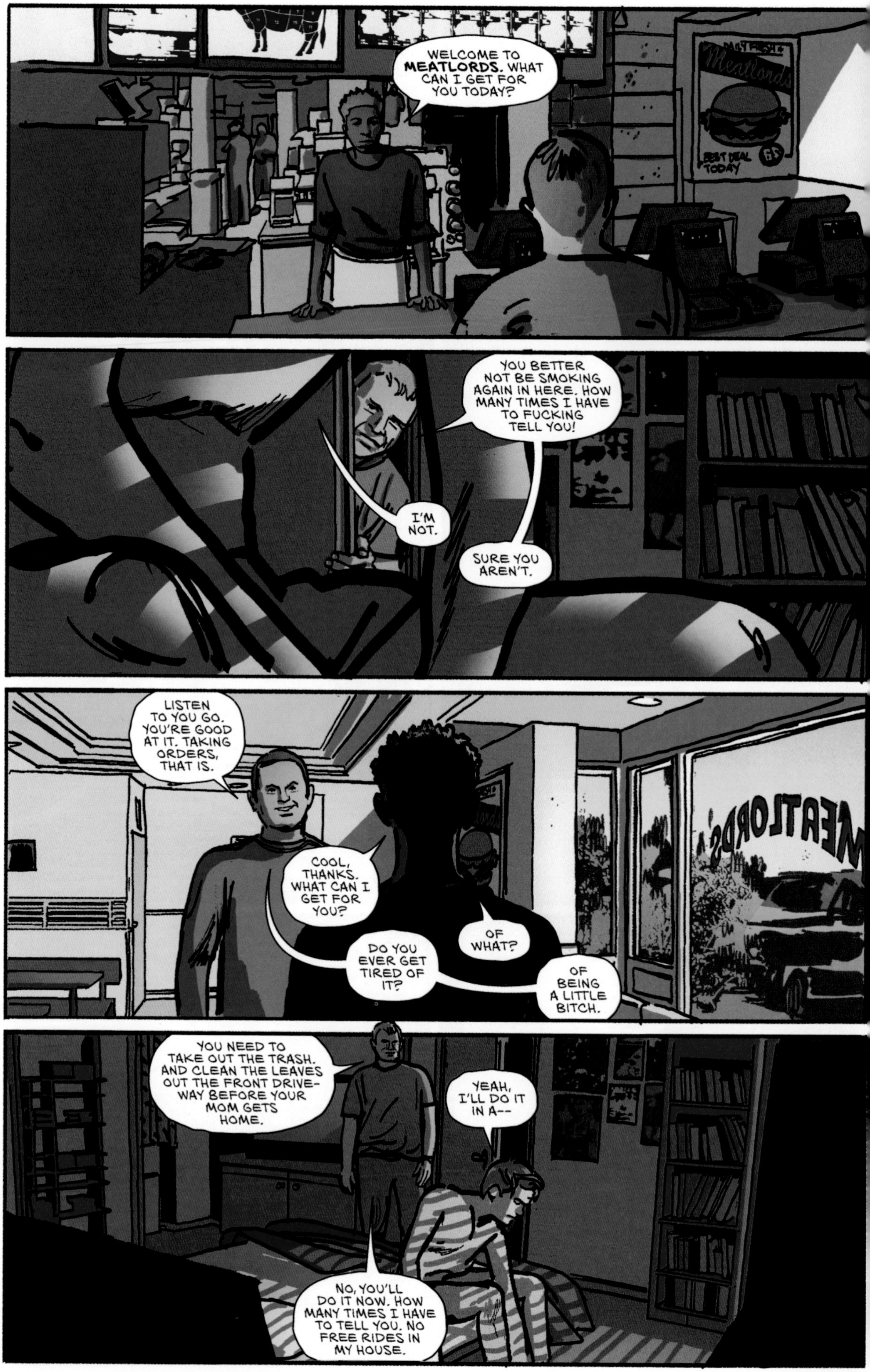
WELCOME TO MEATLORDS. WHAT CAN I GET FOR YOU TODAY?
Meatlords
BEST DEAL TODAY
YOU BETTER NOT BE SMOKING AGAIN IN HERE. HOW MANY TIMES I HAVE TO FUCKING TELL YOU!
I'M NOT.
SURE YOU AREN'T.
LISTEN TO YOU GO. YOU'RE GOOD AT IT. TAKING ORDERS, THAT IS.
COOL, THANKS. WHAT CAN I GET FOR YOU?
DO YOU EVER GET TIRED OF IT?
OF WHAT?
OF BEING A LITTLE BITCH.
YOU NEED TO TAKE OUT THE TRASH. AND CLEAN THE LEAVES OUT THE FRONT DRIVE-WAY BEFORE YOUR MOM GETS HOME.
YEAH, I'LL DO IT IN A--
NO, YOU'LL DO IT NOW. HOW MANY TIMES I HAVE TO TELL YOU. NO FREE RIDES IN MY HOUSE.

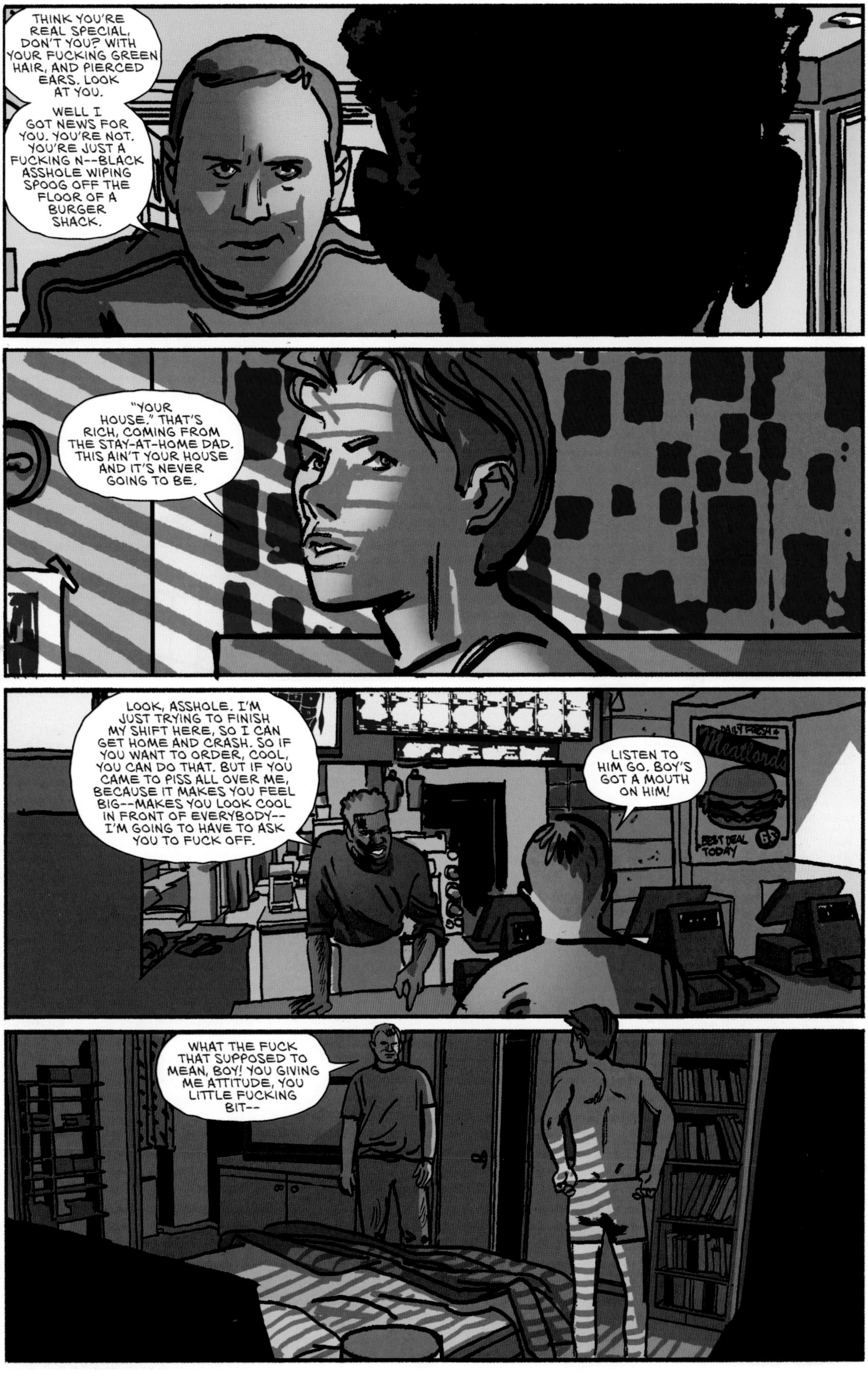

THINK YOU'RE REAL SPECIAL, DON'T YOU? WITH YOUR FUCKING GREEN HAIR, AND PIERCED EARS. LOOK AT YOU.
WELL I GOT NEWS FOR YOU. YOU'RE NOT. YOU'RE JUST A FUCKING N--BLACK ASSHOLE WIPING SPOOG OFF THE FLOOR OF A BURGER SHACK.
"YOUR HOUSE." THAT'S RICH, COMING FROM THE STAY-AT-HOME DAD. THIS AIN'T YOUR HOUSE AND IT'S NEVER GOING TO BE.
LOOK, ASSHOLE. I'M JUST TRYING TO FINISH MY SHIFT HERE, SO I CAN GET HOME AND CRASH. SO IF YOU WANT TO ORDER, COOL, YOU CAN DO THAT. BUT IF YOU CAME TO PISS ALL OVER ME, BECAUSE IT MAKES YOU FEEL BIG--MAKES YOU LOOK COOL IN FRONT OF EVERYBODY-- I'M GOING TO HAVE TO ASK YOU TO FUCK OFF.
LISTEN TO HIM GO. BOY'S GOT A MOUTH ON HIM!
Meatlords
BEST DEAL TODAY
WHAT THE FUCK THAT SUPPOSED TO MEAN, BOY! YOU GIVING ME ATTITUDE, YOU LITTLE FUCKING BIT--

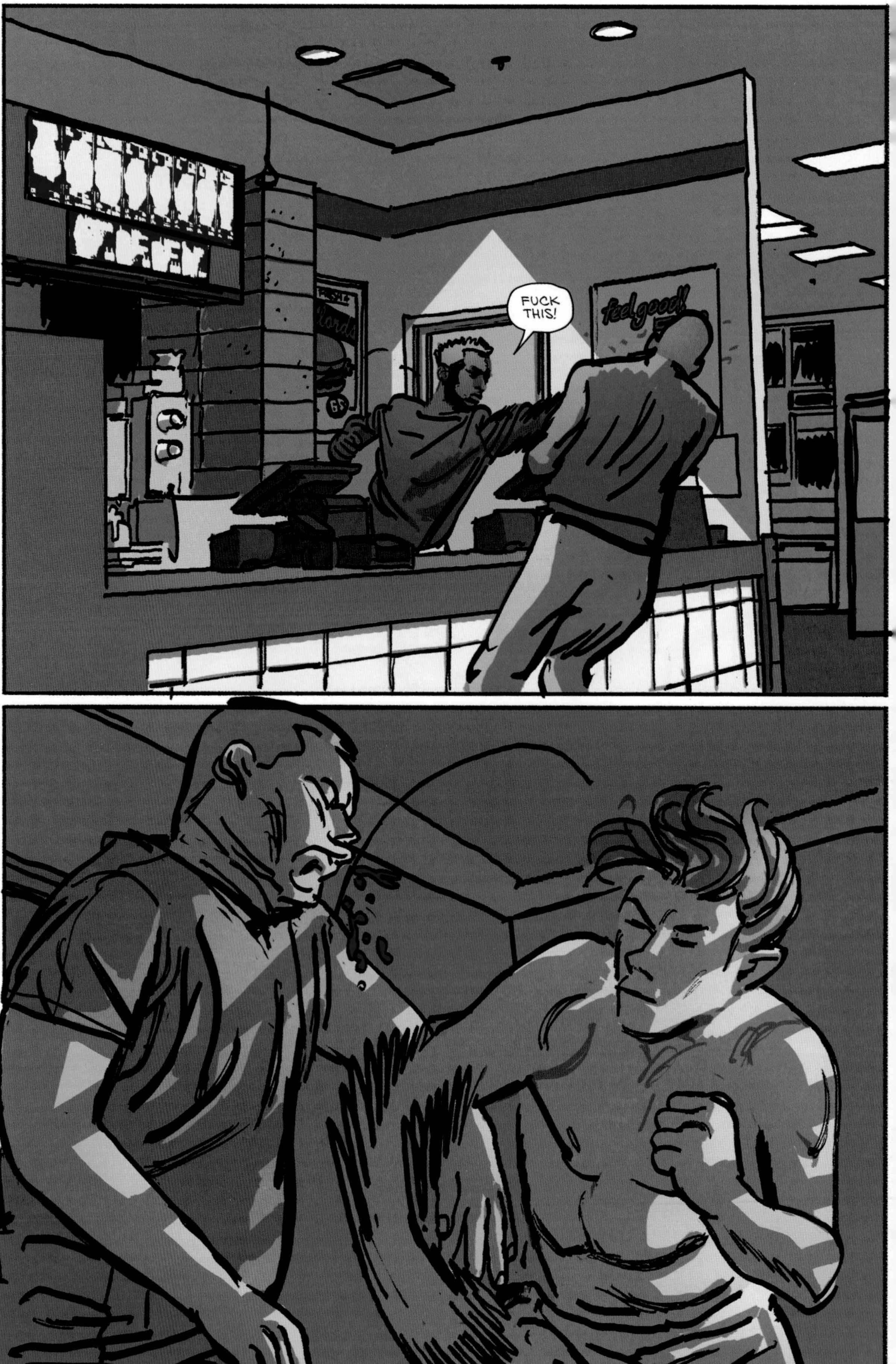
FUCK THIS!
feel good!

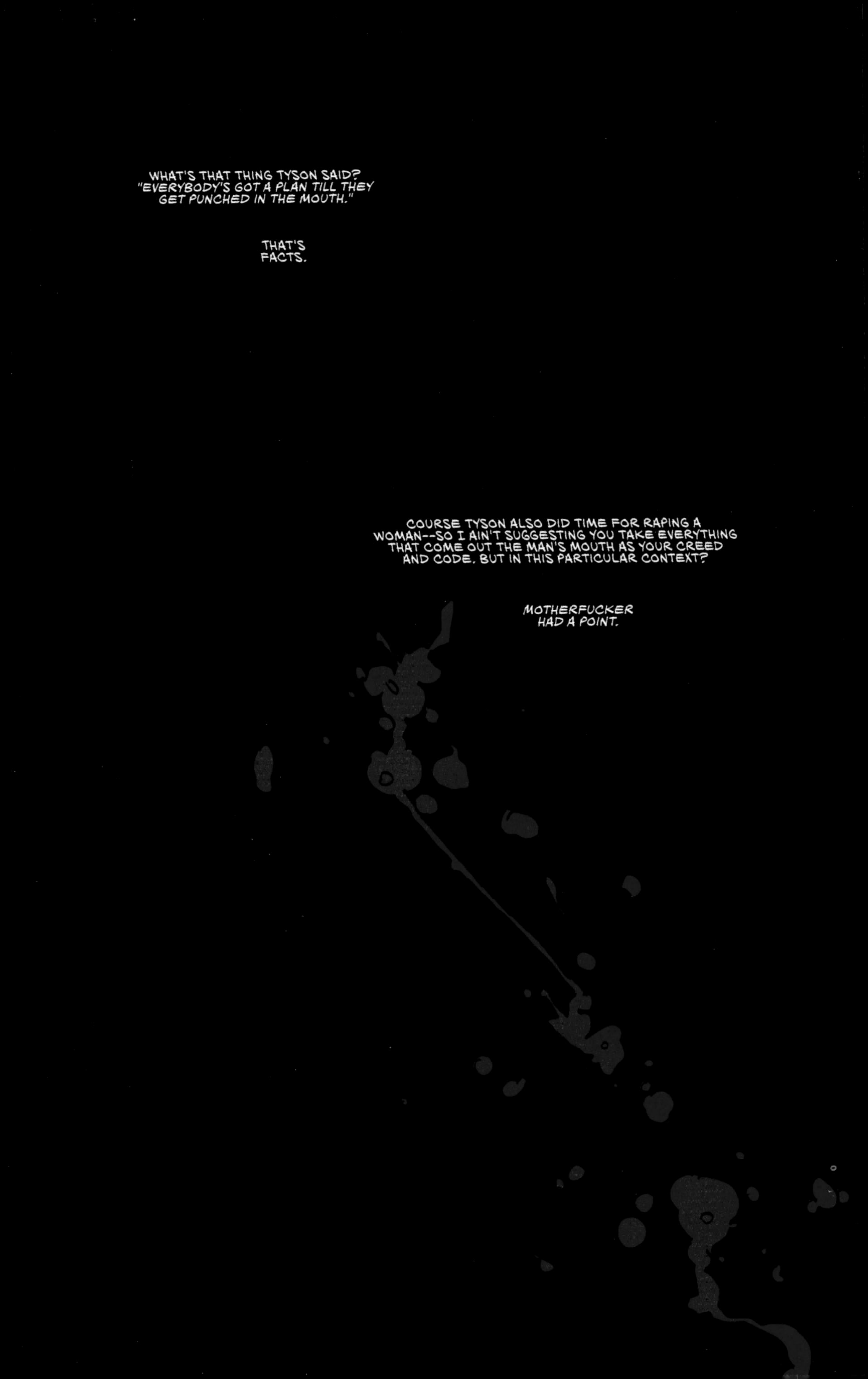
WHAT'S THAT THING TYSON SAID? "EVERYBODY'S GOT A PLAN TILL THEY GET PUNCHED IN THE MOUTH."
THAT'S FACTS.
COURSE TYSON ALSO DID TIME FOR RAPING A WOMAN--SO I AIN'T SUGGESTING YOU TAKE EVERYTHING THAT COME OUT THE MAN'S MOUTH AS YOUR CREED AND CODE. BUT IN THIS PARTICULAR CONTEXT?
MOTHERFUCKER HAD A POINT.

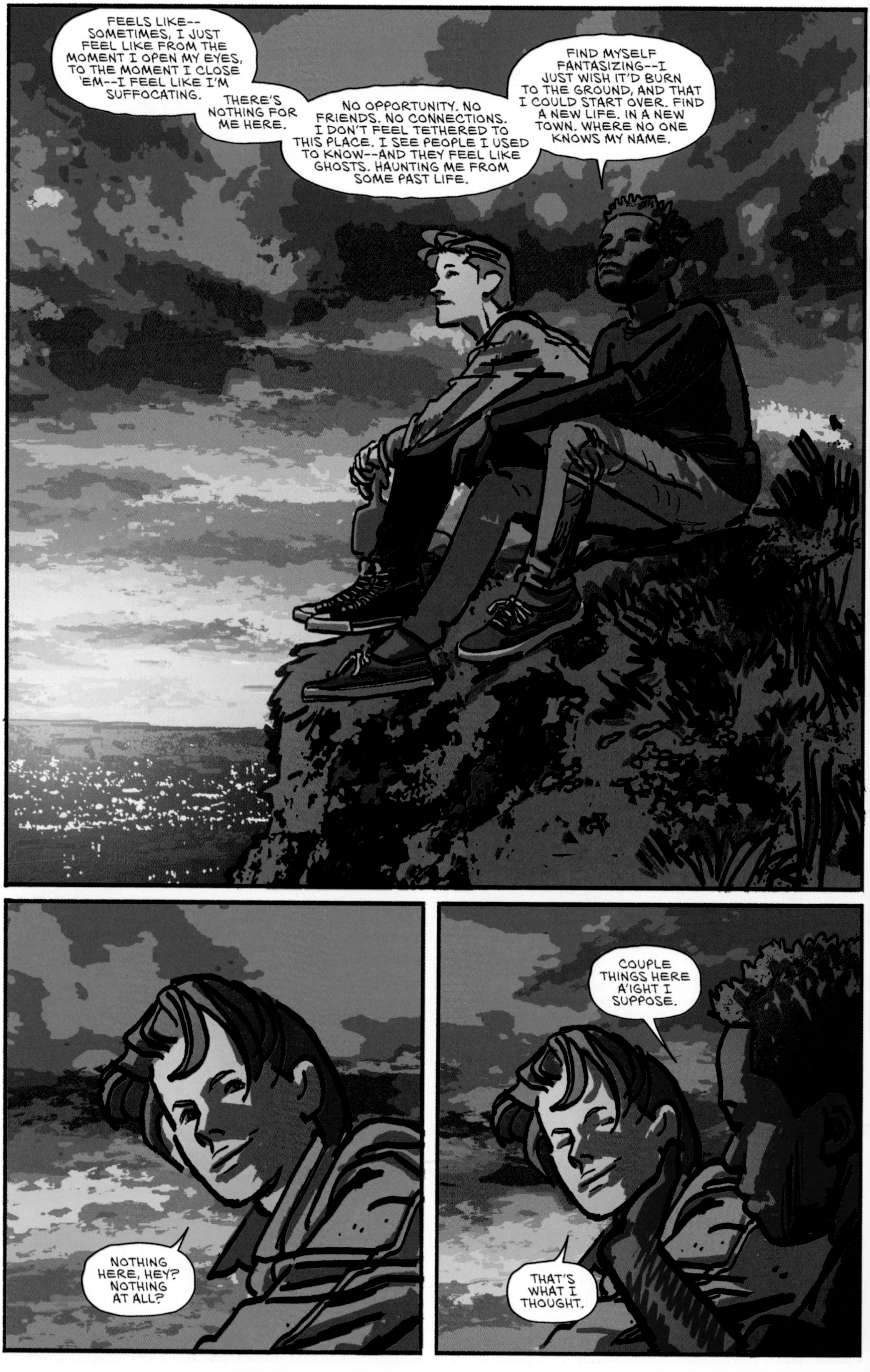
FEELS LIKE-- SOMETIMES, I JUST FEEL LIKE FROM THE MOMENT I OPEN MY EYES, TO THE MOMENT I CLOSE 'EM--I FEEL LIKE I'M SUFFOCATING.
THERE'S NOTHING FOR ME HERE.
NO OPPORTUNITY. NO FRIENDS. NO CONNECTIONS. I DON'T FEEL TETHERED TO THIS PLACE. I SEE PEOPLE I USED TO KNOW--AND THEY FEEL LIKE GHOSTS. HAUNTING ME FROM SOME PAST LIFE.
FIND MYSELF FANTASIZING--I JUST WISH IT'D BURN TO THE GROUND, AND THAT I COULD START OVER. FIND A NEW LIFE. IN A NEW TOWN. WHERE NO ONE KNOWS MY NAME.
NOTHING HERE, HEY? NOTHING AT ALL?
COUPLE THINGS HERE A'IGHT I SUPPOSE.
THAT'S WHAT I THOUGHT.

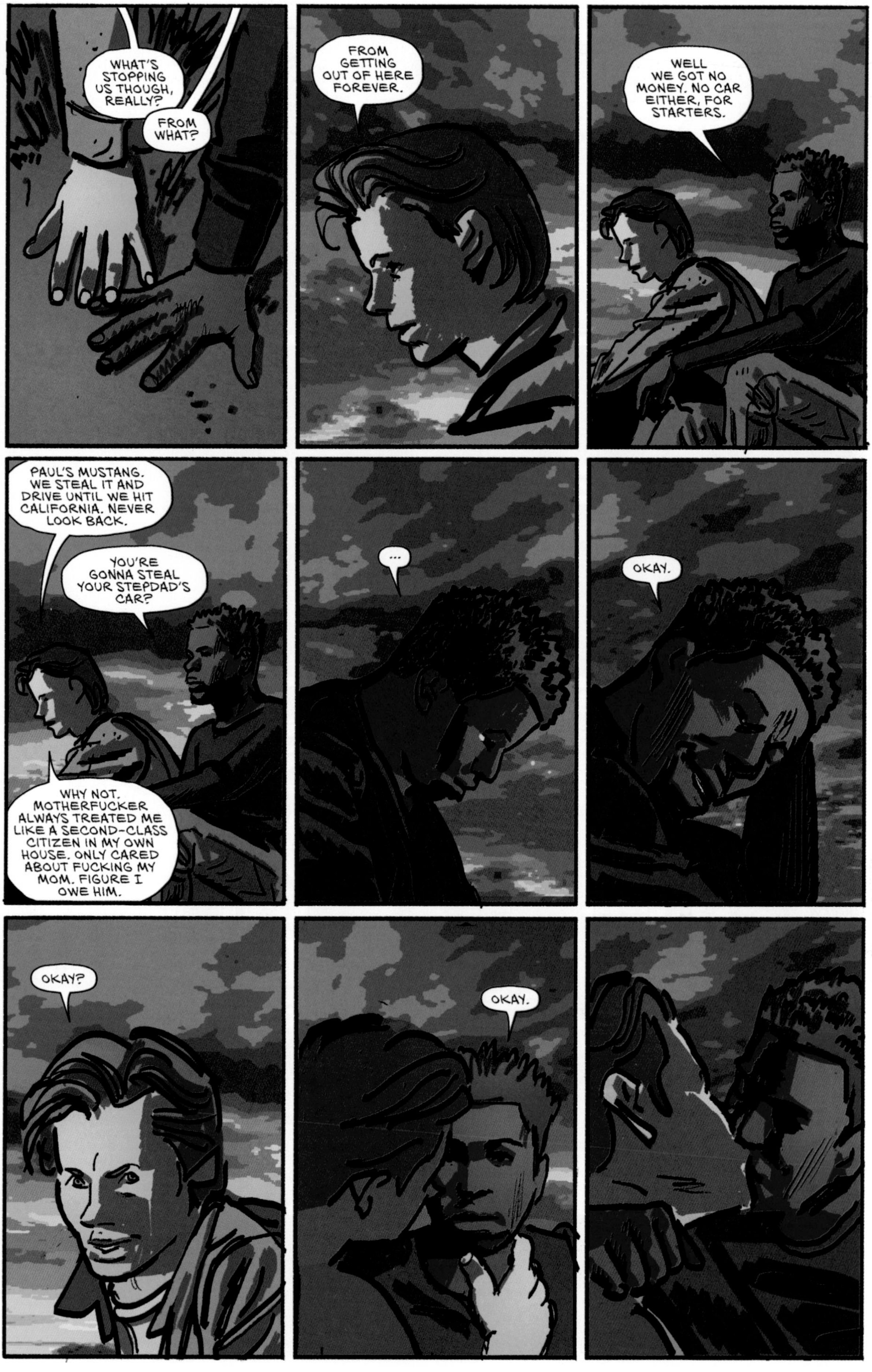
WHAT'S STOPPING US THOUGH, REALLY?
FROM WHAT?
FROM GETTING OUT OF HERE FOREVER.
WELL WE GOT NO MONEY. NO CAR EITHER, FOR STARTERS.
PAUL'S MUSTANG. WE STEAL IT AND DRIVE UNTIL WE HIT CALIFORNIA. NEVER LOOK BACK.
YOU'RE GONNA STEAL YOUR STEPDAD'S CAR?
WHY NOT. MOTHERFUCKER ALWAYS TREATED ME LIKE A SECOND-CLASS CITIZEN IN MY OWN HOUSE. ONLY CARED ABOUT FUCKING MY MOM. FIGURE I OWE HIM.
...
OKAY.
OKAY?
OKAY.

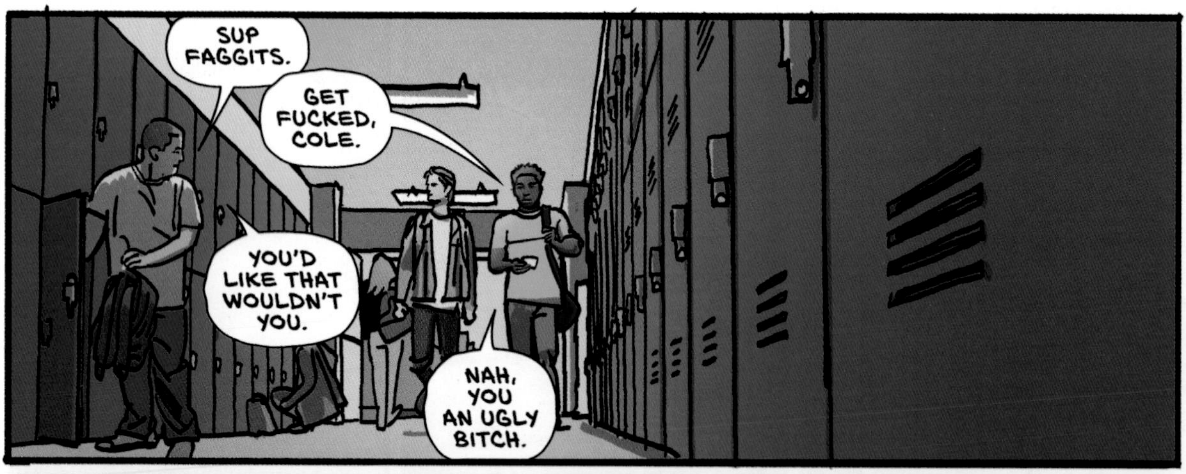
SUP FAGGITS.
GET FUCKED, COLE.
YOU'D LIKE THAT WOULDN'T YOU.
NAH, YOU AN UGLY BITCH.

TECC CONTENT
PRESENTS

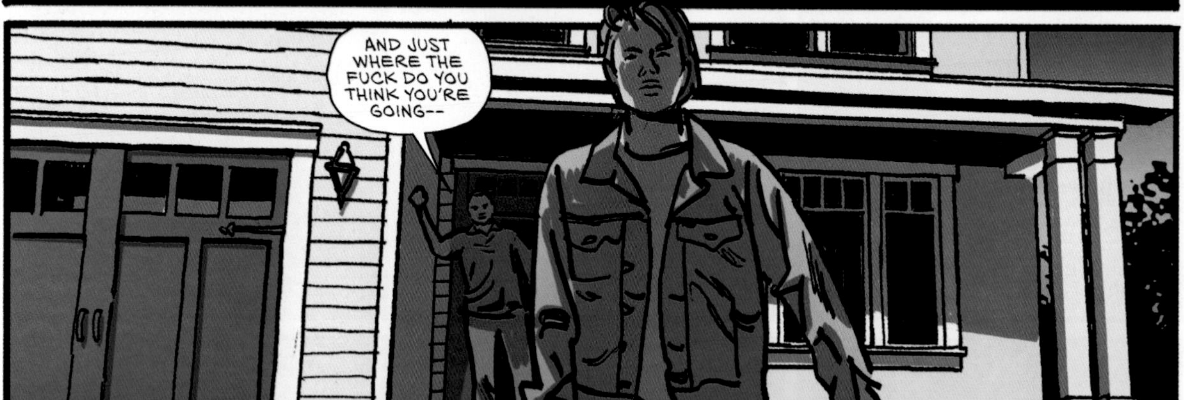
AND JUST WHERE THE FUCK DO YOU THINK YOU'RE GOING--

A
PIRES / DIOTTO / CUNNIFFE
JOINT

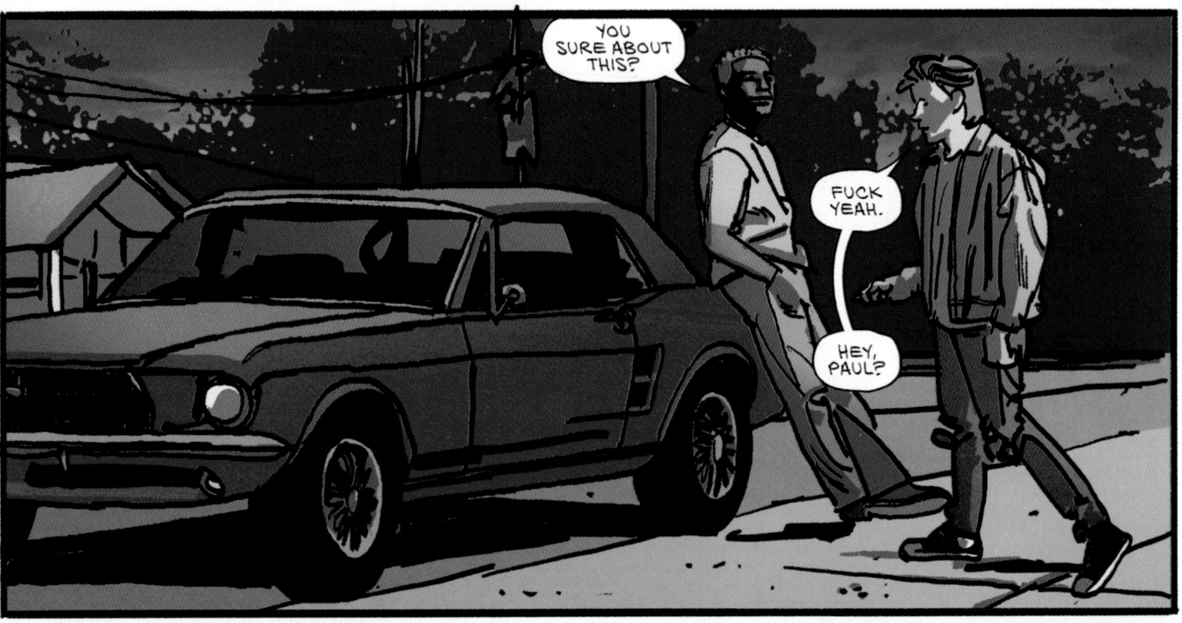
YOU SURE ABOUT THIS?
FUCK YEAH.
HEY, PAUL?

IN COLLABORATION WITH MICAH MYERS

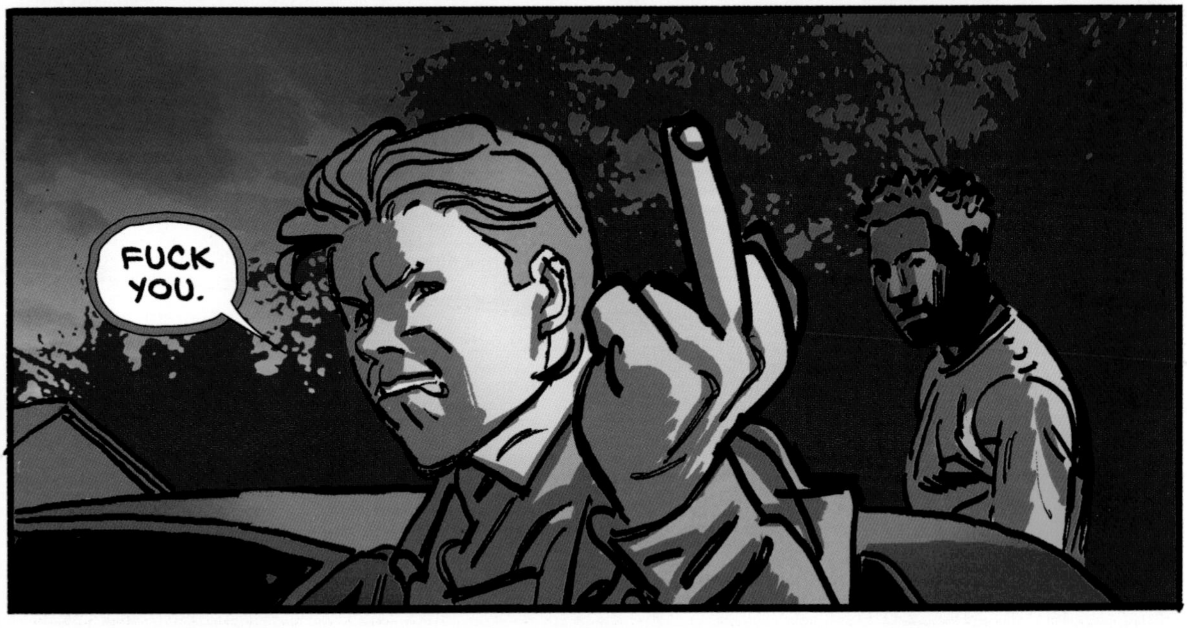
FUCK YOU.

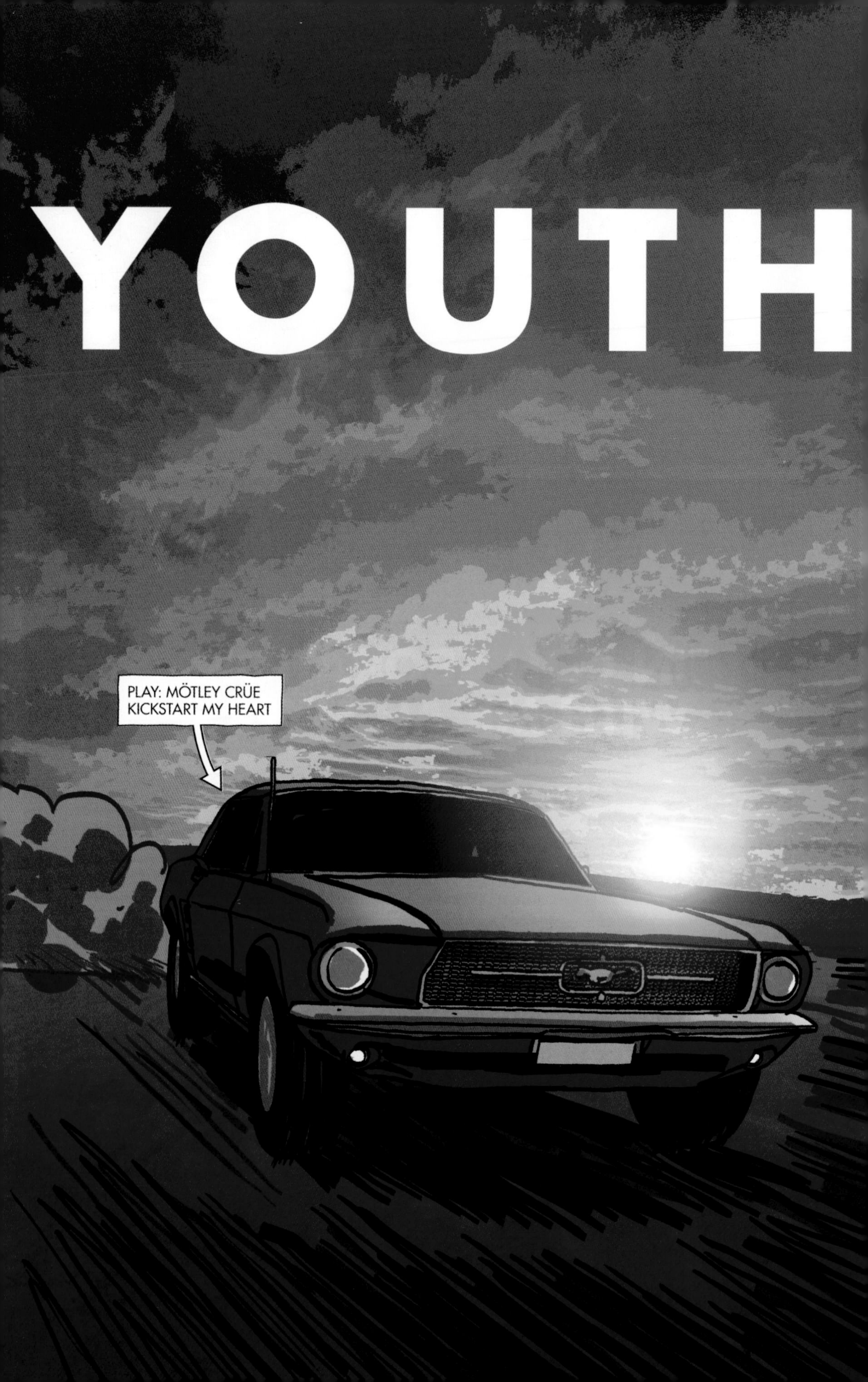
YOUTH
PLAY: MÖTLEY CRÜE
KICKSTART MY HEART

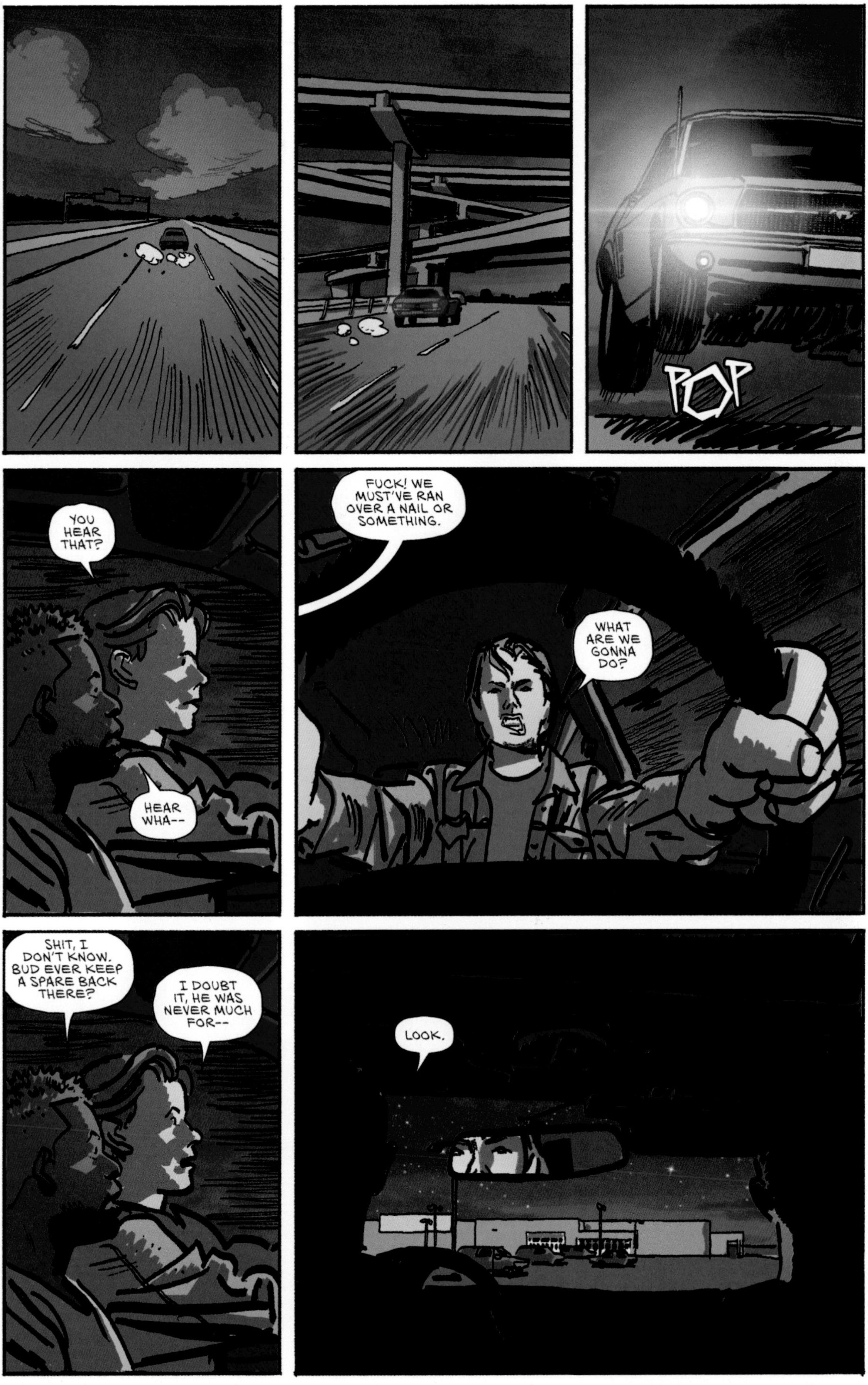
POP
YOU HEAR THAT?
HEAR WHA--
FUCK! WE MUST'VE RAN OVER A NAIL OR SOMETHING.
WHAT ARE WE GONNA DO?
SHIT, I DON'T KNOW. BUD EVER KEEP A SPARE BACK THERE?
I DOUBT IT, HE WAS NEVER MUCH FOR--
LOOK.

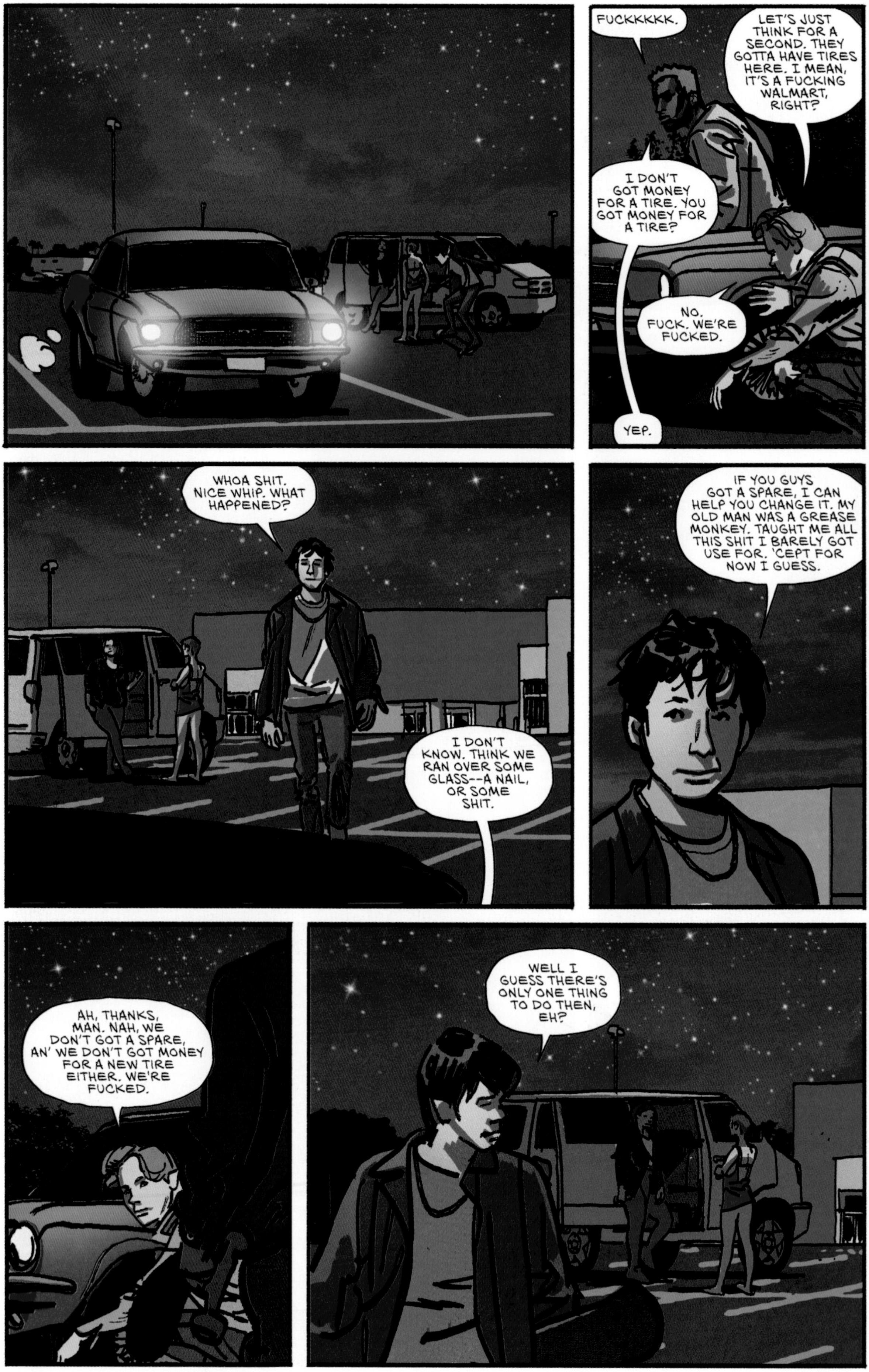
FUCKKKKK.
LET'S JUST THINK FOR A SECOND. THEY GOTTA HAVE TIRES HERE. I MEAN, IT'S A FUCKING WALMART, RIGHT?
I DON'T GOT MONEY FOR A TIRE. YOU GOT MONEY FOR A TIRE?
NO. FUCK. WE'RE FUCKED.
YEP.
WHOA SHIT. NICE WHIP. WHAT HAPPENED?
I DON'T KNOW. THINK WE RAN OVER SOME GLASS--A NAIL, OR SOME SHIT.
IF YOU GUYS GOT A SPARE, I CAN HELP YOU CHANGE IT. MY OLD MAN WAS A GREASE MONKEY. TAUGHT ME ALL THIS SHIT I BARELY GOT USE FOR. 'CEPT FOR NOW I GUESS.
AH, THANKS, MAN. NAH, WE DON'T GOT A SPARE, AN' WE DON'T GOT MONEY FOR A NEW TIRE EITHER. WE'RE FUCKED.
WELL I GUESS THERE'S ONLY ONE THING TO DO THEN, EH?

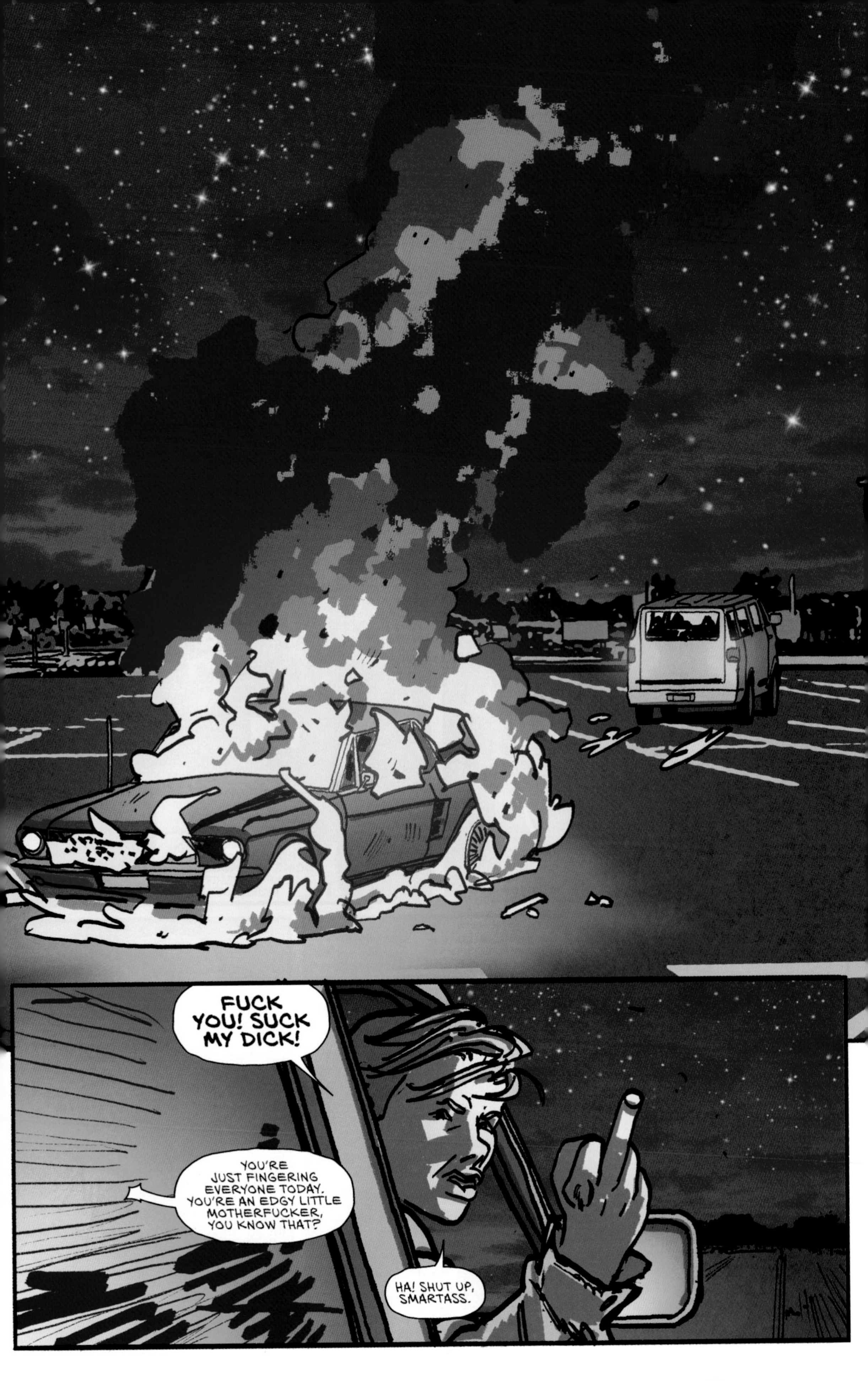
FUCK YOU! SUCK MY DICK!
YOU'RE JUST FINGERING EVERYONE TODAY. YOU'RE AN EDGY LITTLE MOTHERFUCKER, YOU KNOW THAT?
HA! SHUT UP, SMARTASS.

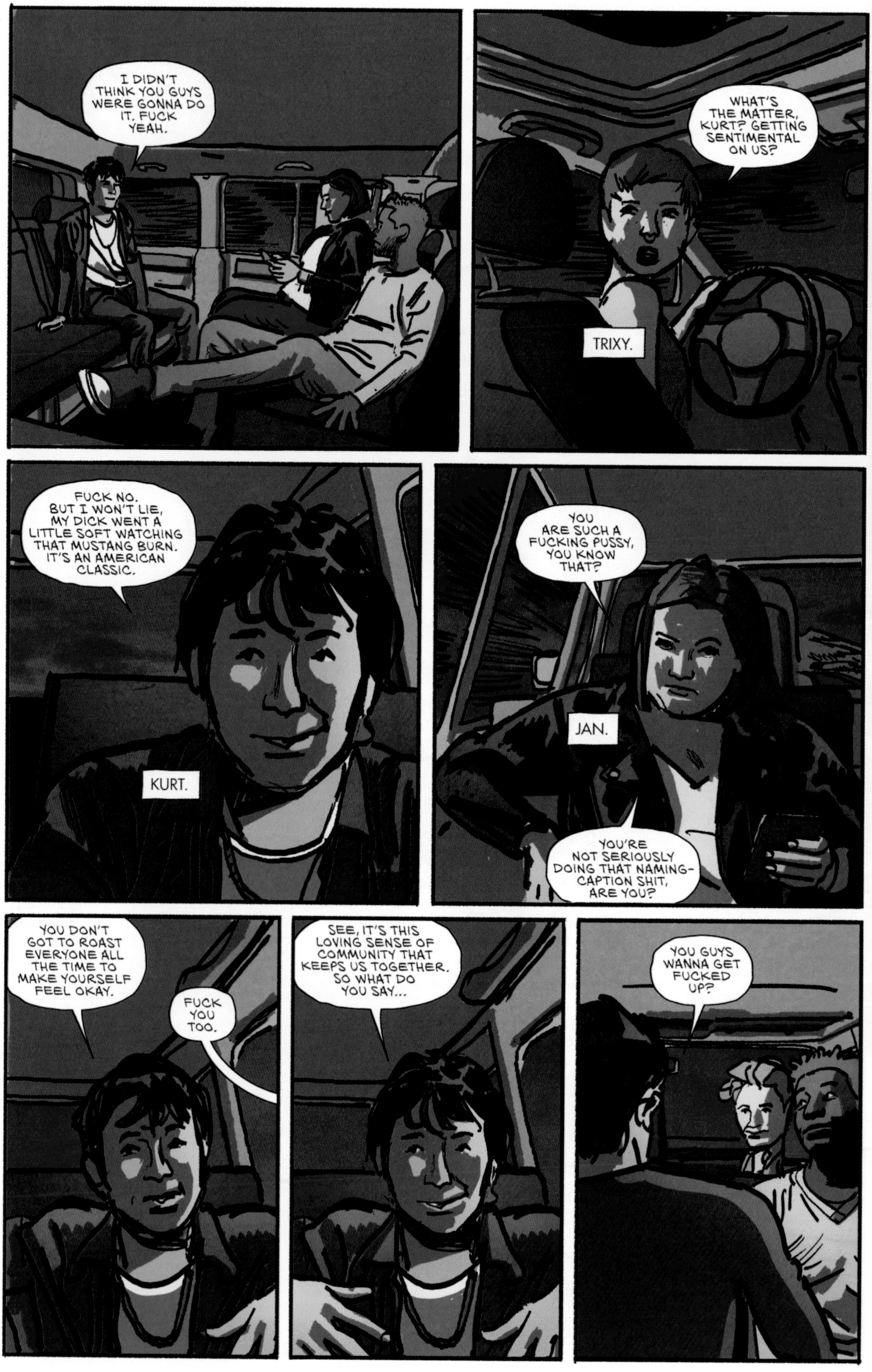
I DIDN'T THINK YOU GUYS WERE GONNA DO IT. FUCK YEAH.
WHAT'S THE MATTER, KURT? GETTING SENTIMENTAL ON US?
TRIXY.
FUCK NO. BUT I WON'T LIE, MY DICK WENT A LITTLE SOFT WATCHING THAT MUSTANG BURN. IT'S AN AMERICAN CLASSIC.
KURT.
YOU ARE SUCH A FUCKING PUSSY, YOU KNOW THAT?
JAN.
YOU'RE NOT SERIOUSLY DOING THAT NAMING-CAPTION SHIT, ARE YOU?
YOU DON'T GOT TO ROAST EVERYONE ALL THE TIME TO MAKE YOURSELF FEEL OKAY.
FUCK YOU TOO.
SEE, IT'S THIS LOVING SENSE OF COMMUNITY THAT KEEPS US TOGETHER. SO WHAT DO YOU SAY...
YOU GUYS WANNA GET FUCKED UP?

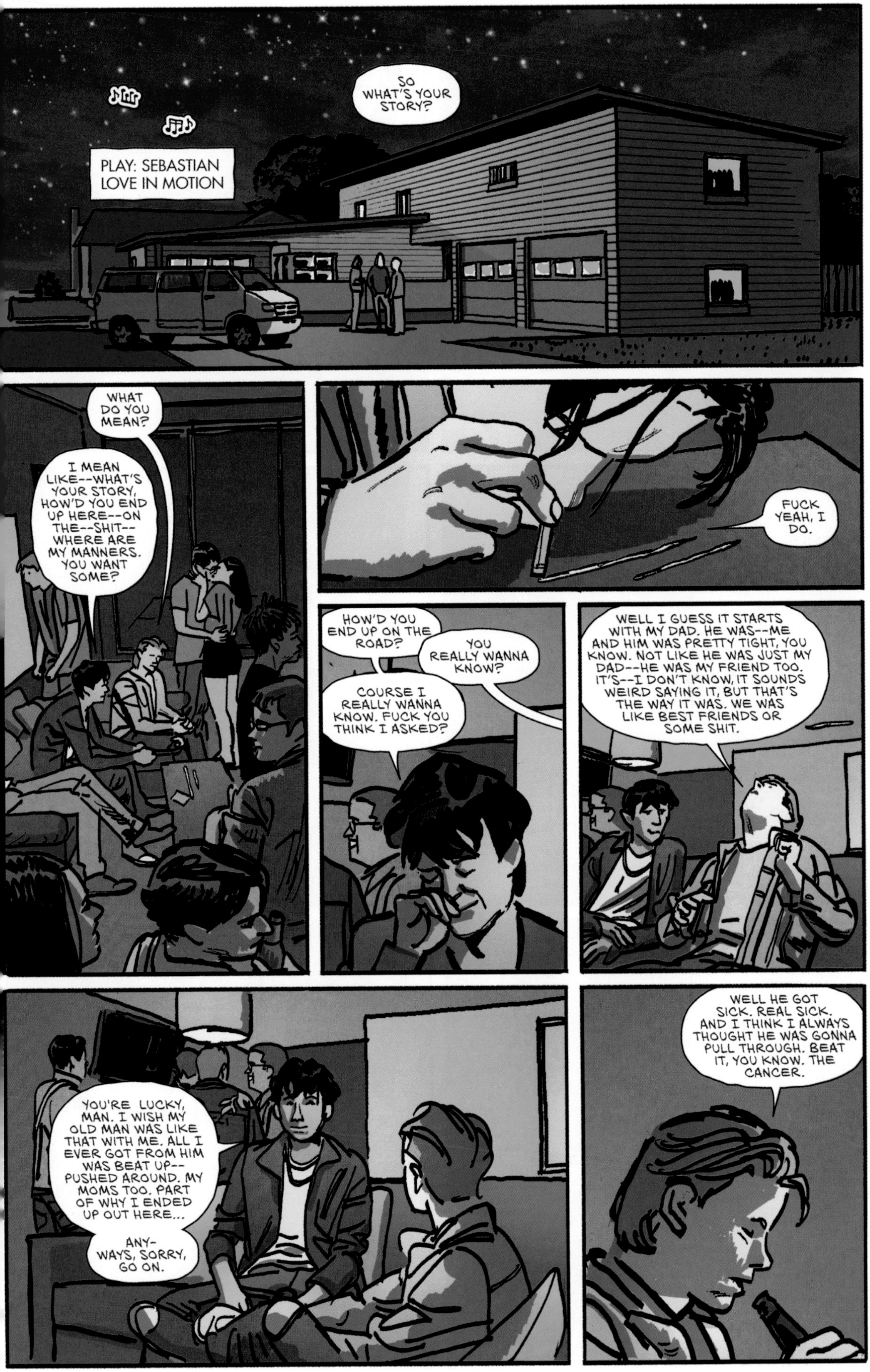
PLAY: SEBASTIAN
LOVE IN MOTION
SO WHAT'S YOUR STORY?
WHAT DO YOU MEAN?
I MEAN LIKE--WHAT'S YOUR STORY, HOW'D YOU END UP HERE--ON THE--SHIT--WHERE ARE MY MANNERS. YOU WANT SOME?
FUCK YEAH, I DO.
HOW'D YOU END UP ON THE ROAD?
YOU REALLY WANNA KNOW?
COURSE I REALLY WANNA KNOW. FUCK YOU THINK I ASKED?
WELL I GUESS IT STARTS WITH MY DAD. HE WAS--ME AND HIM WAS PRETTY TIGHT, YOU KNOW. NOT LIKE HE WAS JUST MY DAD--HE WAS MY FRIEND TOO. IT'S--I DON'T KNOW, IT SOUNDS WEIRD SAYING IT, BUT THAT'S THE WAY IT WAS. WE WAS LIKE BEST FRIENDS OR SOME SHIT.
YOU'RE LUCKY, MAN. I WISH MY OLD MAN WAS LIKE THAT WITH ME. ALL I EVER GOT FROM HIM WAS BEAT UP--PUSHED AROUND. MY MOMS TOO. PART OF WHY I ENDED UP OUT HERE...
ANY-WAYS, SORRY, GO ON.
WELL HE GOT SICK. REAL SICK. AND I THINK I ALWAYS THOUGHT HE WAS GONNA PULL THROUGH. BEAT IT, YOU KNOW. THE CANCER.

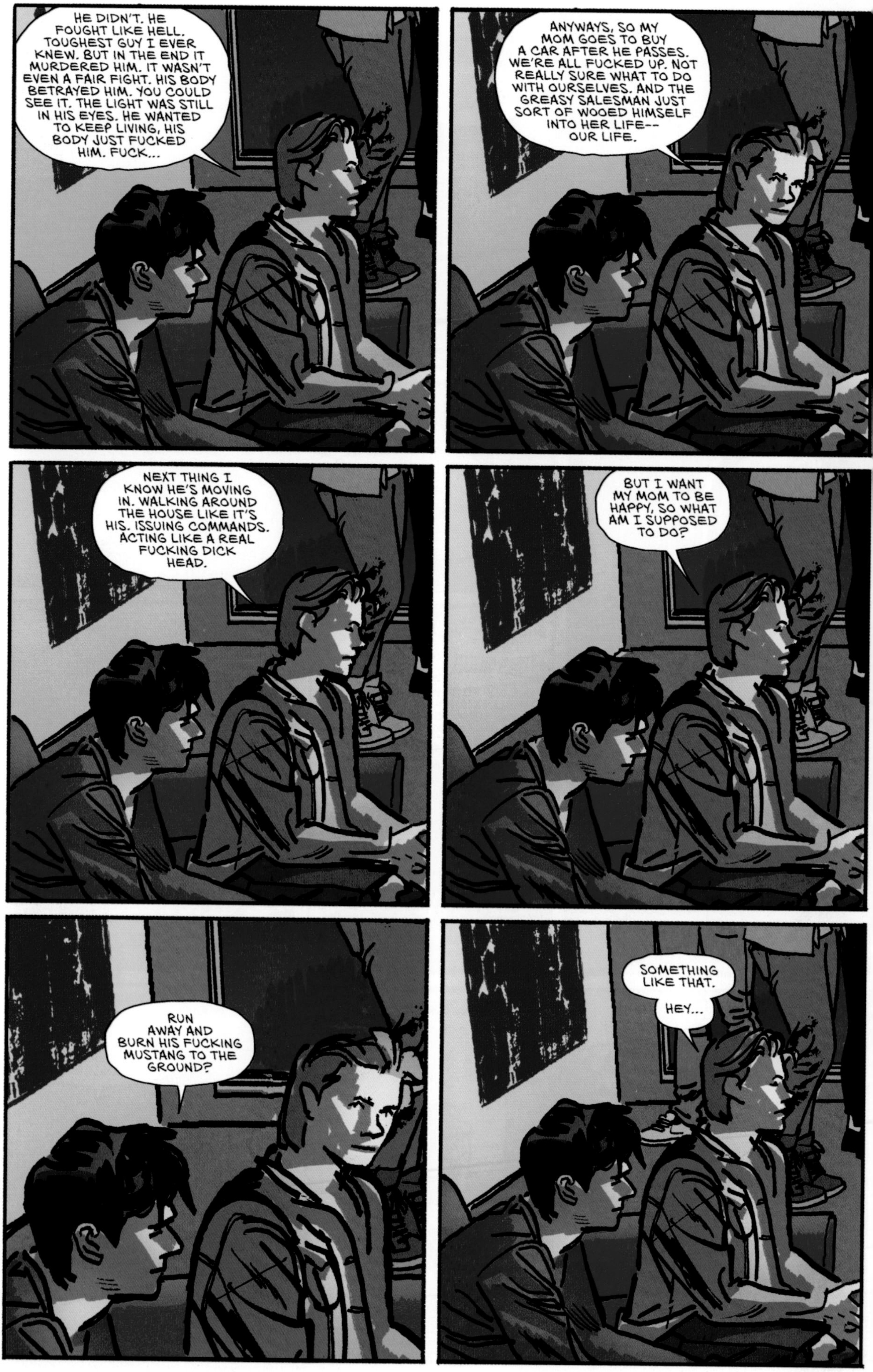
HE DIDN'T. HE FOUGHT LIKE HELL. TOUGHEST GUY I EVER KNEW. BUT IN THE END IT MURDERED HIM. IT WASN'T EVEN A FAIR FIGHT. HIS BODY BETRAYED HIM. YOU COULD SEE IT. THE LIGHT WAS STILL IN HIS EYES. HE WANTED TO KEEP LIVING, HIS BODY JUST FUCKED HIM. FUCK...
ANYWAYS, SO MY MOM GOES TO BUY A CAR AFTER HE PASSES. WE'RE ALL FUCKED UP. NOT REALLY SURE WHAT TO DO WITH OURSELVES. AND THE GREASY SALESMAN JUST SORT OF WOOED HIMSELF INTO HER LIFE-- OUR LIFE.
NEXT THING I KNOW HE'S MOVING IN. WALKING AROUND THE HOUSE LIKE IT'S HIS. ISSUING COMMANDS. ACTING LIKE A REAL FUCKING DICK HEAD.
BUT I WANT MY MOM TO BE HAPPY, SO WHAT AM I SUPPOSED TO DO?
RUN AWAY AND BURN HIS FUCKING MUSTANG TO THE GROUND?
SOMETHING LIKE THAT.
HEY...

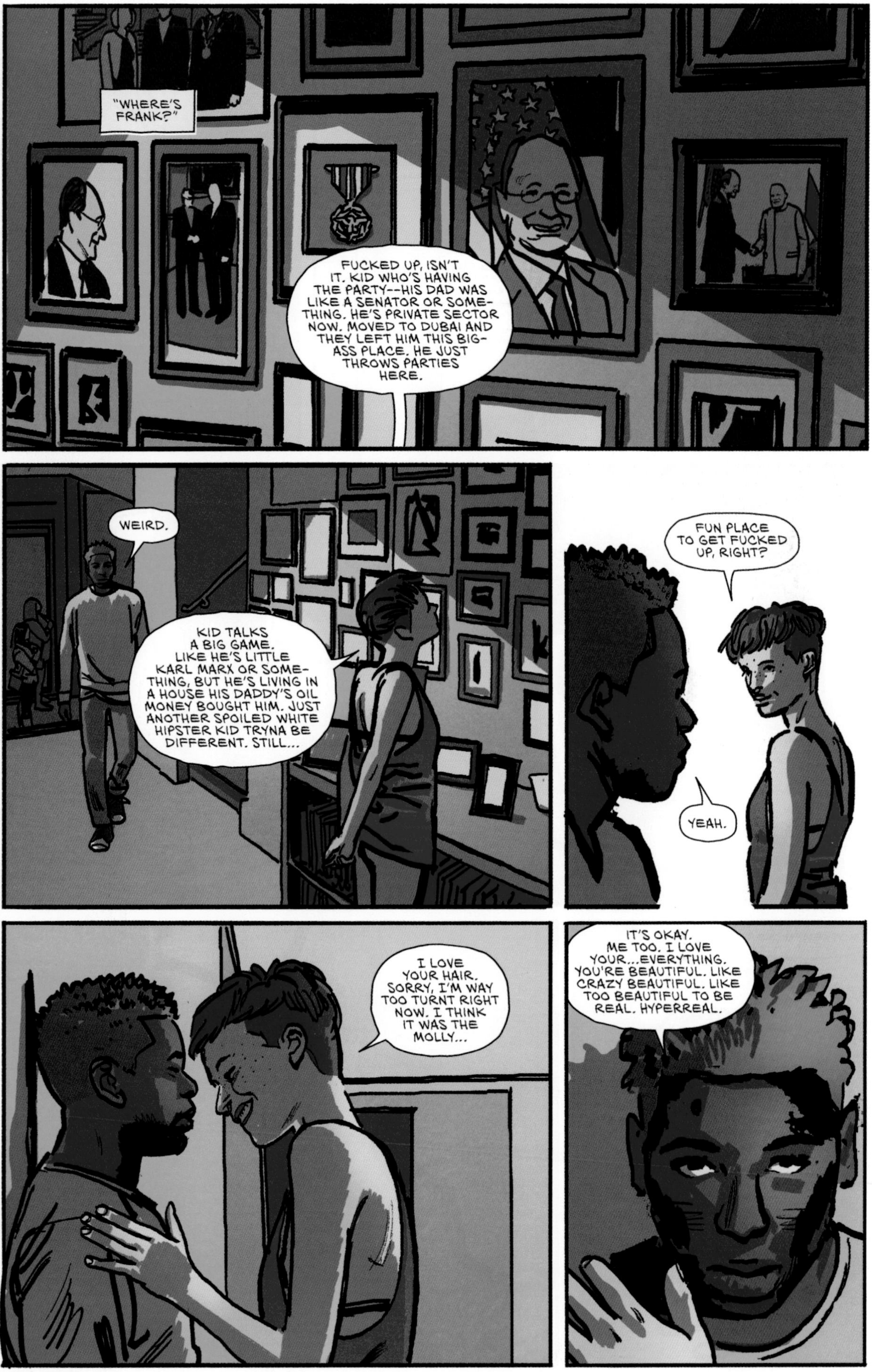
"WHERE'S FRANK?"
FUCKED UP, ISN'T IT. KID WHO'S HAVING THE PARTY--HIS DAD WAS LIKE A SENATOR OR SOMETHING. HE'S PRIVATE SECTOR NOW. MOVED TO DUBAI AND THEY LEFT HIM THIS BIG-ASS PLACE. HE JUST THROWS PARTIES HERE.
WEIRD.
KID TALKS A BIG GAME. LIKE HE'S LITTLE KARL MARX OR SOMETHING, BUT HE'S LIVING IN A HOUSE HIS DADDY'S OIL MONEY BOUGHT HIM. JUST ANOTHER SPOILED WHITE HIPSTER KID TRYNA BE DIFFERENT. STILL...
FUN PLACE TO GET FUCKED UP, RIGHT?
YEAH.
I LOVE YOUR HAIR. SORRY, I'M WAY TOO TURNT RIGHT NOW. I THINK IT WAS THE MOLLY...
IT'S OKAY. ME TOO. I LOVE YOUR...EVERYTHING. YOU'RE BEAUTIFUL. LIKE CRAZY BEAUTIFUL. LIKE TOO BEAUTIFUL TO BE REAL. HYPERREAL.

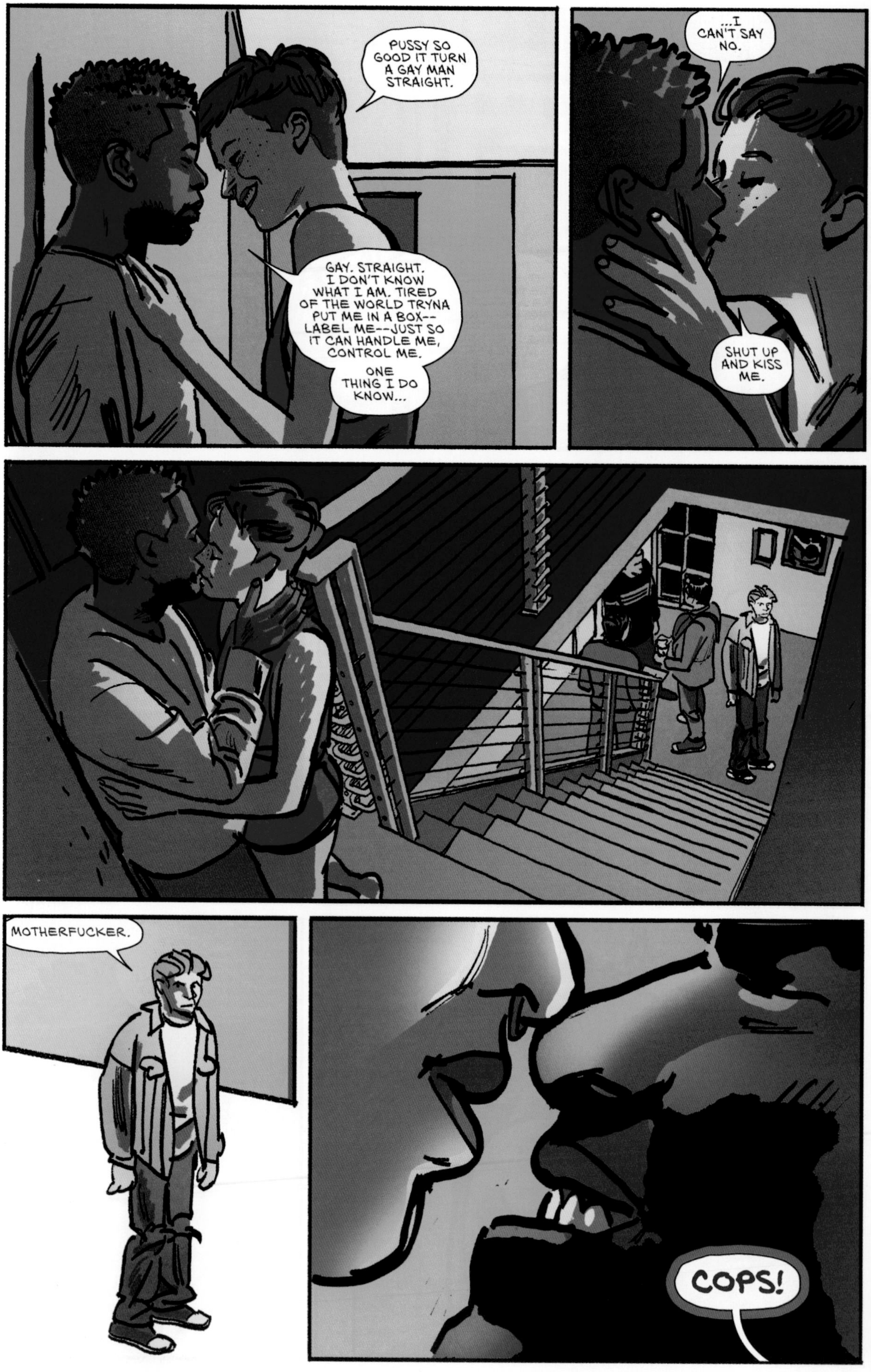
PUSSY SO GOOD IT TURN A GAY MAN STRAIGHT.
GAY. STRAIGHT. I DON'T KNOW WHAT I AM. TIRED OF THE WORLD TRYNA PUT ME IN A BOX--LABEL ME--JUST SO IT CAN HANDLE ME, CONTROL ME.
ONE THING I DO KNOW...
...I CAN'T SAY NO.
SHUT UP AND KISS ME.
MOTHERFUCKER.
COPS!

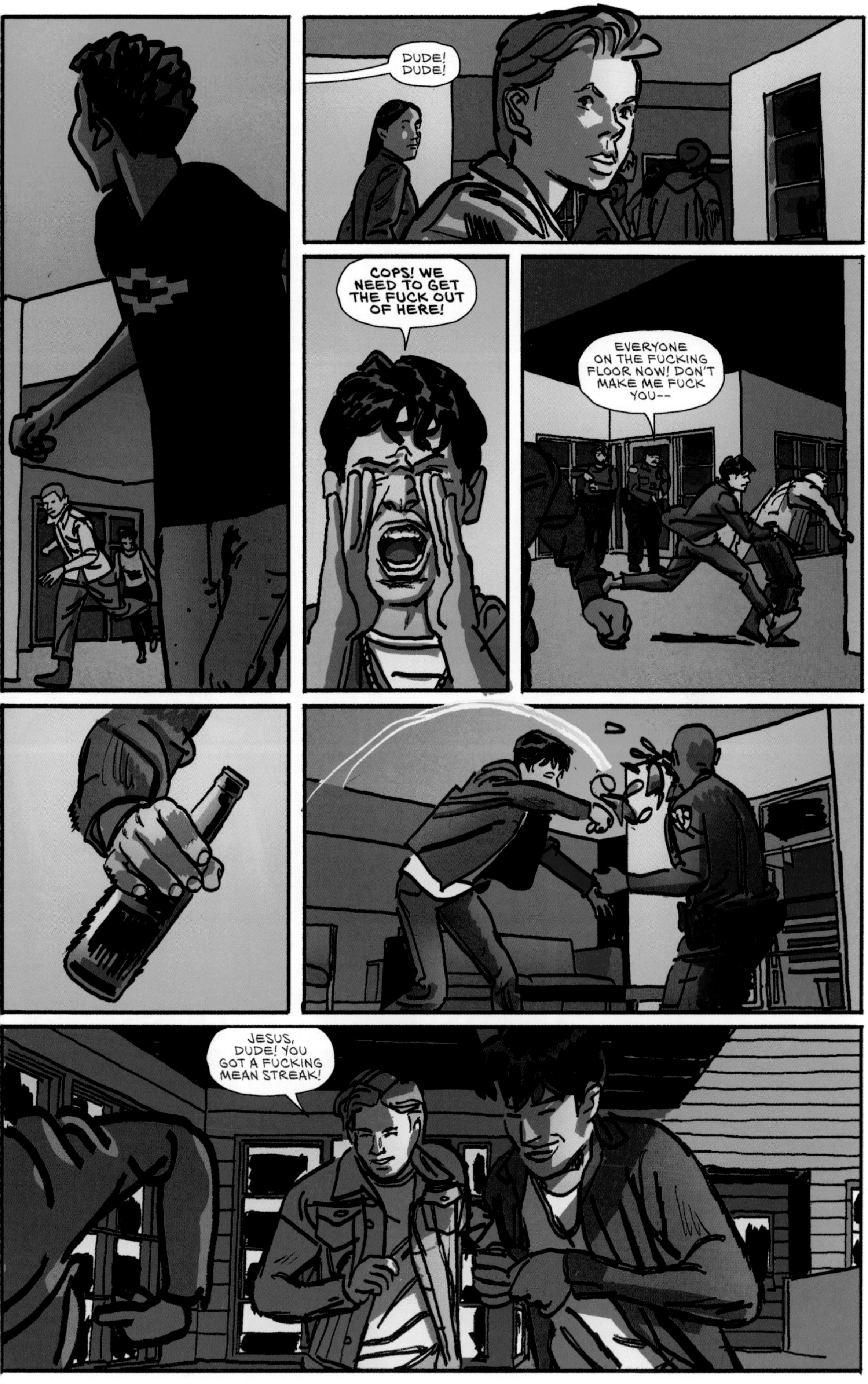
DUDE! DUDE!
COPS! WE NEED TO GET THE FUCK OUT OF HERE!
EVERYONE ON THE FUCKING FLOOR NOW! DON'T MAKE ME FUCK YOU--
JESUS, DUDE! YOU GOT A FUCKING MEAN STREAK!

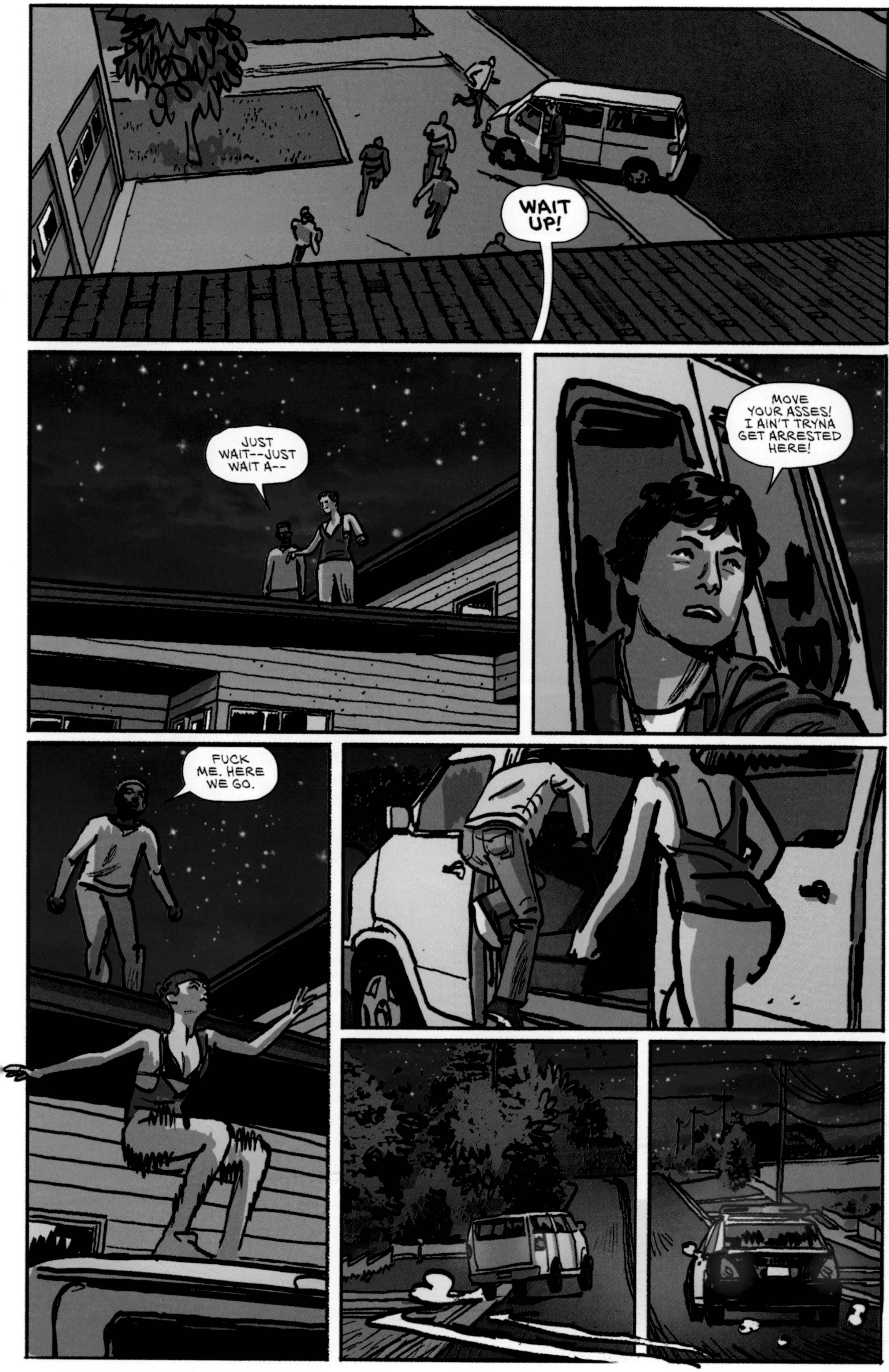
WAIT UP!
JUST WAIT--JUST WAIT A--
MOVE YOUR ASSES! I AIN'T TRYNA GET ARRESTED HERE!
FUCK ME. HERE WE GO.

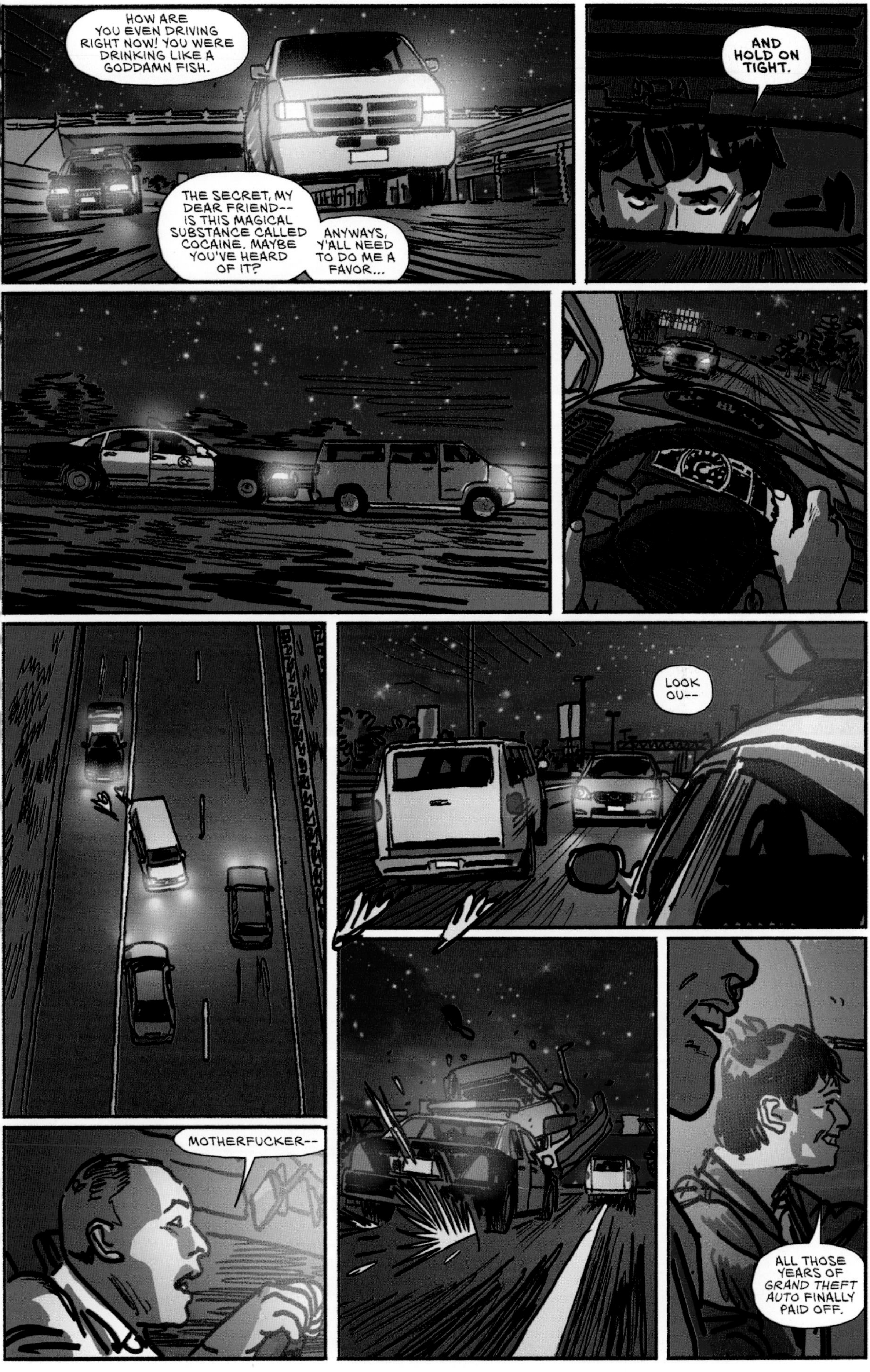
HOW ARE YOU EVEN DRIVING RIGHT NOW! YOU WERE DRINKING LIKE A GODDAMN FISH.
THE SECRET, MY DEAR FRIEND-- IS THIS MAGICAL SUBSTANCE CALLED COCAINE. MAYBE YOU'VE HEARD OF IT?
ANYWAYS, Y'ALL NEED TO DO ME A FAVOR...
AND HOLD ON TIGHT.
LOOK OU--
MOTHERFUCKER--
ALL THOSE YEARS OF GRAND THEFT AUTO FINALLY PAID OFF.

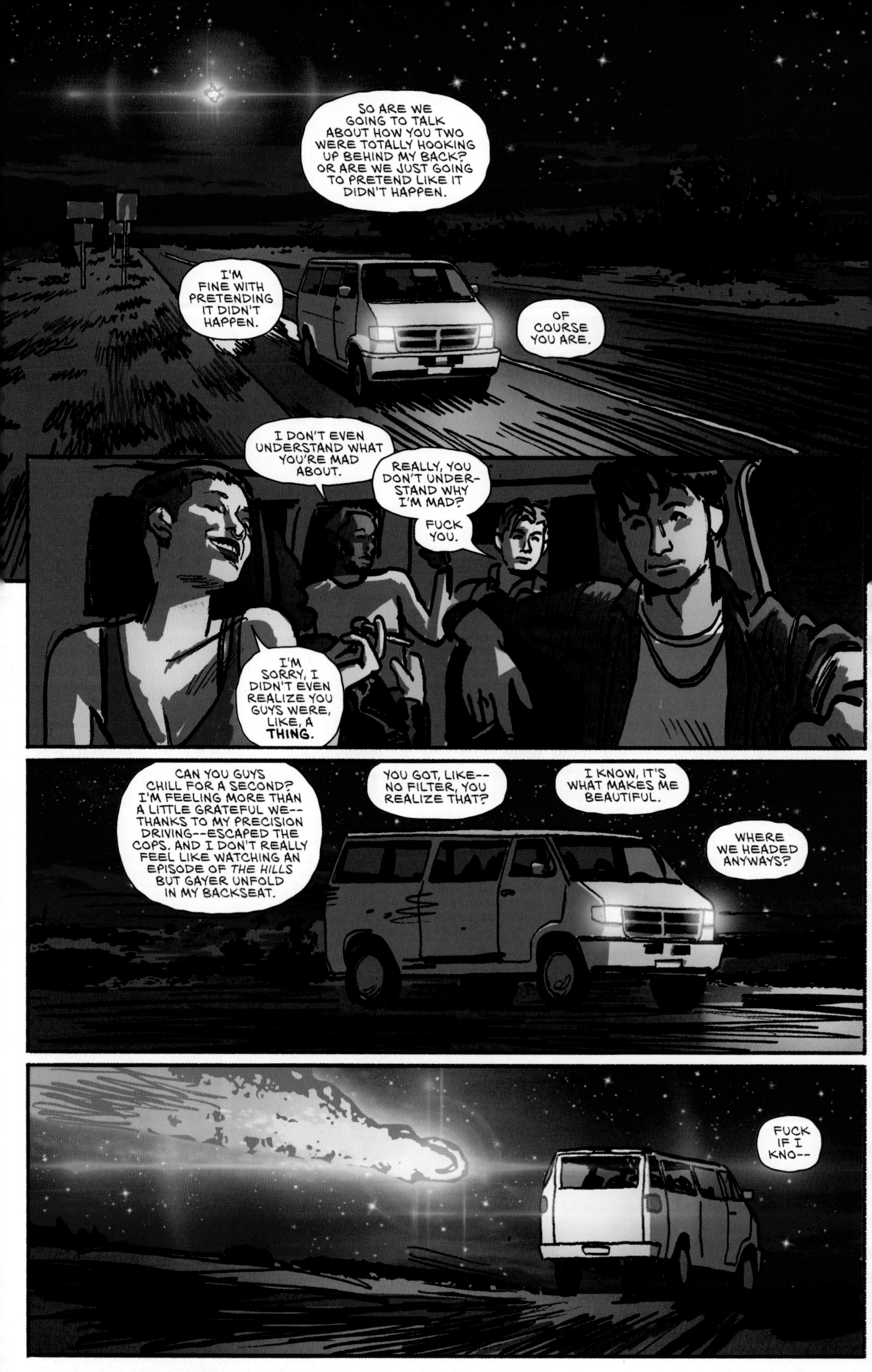
SO ARE WE GOING TO TALK ABOUT HOW YOU TWO WERE TOTALLY HOOKING UP BEHIND MY BACK? OR ARE WE JUST GOING TO PRETEND LIKE IT DIDN'T HAPPEN.
I'M FINE WITH PRETENDING IT DIDN'T HAPPEN.
OF COURSE YOU ARE.
I DON'T EVEN UNDERSTAND WHAT YOU'RE MAD ABOUT.
REALLY, YOU DON'T UNDERSTAND WHY I'M MAD?
FUCK YOU.
I'M SORRY, I DIDN'T EVEN REALIZE YOU GUYS WERE, LIKE, A **THING**.
CAN YOU GUYS CHILL FOR A SECOND? I'M FEELING MORE THAN A LITTLE GRATEFUL WE--THANKS TO MY PRECISION DRIVING--ESCAPED THE COPS. AND I DON'T REALLY FEEL LIKE WATCHING AN EPISODE OF *THE HILLS* BUT GAYER UNFOLD IN MY BACKSEAT.
YOU GOT, LIKE--NO FILTER, YOU REALIZE THAT?
I KNOW, IT'S WHAT MAKES ME BEAUTIFUL.
WHERE WE HEADED ANYWAYS?
FUCK IF I KNO--

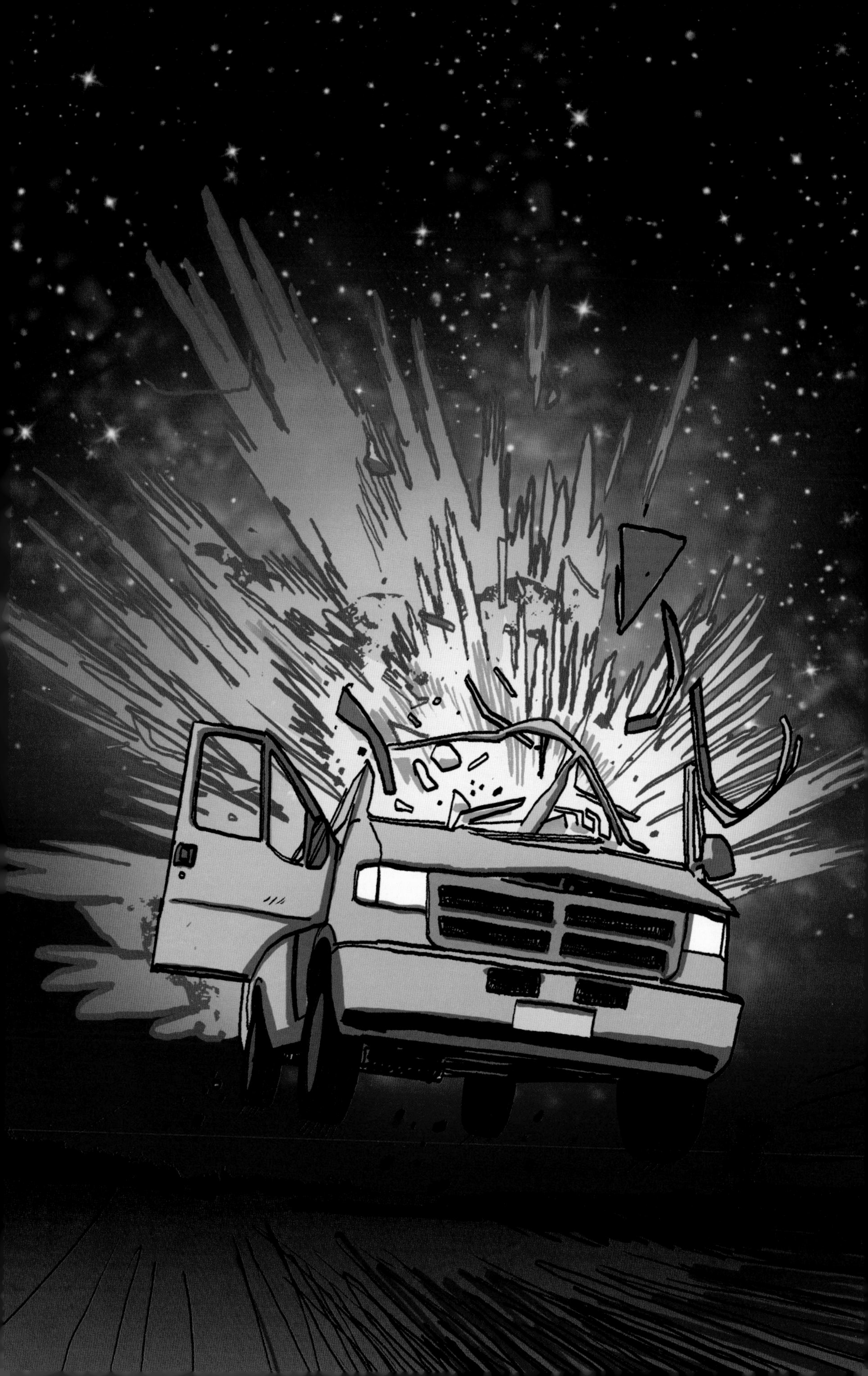

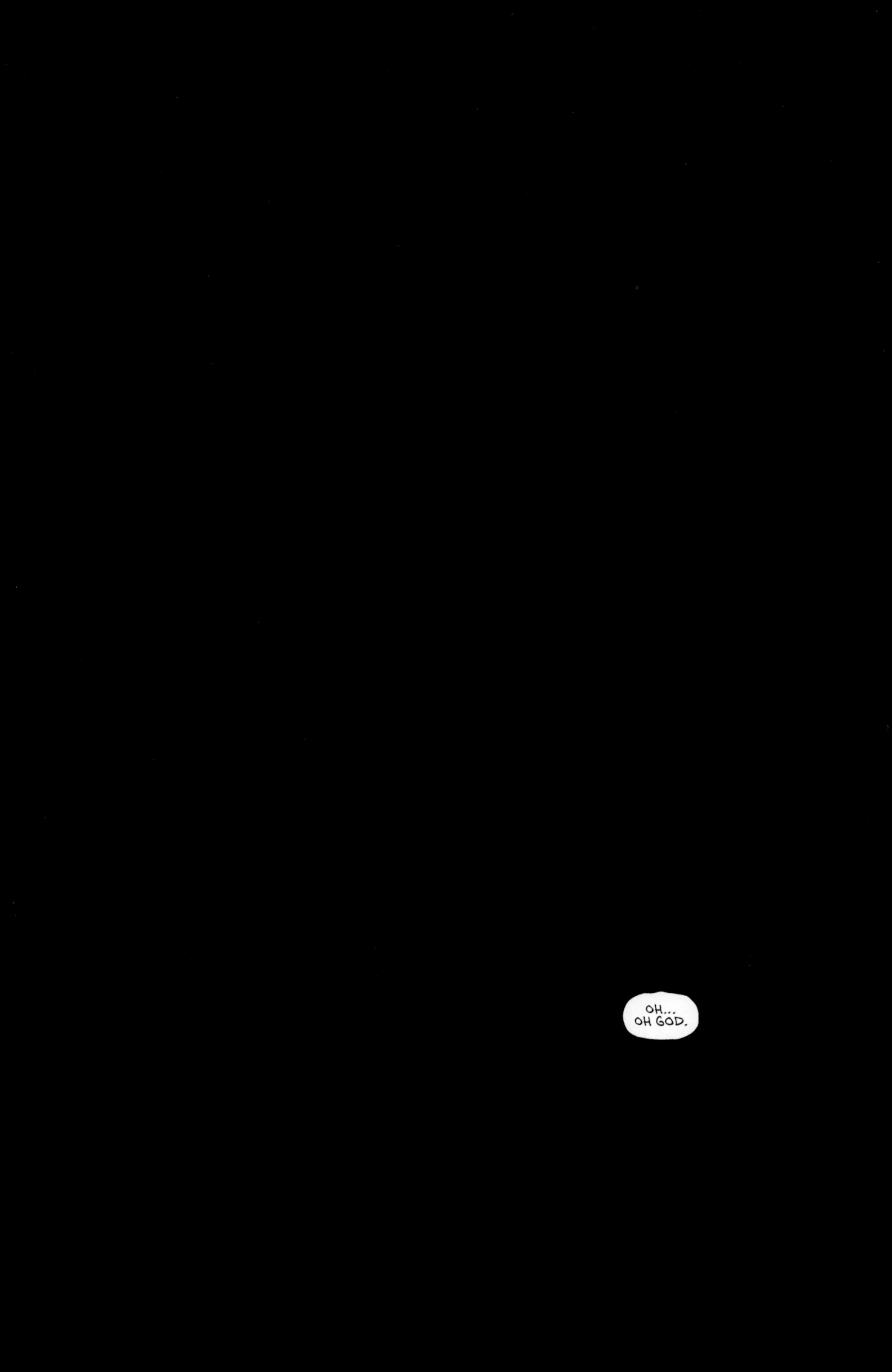
OH... OH GOD.

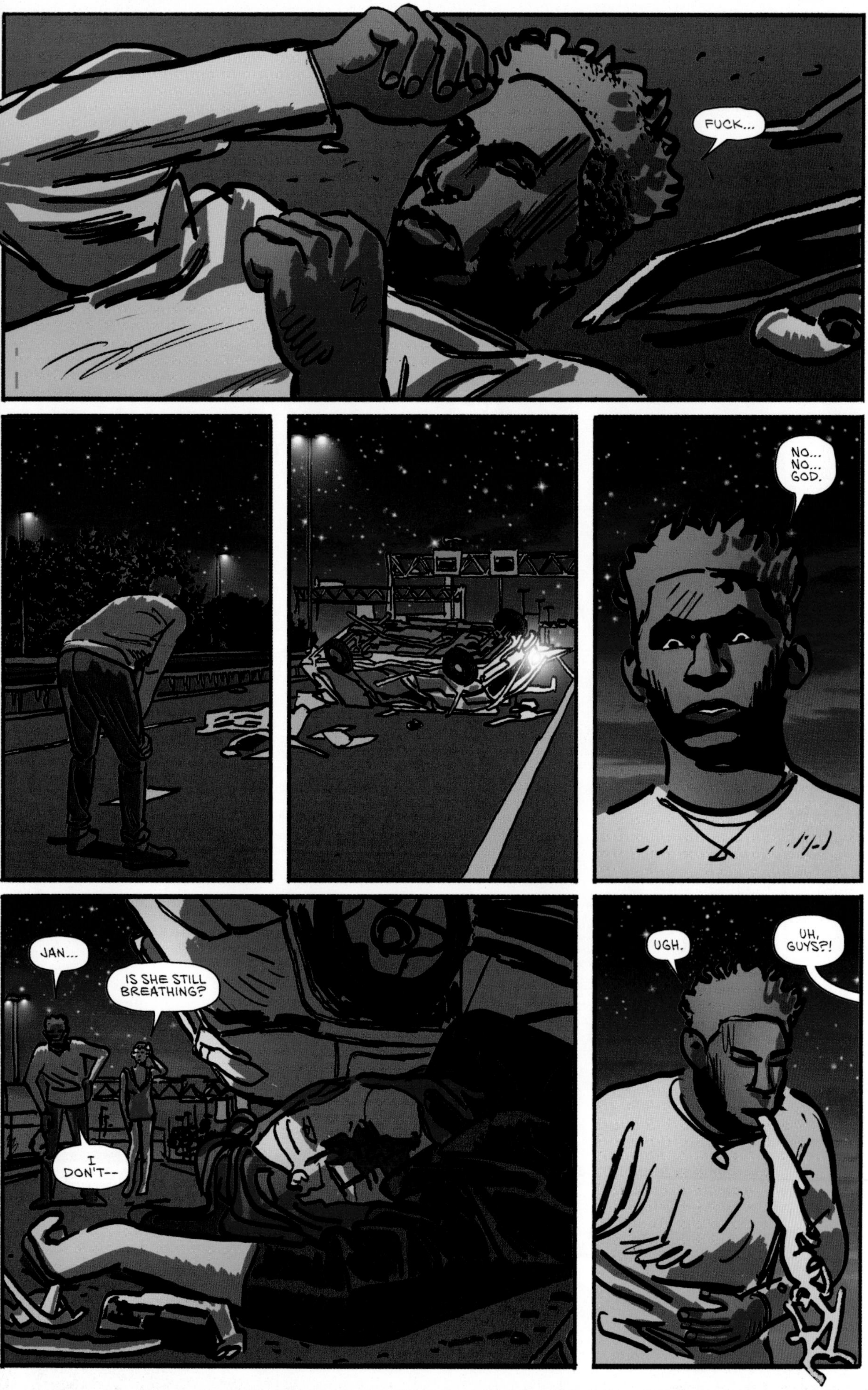
FUCK...
NO... NO... GOD.
JAN...
IS SHE STILL BREATHING?
I DON'T--
UGH.
UH, GUYS?!

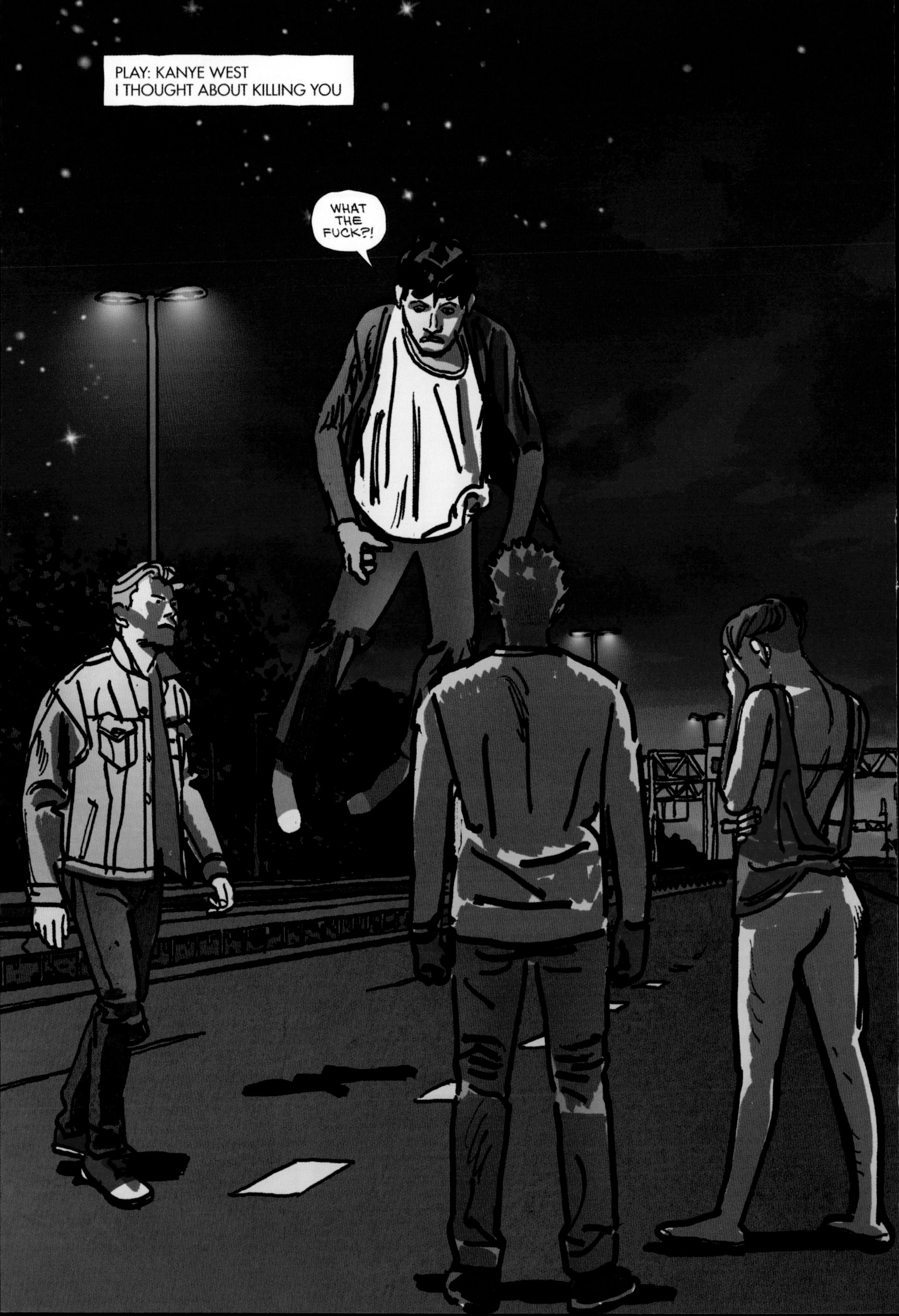
PLAY: KANYE WEST
I THOUGHT ABOUT KILLING YOU
WHAT THE FUCK?!

Youth

Youth

Chapter One

Nostalgia Overdrive

"The violence of love
is as much to be dreaded
as that of hate."
– Henry David Thoreau

SPECIAL THANKS:
Ed Brisson, Lawrence

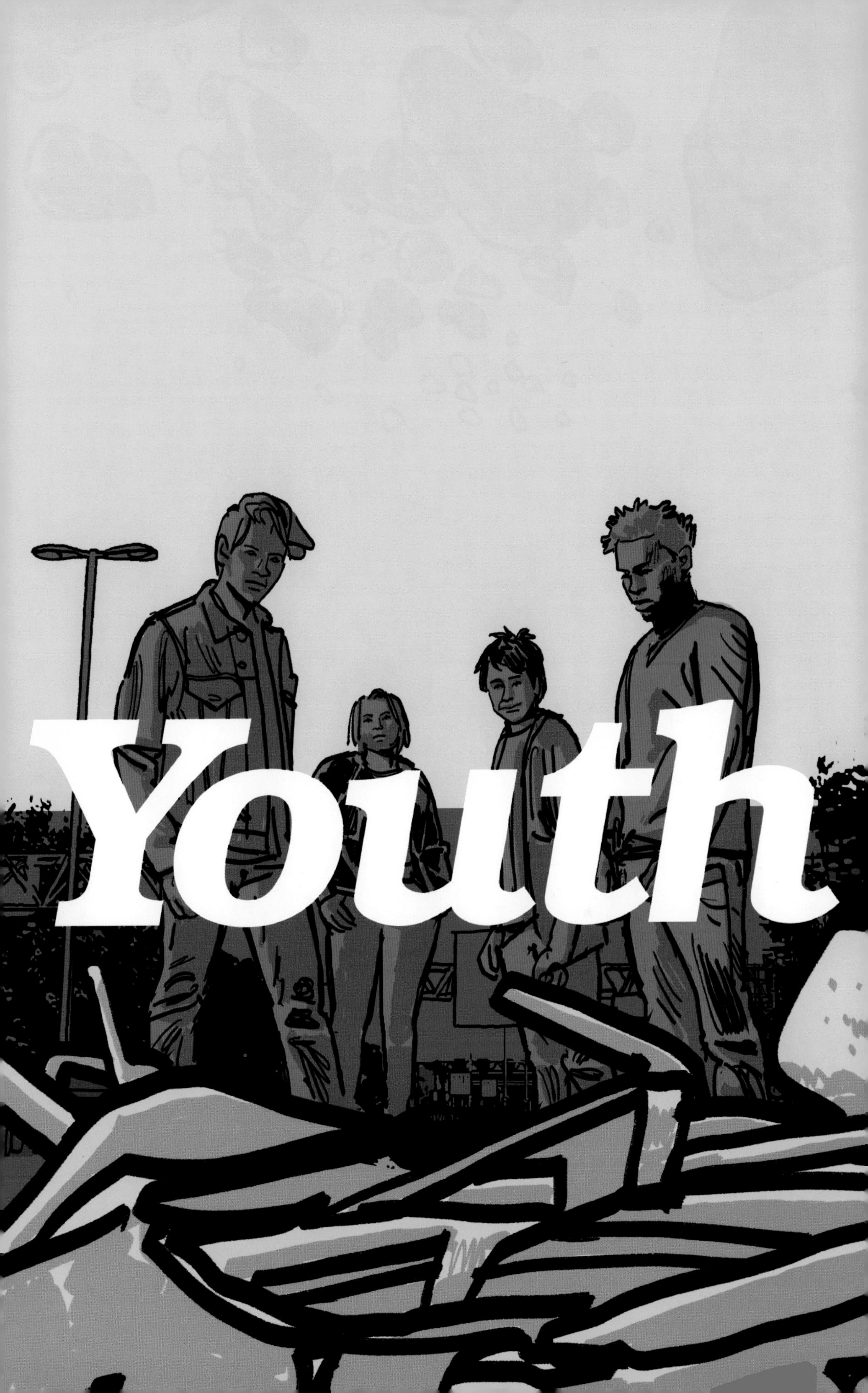
Youth

FIND MYSELF
THINKING 'BOUT THE
START OF THINGS.

NOW, I AIN'T TALKING ABOUT
WHAT HAPPENED TO US.

OR EVEN MYSELF, IN
PARTICULAR. I'M TALKING--
I'M THINKING IN A BROADER
CONTEXT HERE.

I'M TALKING ABOUT
EVERYTHING.

NOW SOME FOLKS, THEY'D HAVE
YOU BELIEVE THE WORLD IS COLD
AND RANDOM. THAT ALL THIS
LIFE--ALL THIS VASTLY COMPLEX
UNIVERSE JUST CAME SPRINGING
INTO BEING THROUGH MILLENNIA OF
MISTAKES AND ACCIDENTS.

OTHER FOLKS LIKE TO
IMAGINE SOME BEARDED
OLD WHITE DUDE, MAKING
SHIT IN SEVEN DAYS.

ME? LIKE MOST THINGS I
THINK THE TRUTH IS
SOMEWHERE IN BETWEEN.

ONE THING'S FOR
CERTAIN THOUGH...

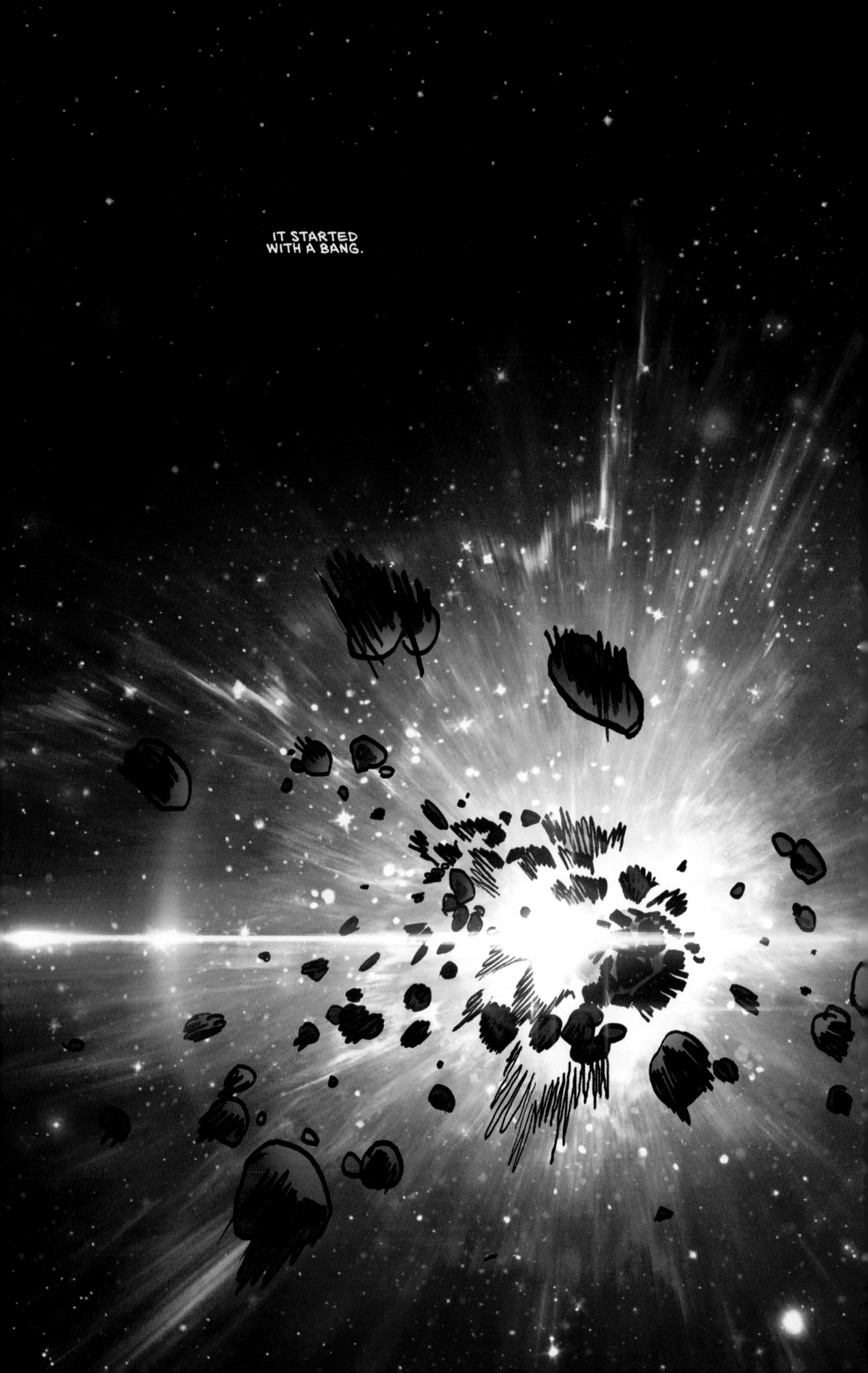
IT STARTED WITH A BANG.

PLAY: DEBUSSY - CLAIR DE LUNE

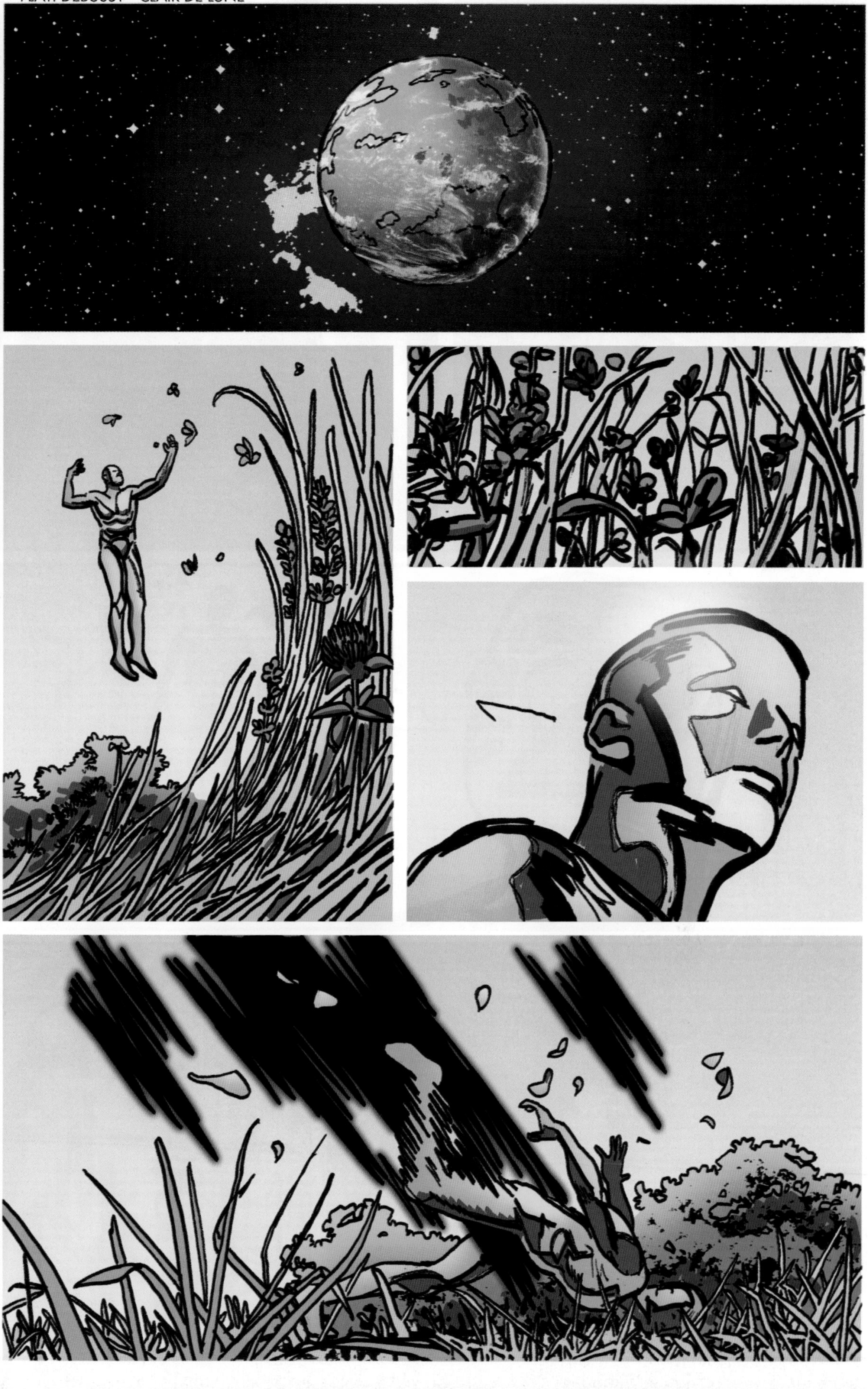

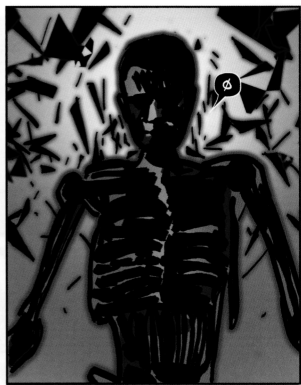

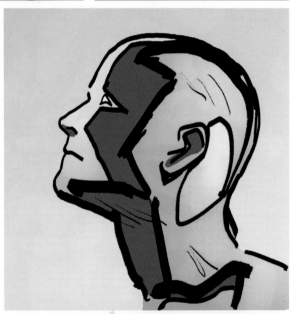

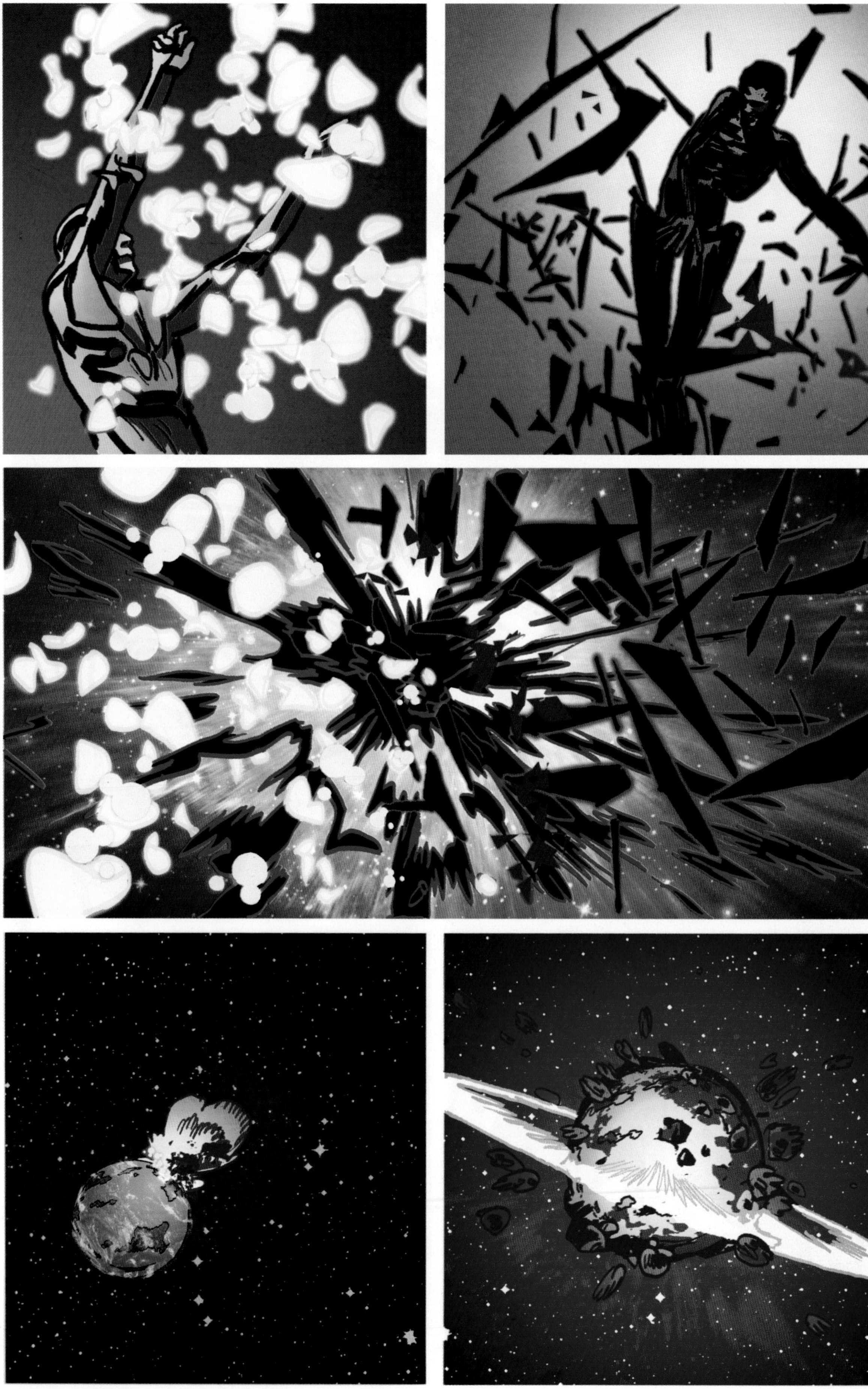

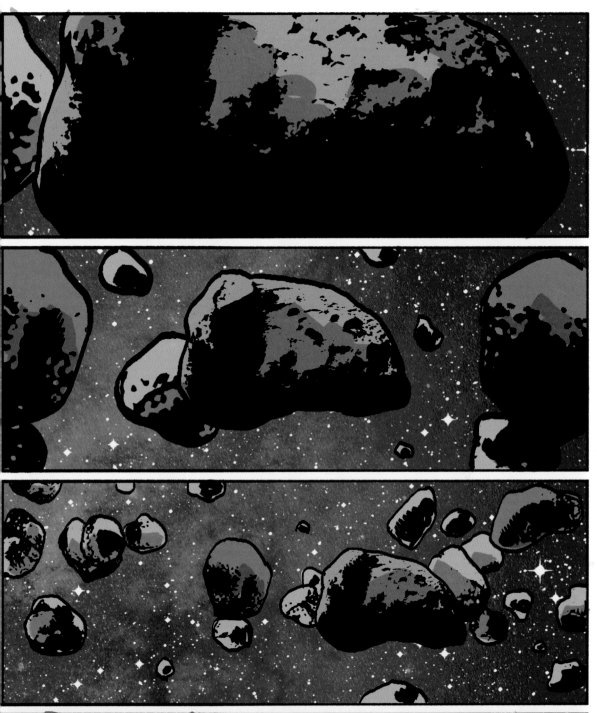

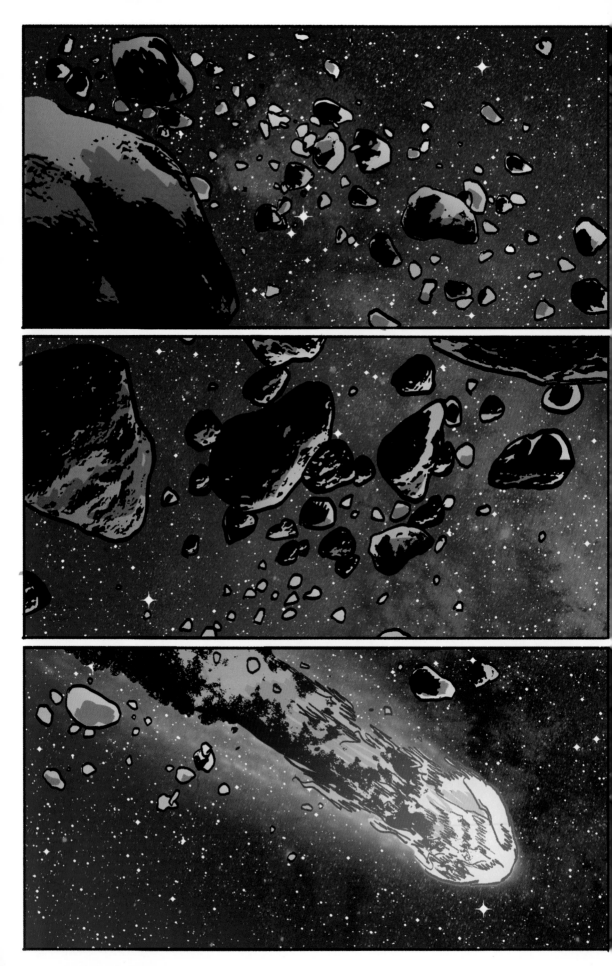

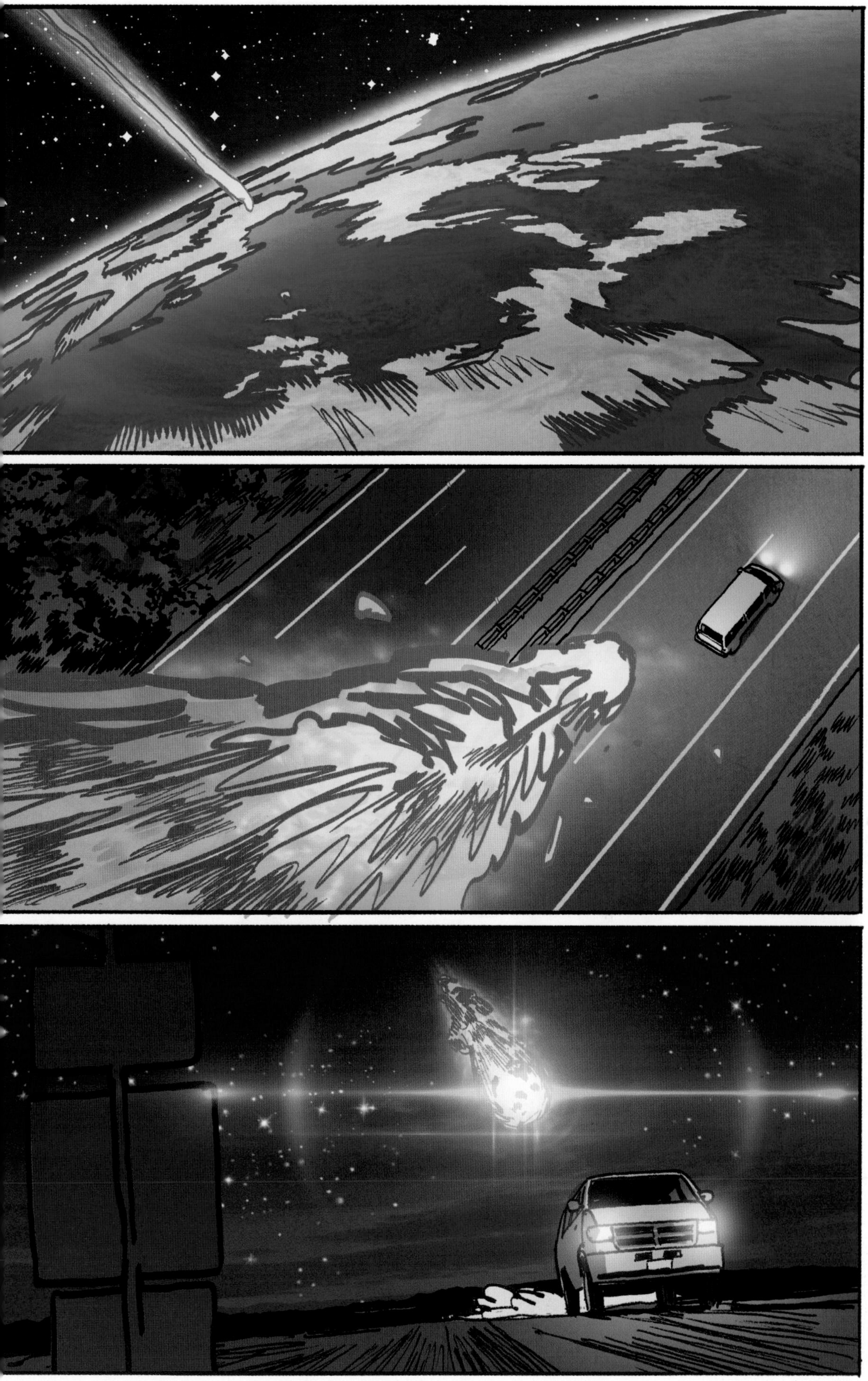

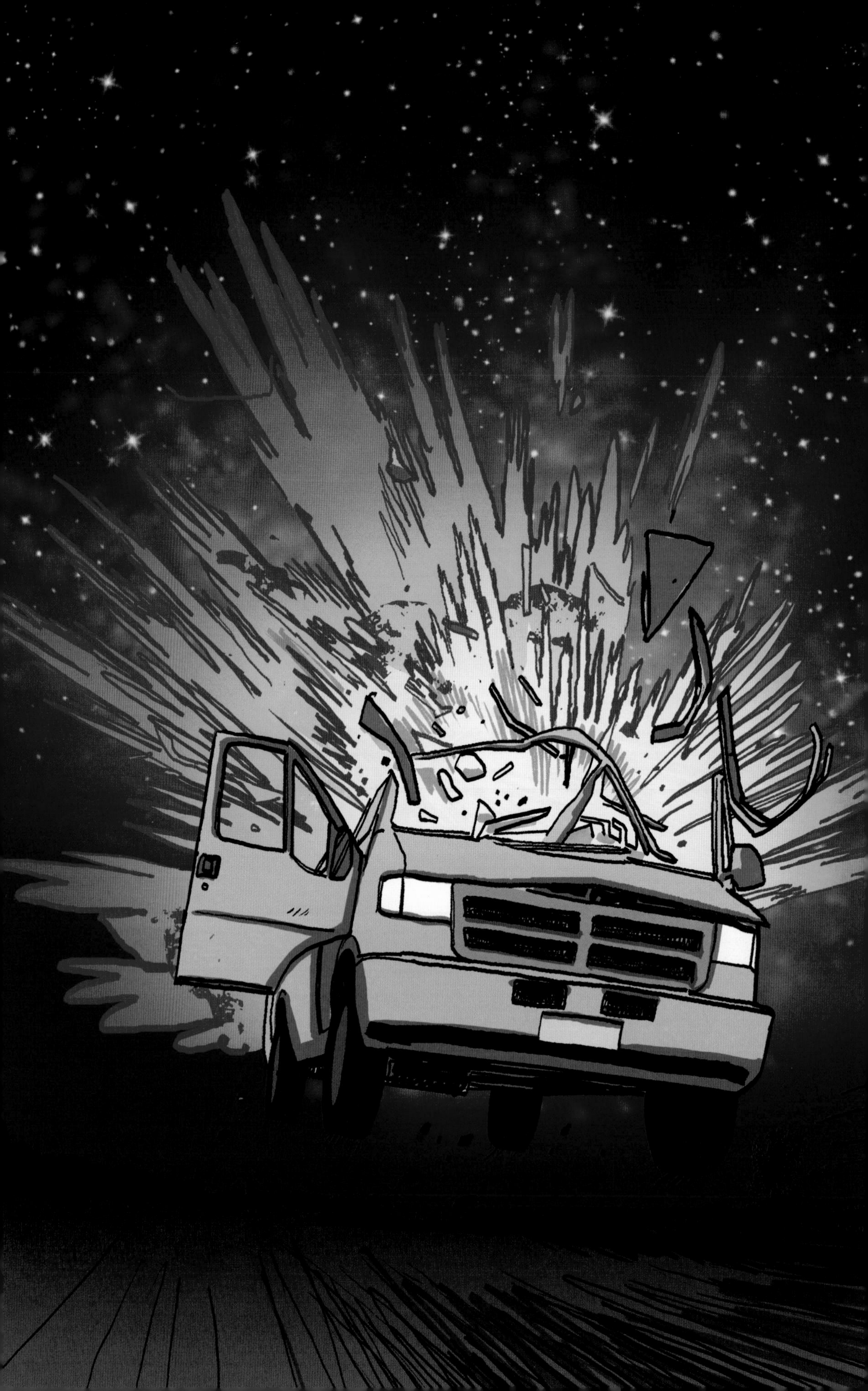

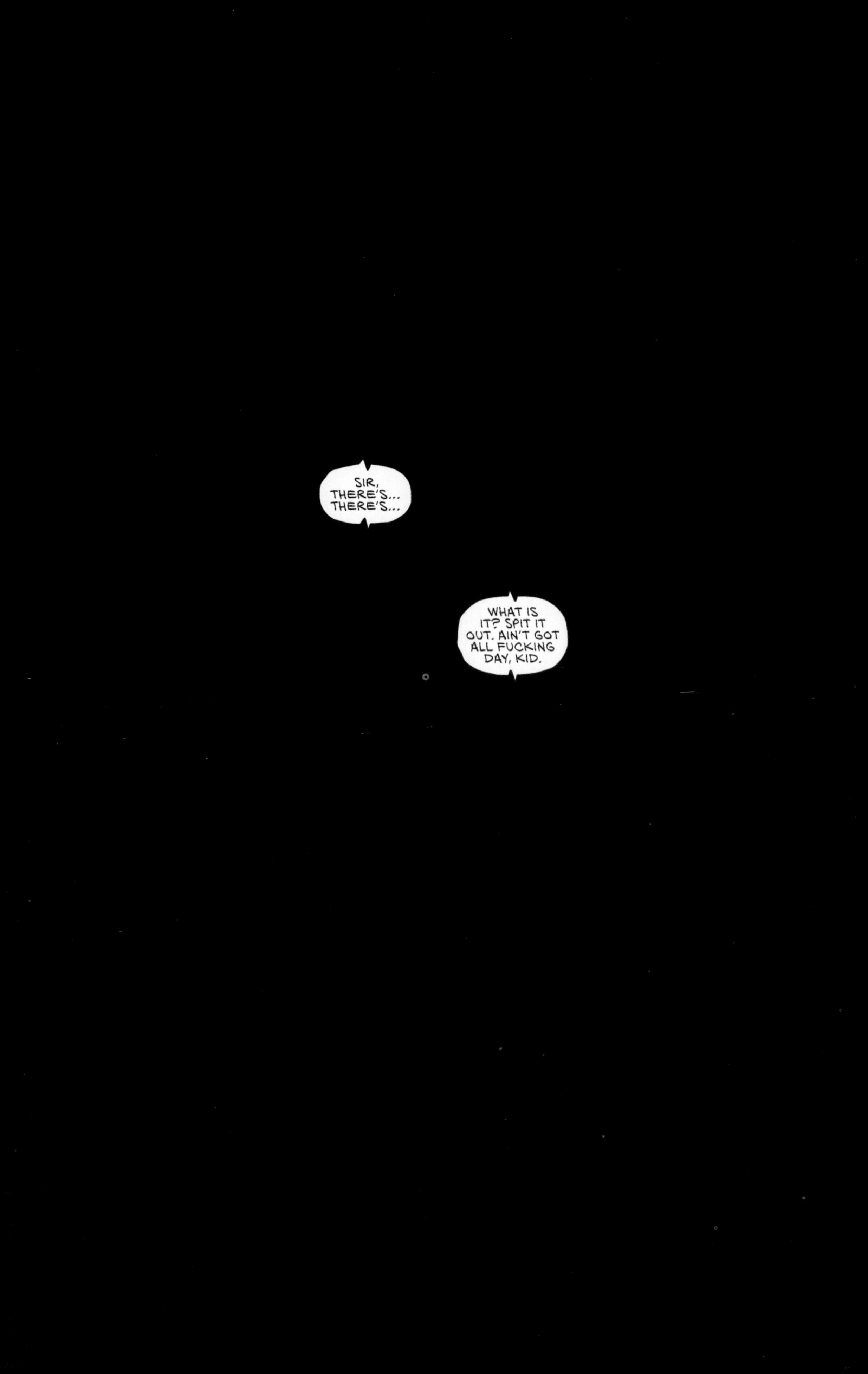
SIR, THERE'S... THERE'S...
WHAT IS IT? SPIT IT OUT. AIN'T GOT ALL FUCKING DAY, KID.

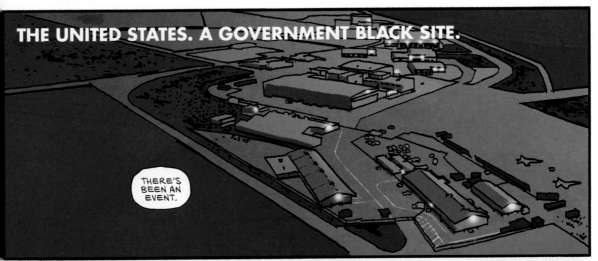

THE UNITED STATES. A GOVERNMENT BLACK SITE.

THERE'S BEEN AN EVENT.

SCRAMBLE A TEAM.

WHAT?

WAS I SPEAKING CHINESE?!

DON THUNDER.
GOVERNMENT SUPERSPY.
Bootleg Nick Fury.

SCRAMBLE A FUCKING TEAM.

WHERE THEY HIRING YOU ASSHOLES, ANYWAYS?

MY DAD WAS A CONGRESSM--

SHUT THE FUCK UP.

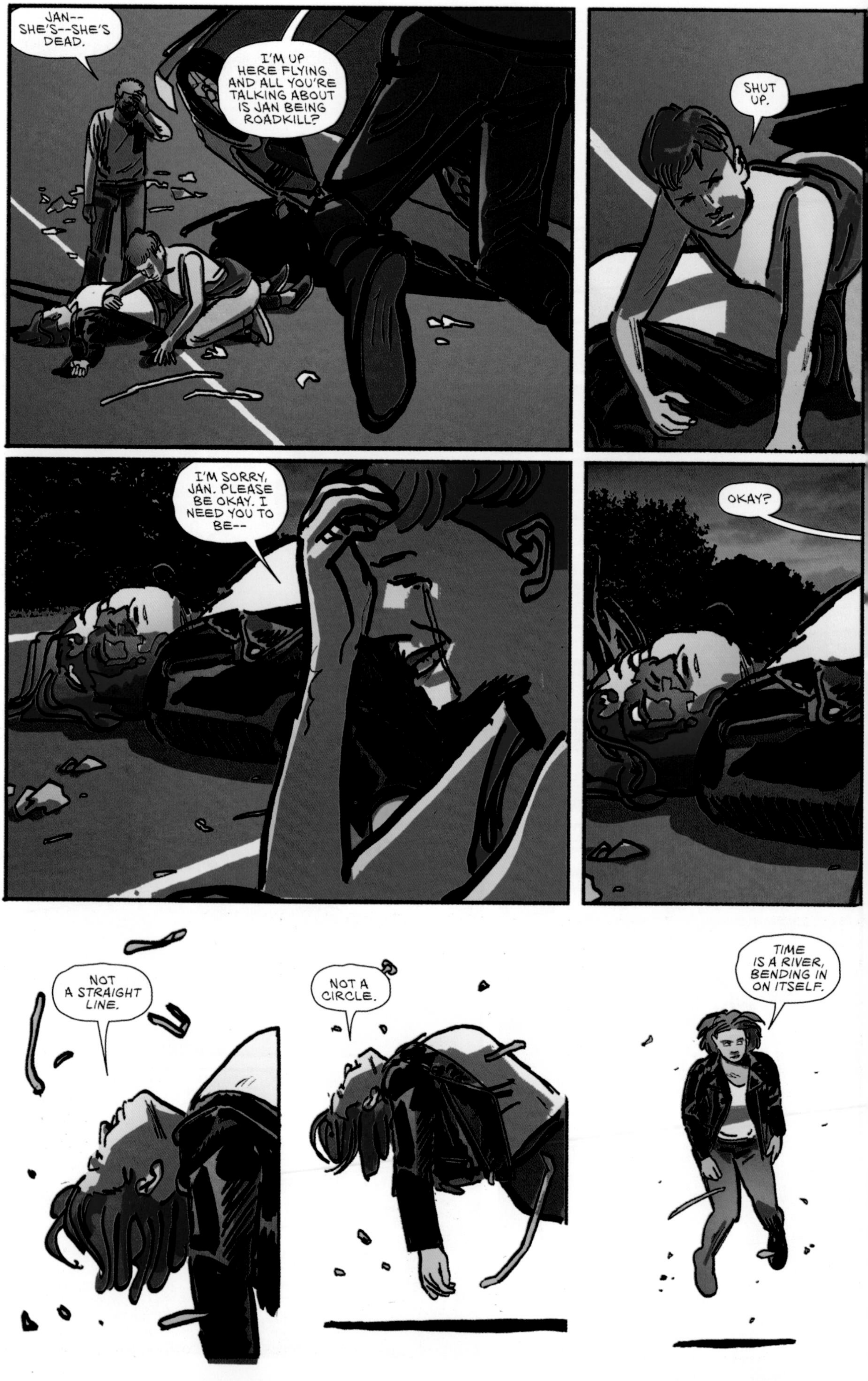
JAN-- SHE'S--SHE'S DEAD.
I'M UP HERE FLYING AND ALL YOU'RE TALKING ABOUT IS JAN BEING ROADKILL?
SHUT UP.
I'M SORRY, JAN. PLEASE BE OKAY. I NEED YOU TO BE--
OKAY?
NOT A STRAIGHT LINE.
NOT A CIRCLE.
TIME IS A RIVER, BENDING IN ON ITSELF.

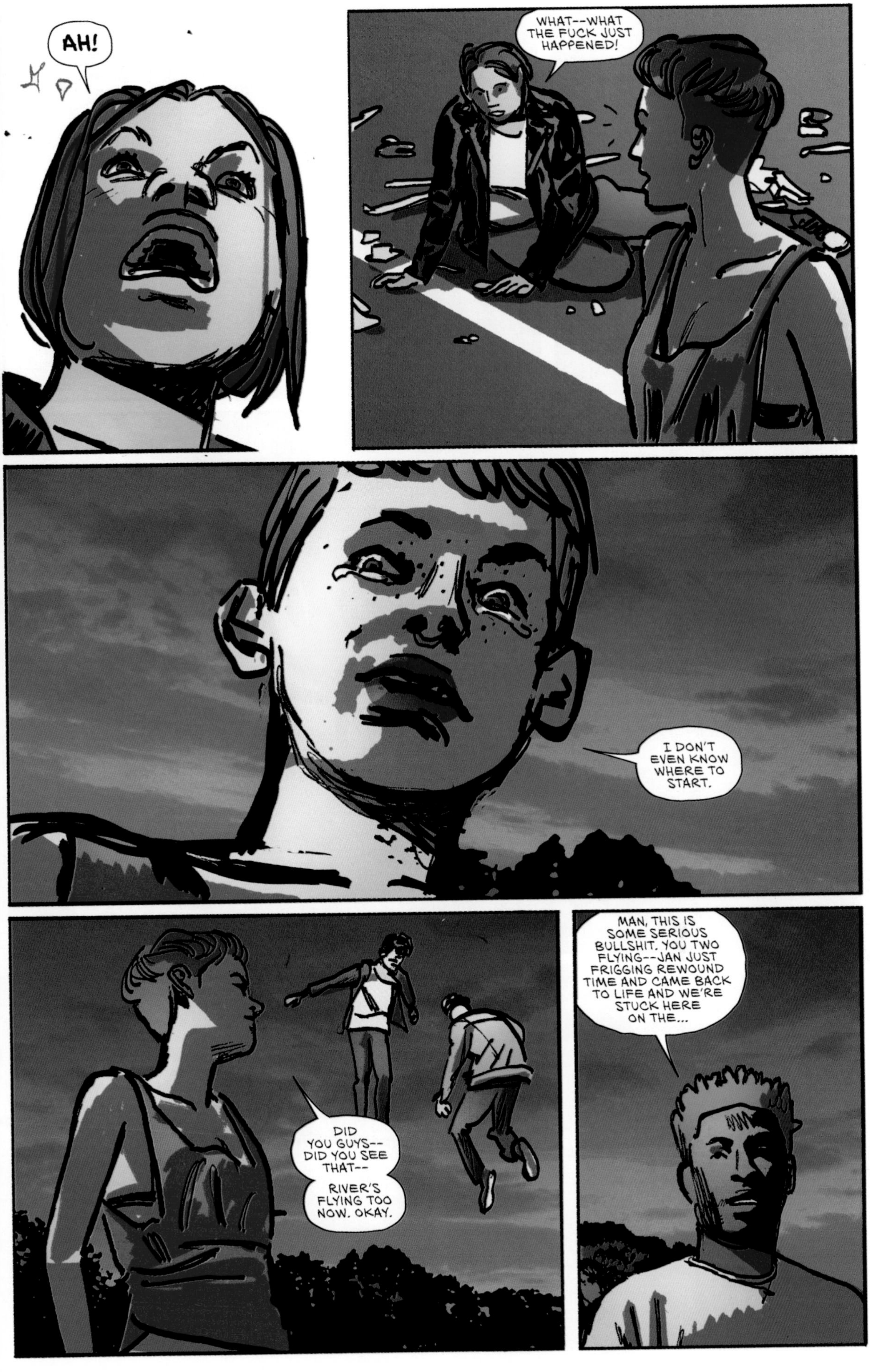
AH!
WHAT--WHAT THE FUCK JUST HAPPENED!
I DON'T EVEN KNOW WHERE TO START.
DID YOU GUYS-- DID YOU SEE THAT--
RIVER'S FLYING TOO NOW. OKAY.
MAN, THIS IS SOME SERIOUS BULLSHIT. YOU TWO FLYING--JAN JUST FRIGGING REWOUND TIME AND CAME BACK TO LIFE AND WE'RE STUCK HERE ON THE...

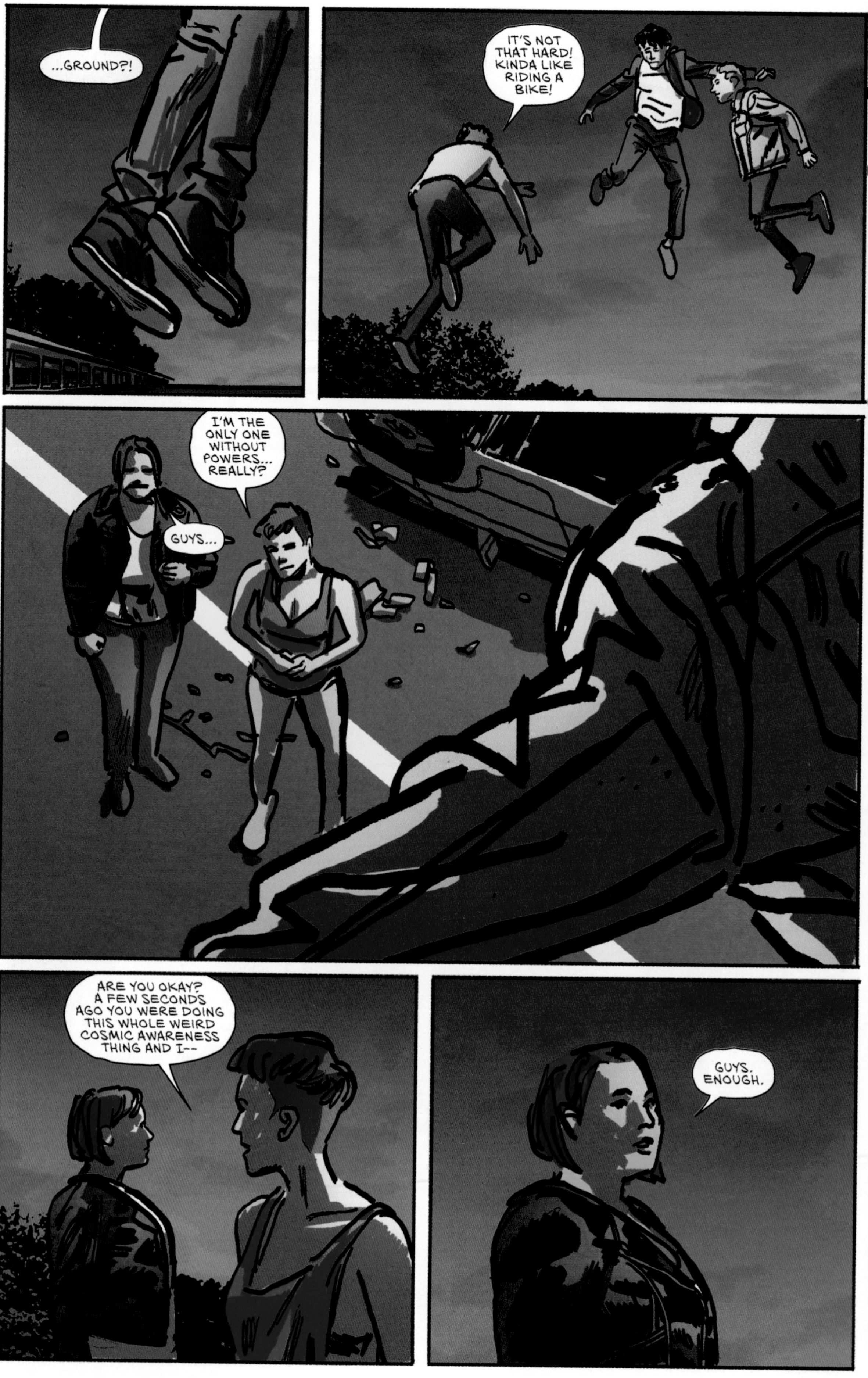
...GROUND?!
IT'S NOT THAT HARD! KINDA LIKE RIDING A BIKE!
I'M THE ONLY ONE WITHOUT POWERS... REALLY?
GUYS...
ARE YOU OKAY? A FEW SECONDS AGO YOU WERE DOING THIS WHOLE WEIRD COSMIC AWARENESS THING AND I--
GUYS. ENOUGH.

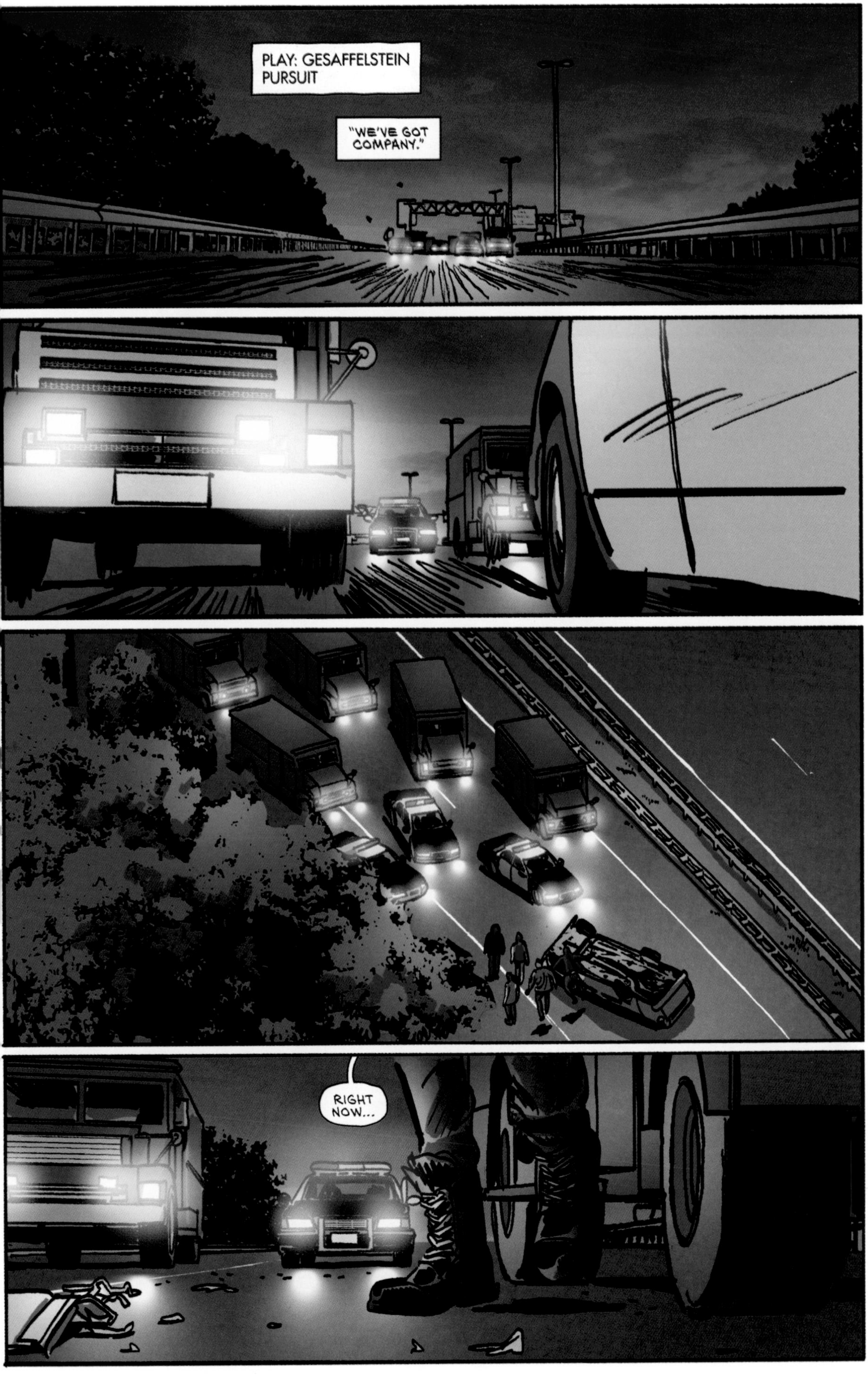
PLAY: GESAFFELSTEIN PURSUIT
"WE'VE GOT COMPANY."
RIGHT NOW...

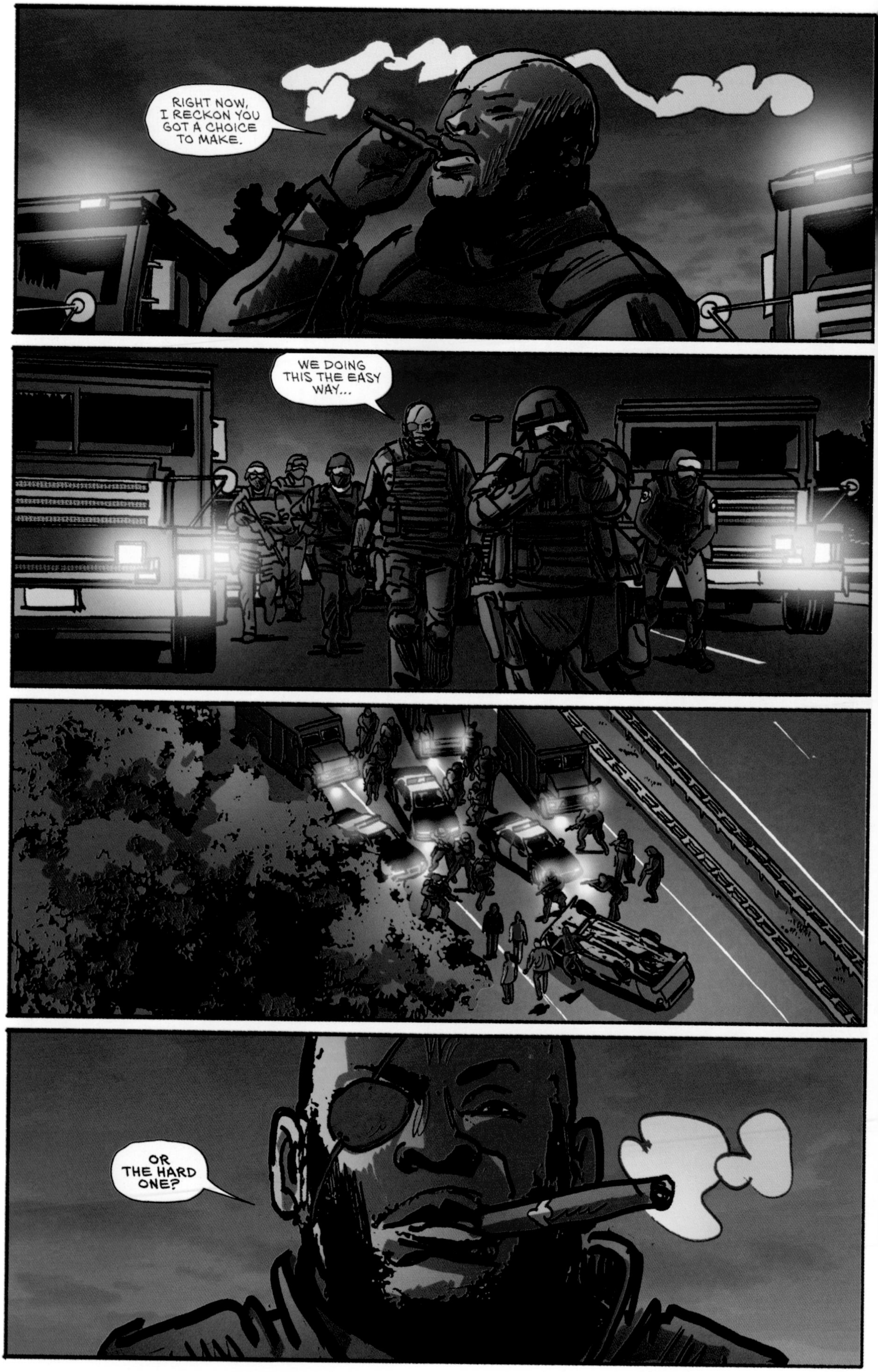
RIGHT NOW, I RECKON YOU GOT A CHOICE TO MAKE.
WE DOING THIS THE EASY WAY...
OR THE HARD ONE?

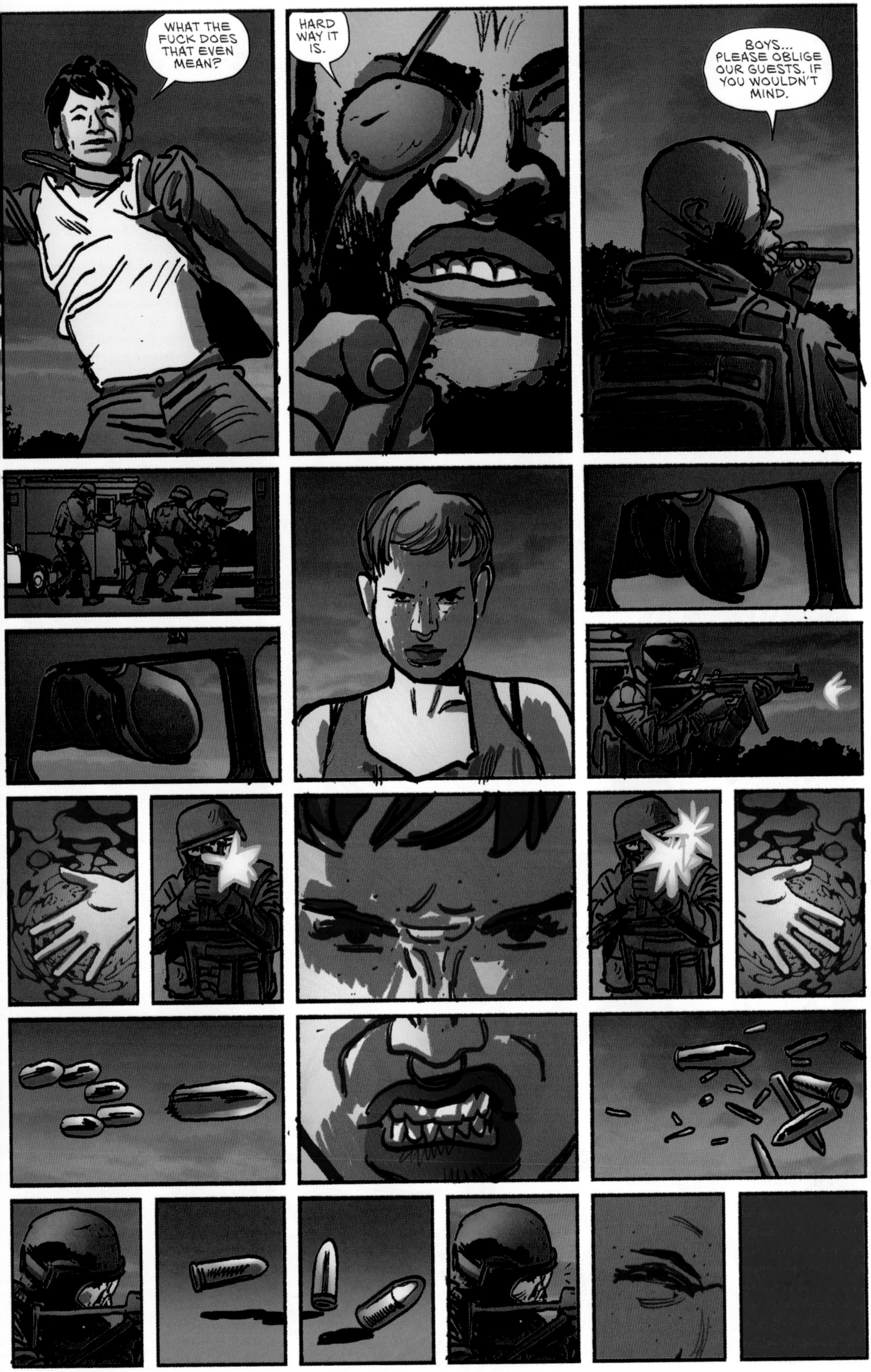
WHAT THE FUCK DOES THAT EVEN MEAN?
HARD WAY IT IS.
BOYS... PLEASE OBLIGE OUR GUESTS. IF YOU WOULDN'T MIND.

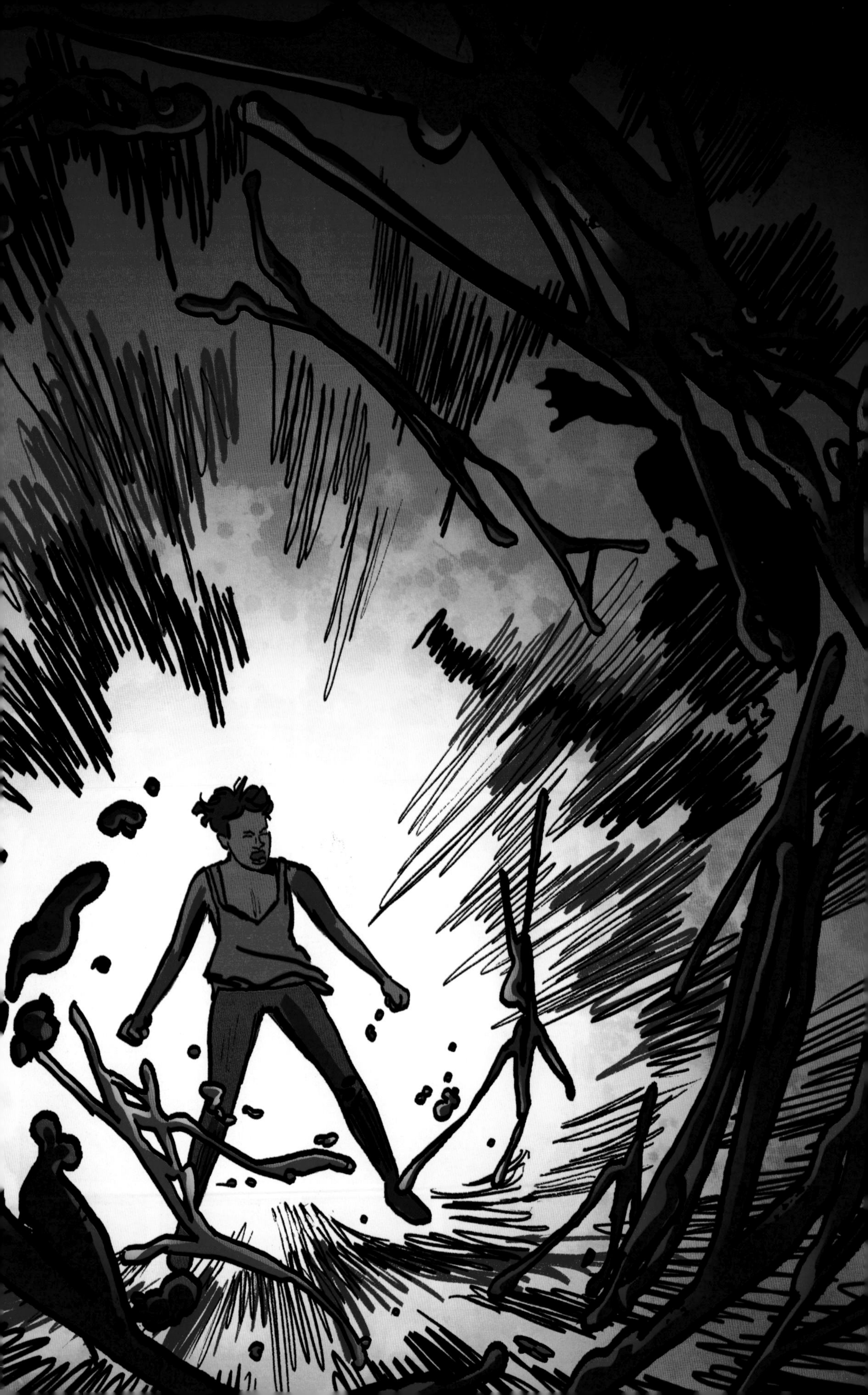

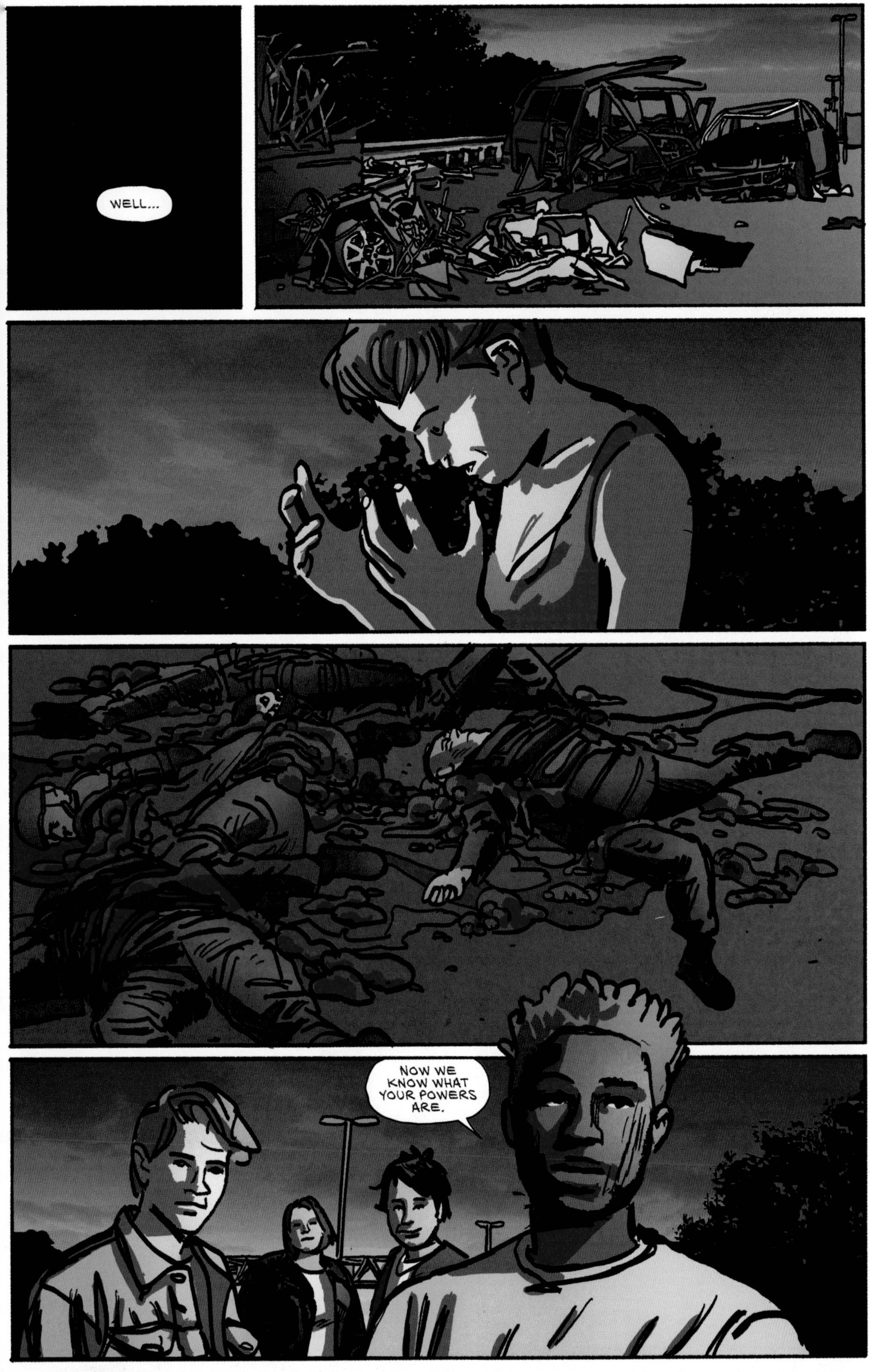
WELL...
NOW WE KNOW WHAT YOUR POWERS ARE.

Youth

Chapter Two

Celestial Navigations

"The nitrogen in our DNA,
the calcium in our teeth, the
iron in our blood, the carbon in
our apple pies were made in the
interiors of collapsing stars.
We are made of starstuff."
– Carl Sagan

Youth

Youth

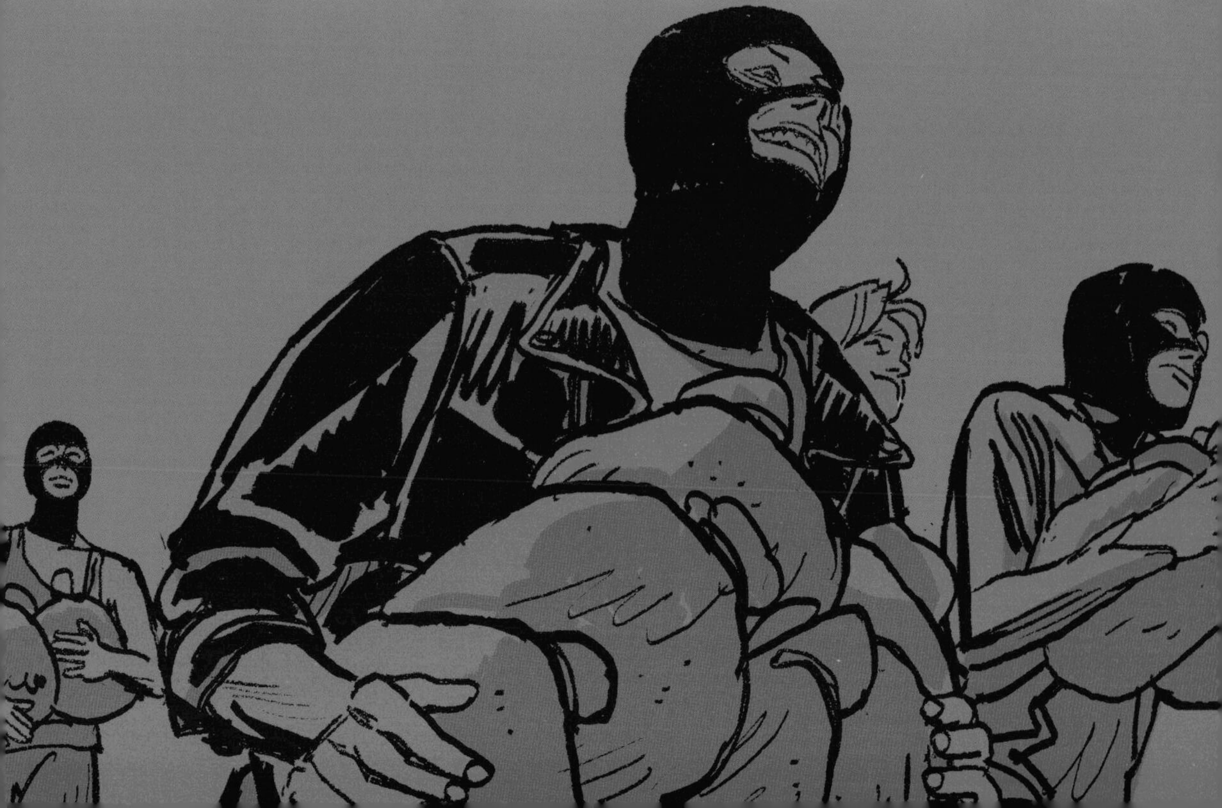

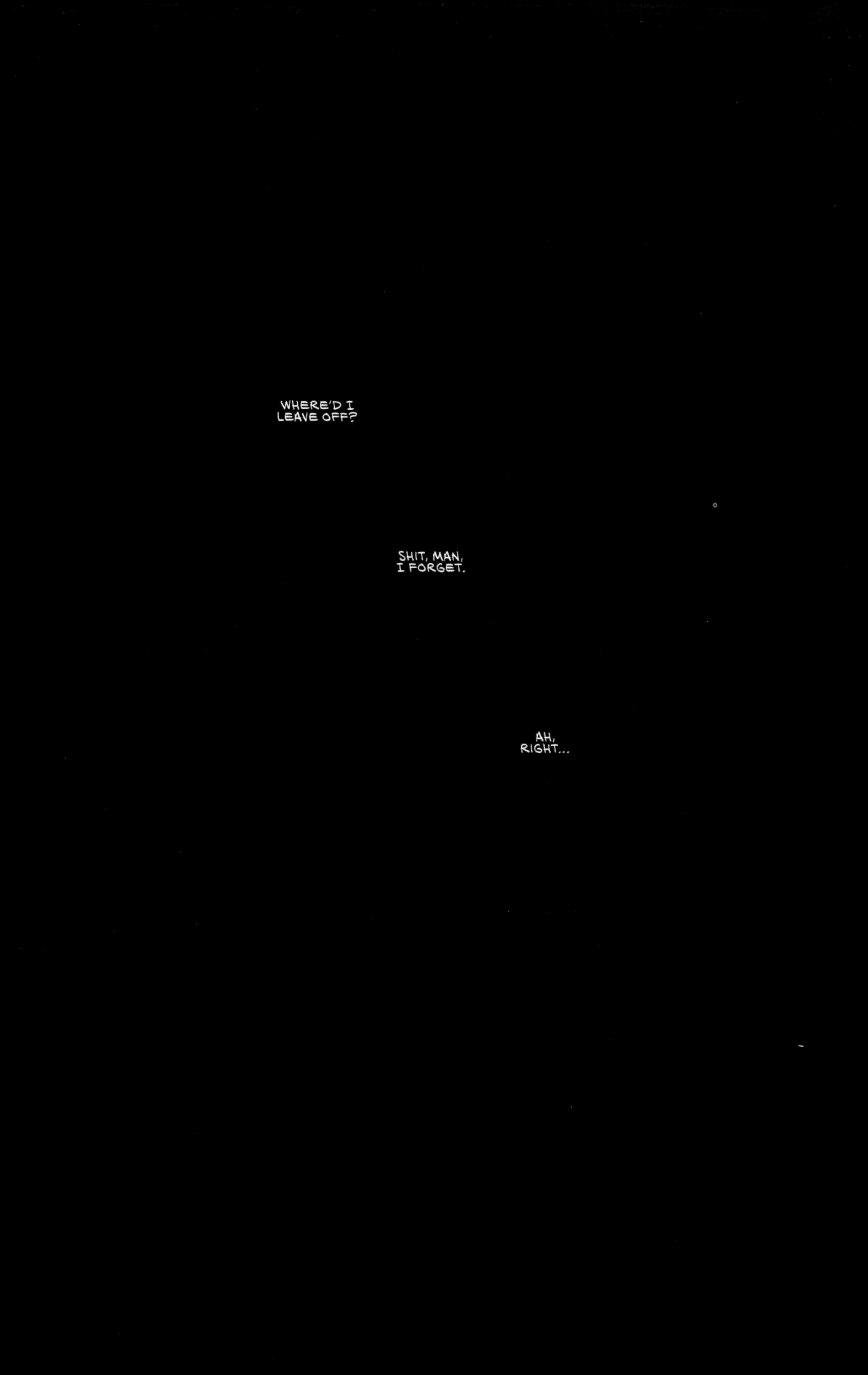
WHERE'D I LEAVE OFF?
SHIT, MAN, I FORGET.
AH, RIGHT...

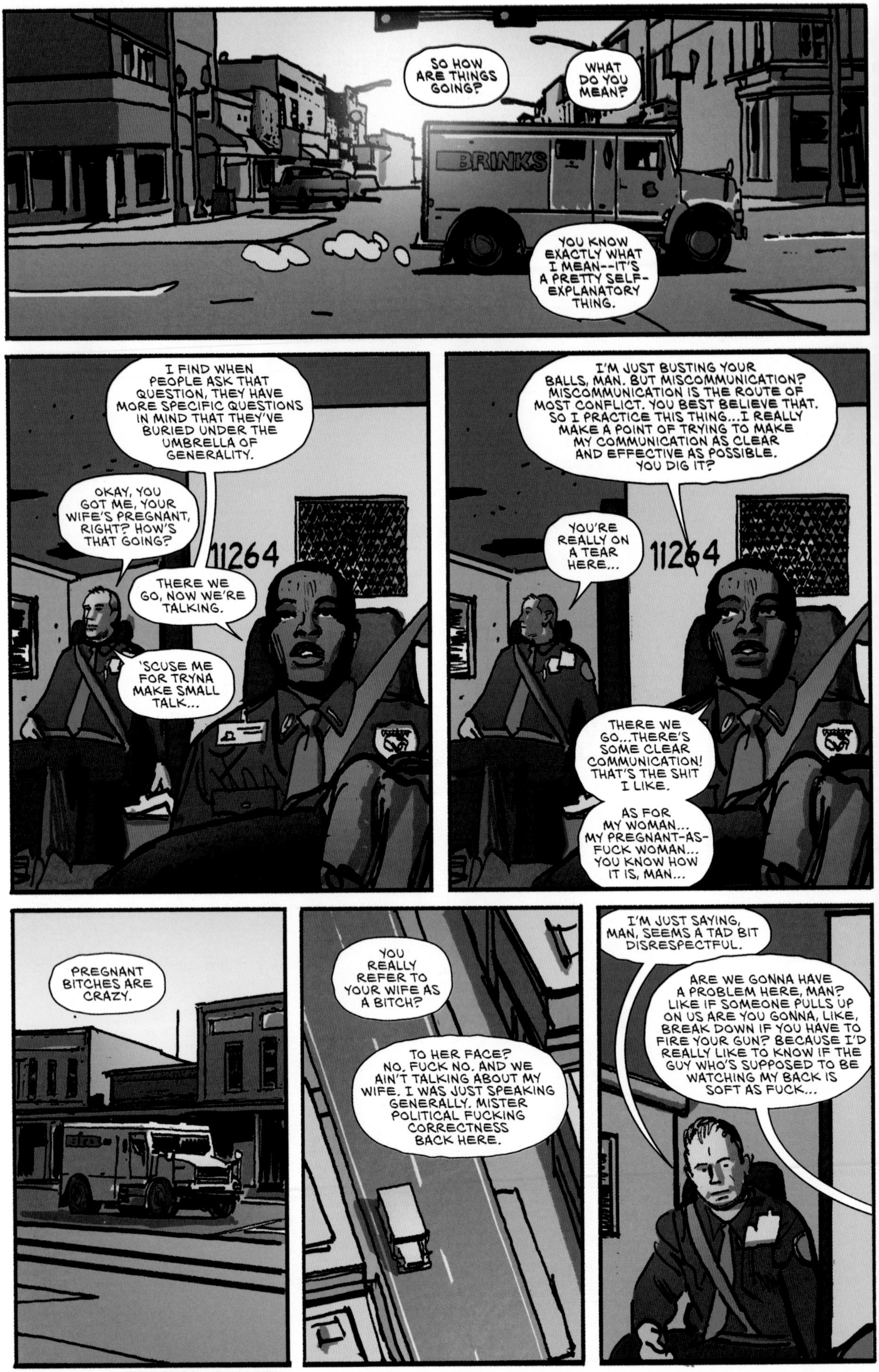

SO HOW ARE THINGS GOING?
WHAT DO YOU MEAN?
YOU KNOW EXACTLY WHAT I MEAN--IT'S A PRETTY SELF-EXPLANATORY THING.
BRINKS
I FIND WHEN PEOPLE ASK THAT QUESTION, THEY HAVE MORE SPECIFIC QUESTIONS IN MIND THAT THEY'VE BURIED UNDER THE UMBRELLA OF GENERALITY.
OKAY, YOU GOT ME, YOUR WIFE'S PREGNANT, RIGHT? HOW'S THAT GOING?
THERE WE GO, NOW WE'RE TALKING.
'SCUSE ME FOR TRYNA MAKE SMALL TALK...
11264
I'M JUST BUSTING YOUR BALLS, MAN. BUT MISCOMMUNICATION? MISCOMMUNICATION IS THE ROUTE OF MOST CONFLICT. YOU BEST BELIEVE THAT. SO I PRACTICE THIS THING...I REALLY MAKE A POINT OF TRYING TO MAKE MY COMMUNICATION AS CLEAR AND EFFECTIVE AS POSSIBLE. YOU DIG IT?
YOU'RE REALLY ON A TEAR HERE...
11264
THERE WE GO...THERE'S SOME CLEAR COMMUNICATION! THAT'S THE SHIT I LIKE.
AS FOR MY WOMAN... MY PREGNANT-AS-FUCK WOMAN... YOU KNOW HOW IT IS, MAN...
PREGNANT BITCHES ARE CRAZY.
YOU REALLY REFER TO YOUR WIFE AS A BITCH?
TO HER FACE? NO. FUCK NO. AND WE AIN'T TALKING ABOUT MY WIFE. I WAS JUST SPEAKING GENERALLY. MISTER POLITICAL FUCKING CORRECTNESS BACK HERE.
I'M JUST SAYING, MAN, SEEMS A TAD BIT DISRESPECTFUL.
ARE WE GONNA HAVE A PROBLEM HERE, MAN? LIKE IF SOMEONE PULLS UP ON US ARE YOU GONNA, LIKE, BREAK DOWN IF YOU HAVE TO FIRE YOUR GUN? BECAUSE I'D REALLY LIKE TO KNOW IF THE GUY WHO'S SUPPOSED TO BE WATCHING MY BACK IS SOFT AS FUCK...

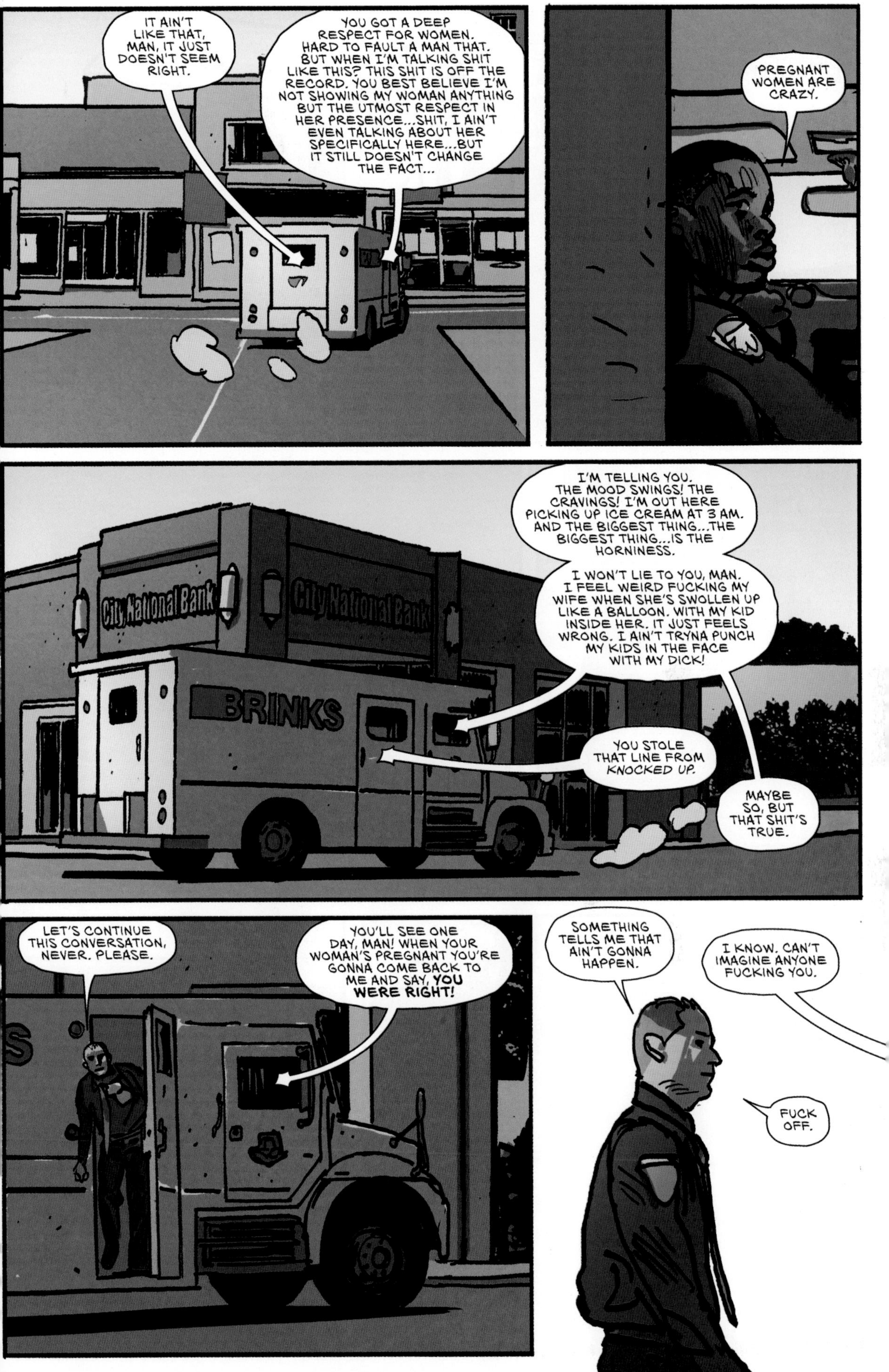
IT AIN'T LIKE THAT, MAN, IT JUST DOESN'T SEEM RIGHT.
YOU GOT A DEEP RESPECT FOR WOMEN. HARD TO FAULT A MAN THAT. BUT WHEN I'M TALKING SHIT LIKE THIS? THIS SHIT IS OFF THE RECORD. YOU BEST BELIEVE I'M NOT SHOWING MY WOMAN ANYTHING BUT THE UTMOST RESPECT IN HER PRESENCE...SHIT, I AIN'T EVEN TALKING ABOUT HER SPECIFICALLY HERE...BUT IT STILL DOESN'T CHANGE THE FACT...
PREGNANT WOMEN ARE CRAZY.
City National Bank
City National Bank
BRINKS
I'M TELLING YOU. THE MOOD SWINGS! THE CRAVINGS! I'M OUT HERE PICKING UP ICE CREAM AT 3 AM. AND THE BIGGEST THING...THE BIGGEST THING...IS THE HORNINESS.
I WON'T LIE TO YOU, MAN. I FEEL WEIRD FUCKING MY WIFE WHEN SHE'S SWOLLEN UP LIKE A BALLOON. WITH MY KID INSIDE HER. IT JUST FEELS WRONG. I AIN'T TRYNA PUNCH MY KIDS IN THE FACE WITH MY DICK!
YOU STOLE THAT LINE FROM *KNOCKED UP*.
MAYBE SO, BUT THAT SHIT'S TRUE.
LET'S CONTINUE THIS CONVERSATION, NEVER. PLEASE.
YOU'LL SEE ONE DAY, MAN! WHEN YOUR WOMAN'S PREGNANT YOU'RE GONNA COME BACK TO ME AND SAY, **YOU WERE RIGHT!**
SOMETHING TELLS ME THAT AIN'T GONNA HAPPEN.
I KNOW. CAN'T IMAGINE ANYONE FUCKING YOU.
FUCK OFF.

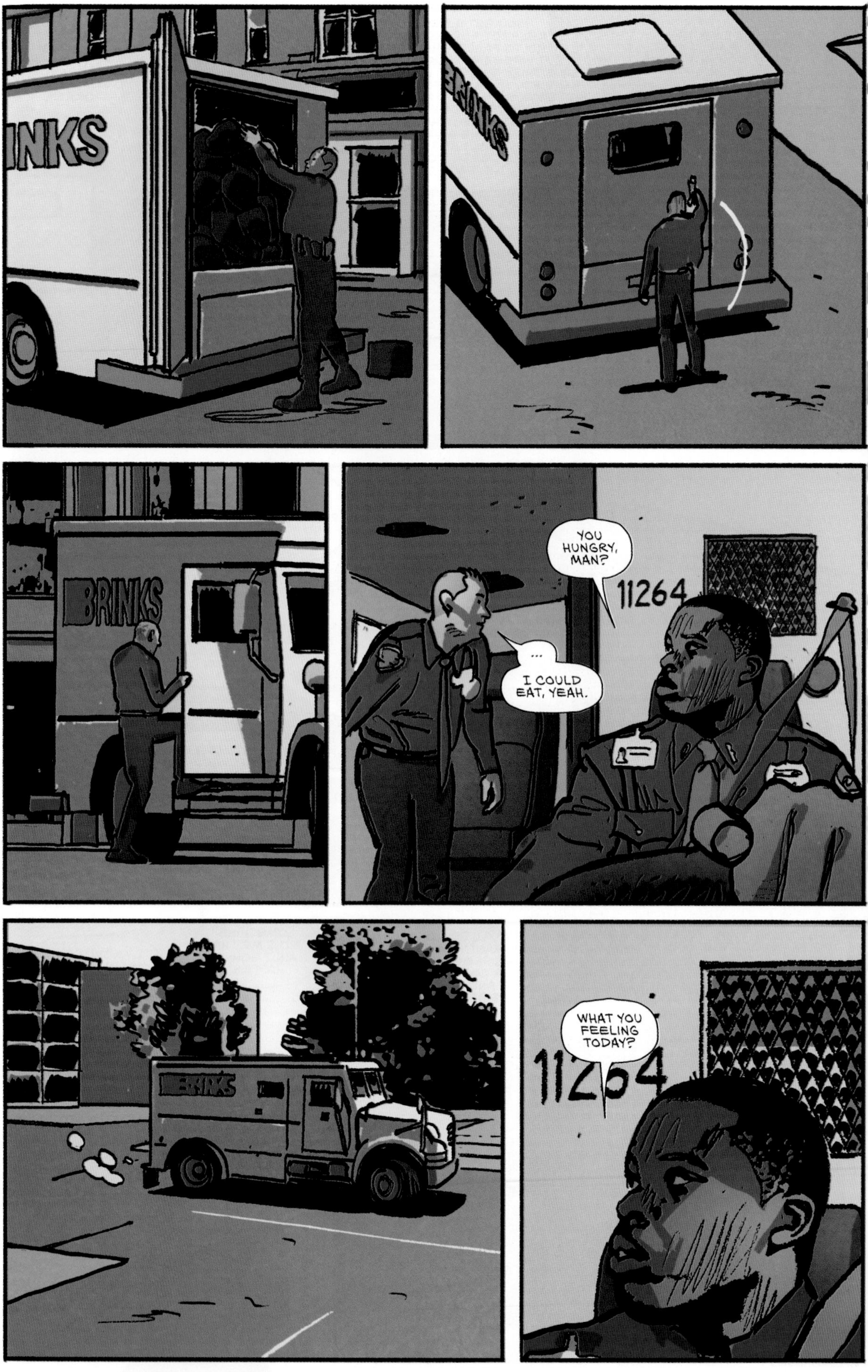
BRINKS
BRINKS
BRINKS
YOU HUNGRY, MAN?
11264
... I COULD EAT, YEAH.
BRINKS
WHAT YOU FEELING TODAY?
11264

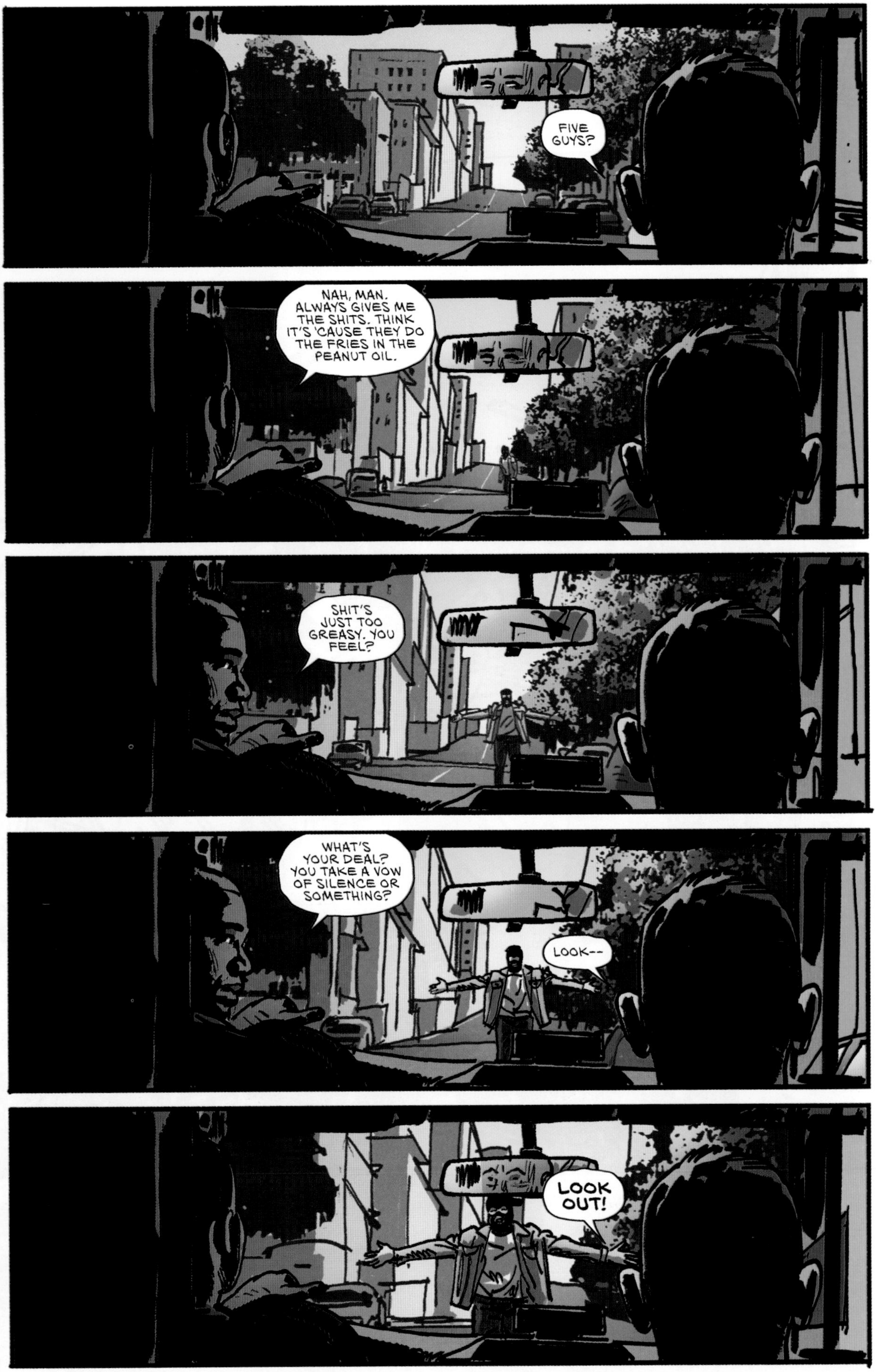
FIVE GUYS?
NAH, MAN. ALWAYS GIVES ME THE SHITS. THINK IT'S 'CAUSE THEY DO THE FRIES IN THE PEANUT OIL.
SHIT'S JUST TOO GREASY. YOU FEEL?
WHAT'S YOUR DEAL? YOU TAKE A VOW OF SILENCE OR SOMETHING?
LOOK--
LOOK OUT!

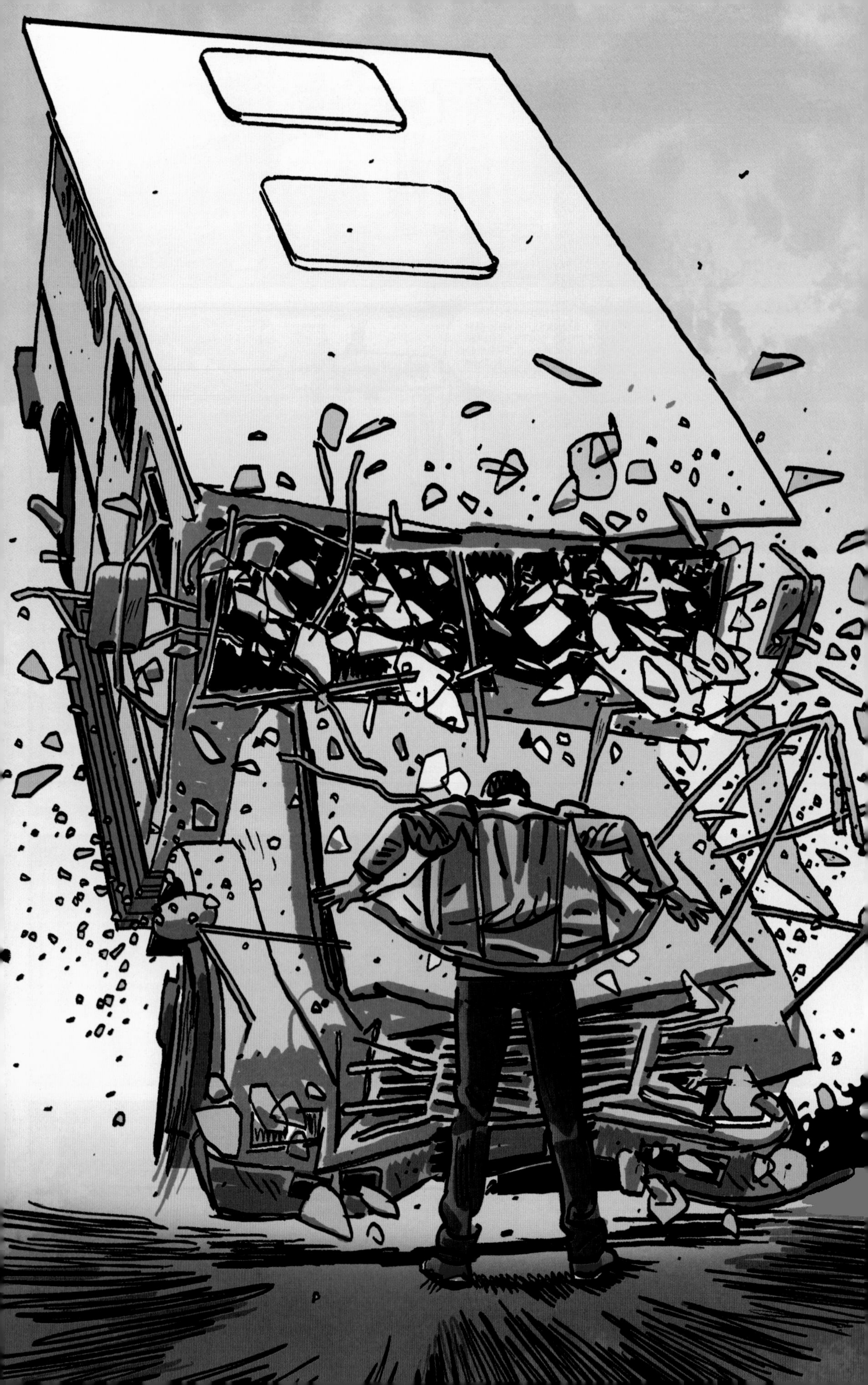

WAIT A MINUTE.
I THINK I FUCKED
THIS UP. I JUMPED
AHEAD.

NEVER
CLAIMED TO
BE SOME MASTER
STORYTELLER...

ANYWAYS...

LET'S
REWIND JUST A
LITTLE BIT.

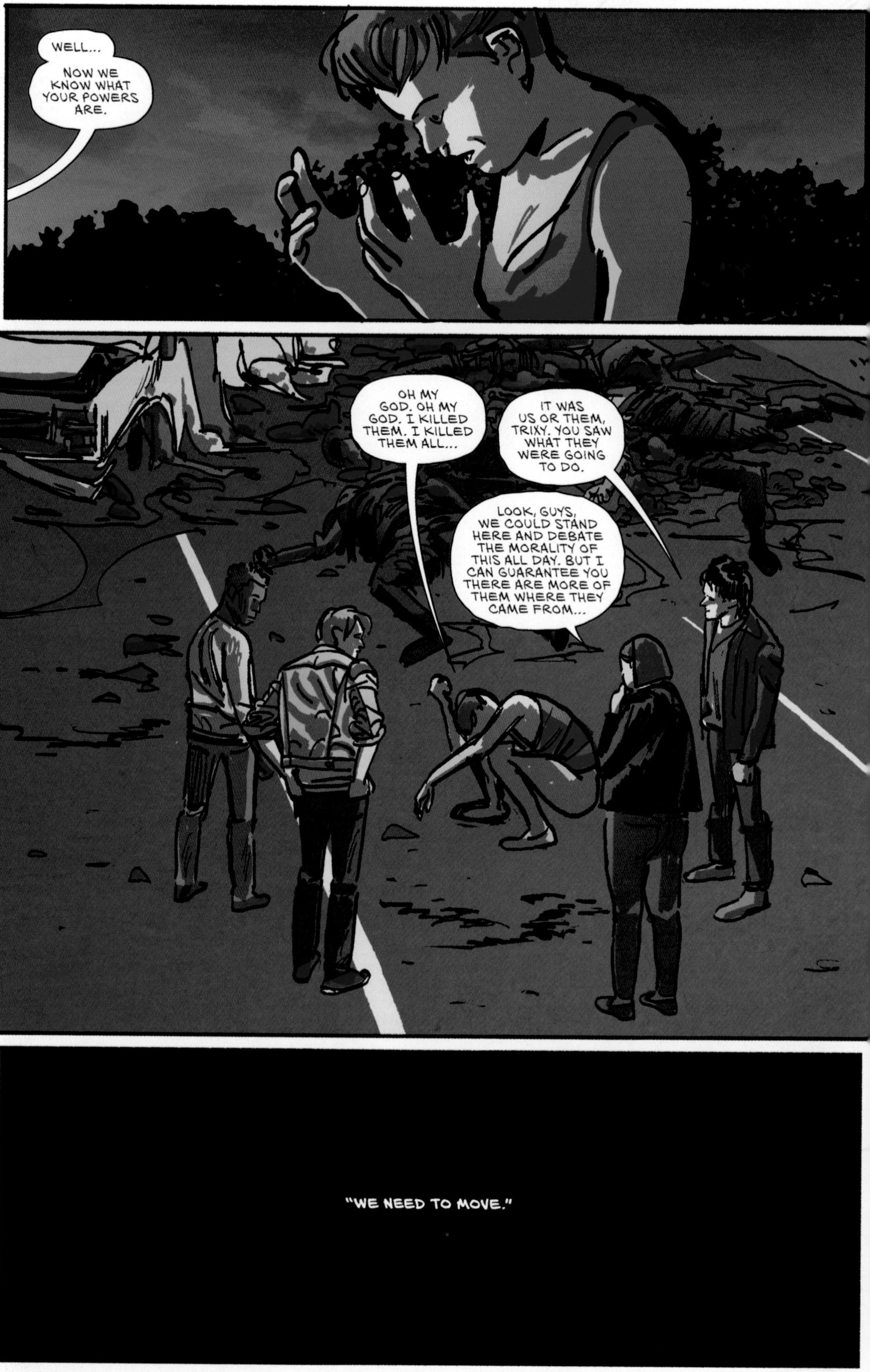
WELL...
NOW WE KNOW WHAT YOUR POWERS ARE.
OH MY GOD. OH MY GOD. I KILLED THEM. I KILLED THEM ALL...
IT WAS US OR THEM, TRIXY. YOU SAW WHAT THEY WERE GOING TO DO.
LOOK, GUYS, WE COULD STAND HERE AND DEBATE THE MORALITY OF THIS ALL DAY. BUT I CAN GUARANTEE YOU THERE ARE MORE OF THEM WHERE THEY CAME FROM...
"WE NEED TO MOVE."

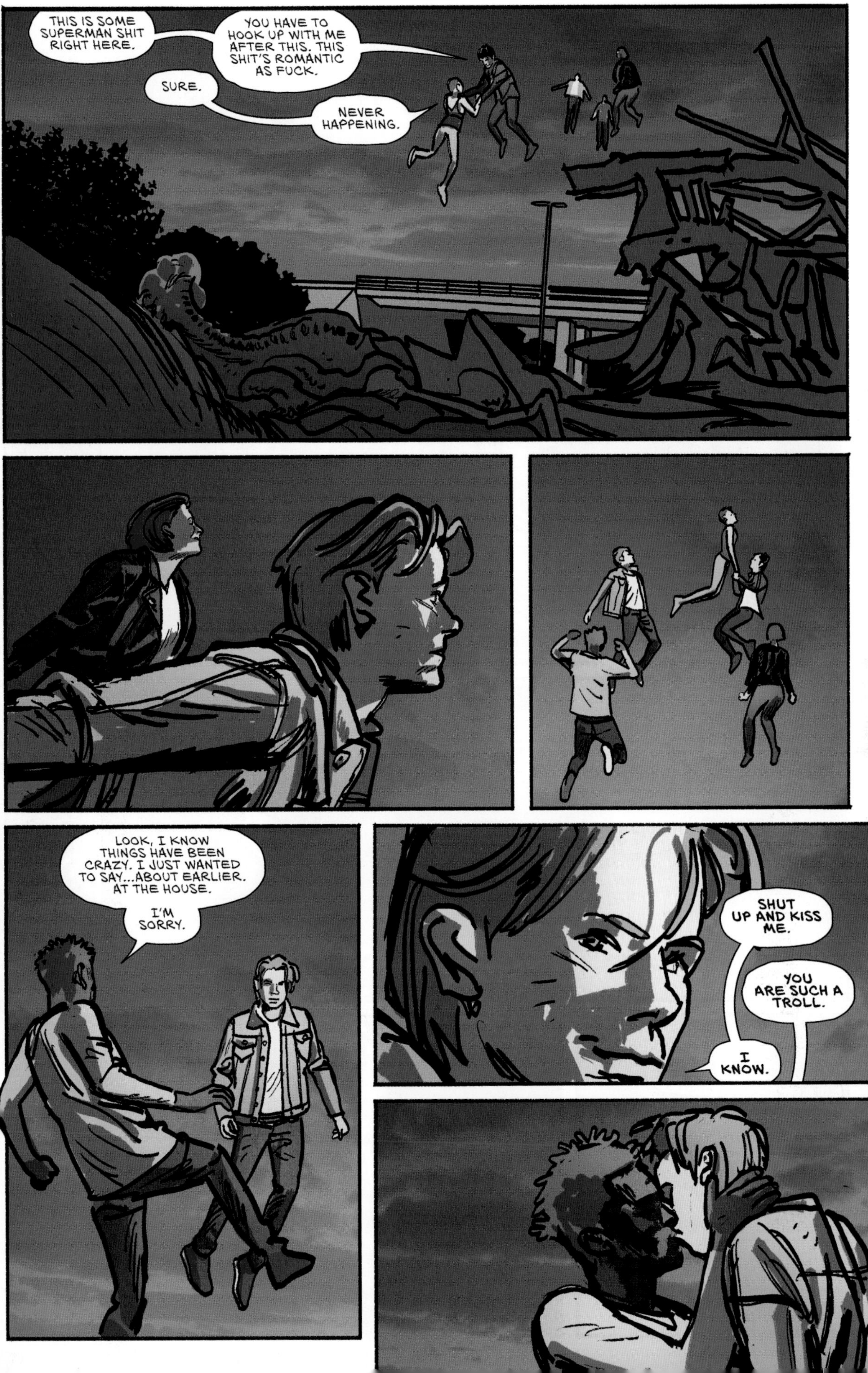
THIS IS SOME SUPERMAN SHIT RIGHT HERE.
YOU HAVE TO HOOK UP WITH ME AFTER THIS. THIS SHIT'S ROMANTIC AS FUCK.
SURE.
NEVER HAPPENING.
LOOK, I KNOW THINGS HAVE BEEN CRAZY. I JUST WANTED TO SAY...ABOUT EARLIER. AT THE HOUSE.
I'M SORRY.
SHUT UP AND KISS ME.
YOU ARE SUCH A TROLL.
I KNOW.

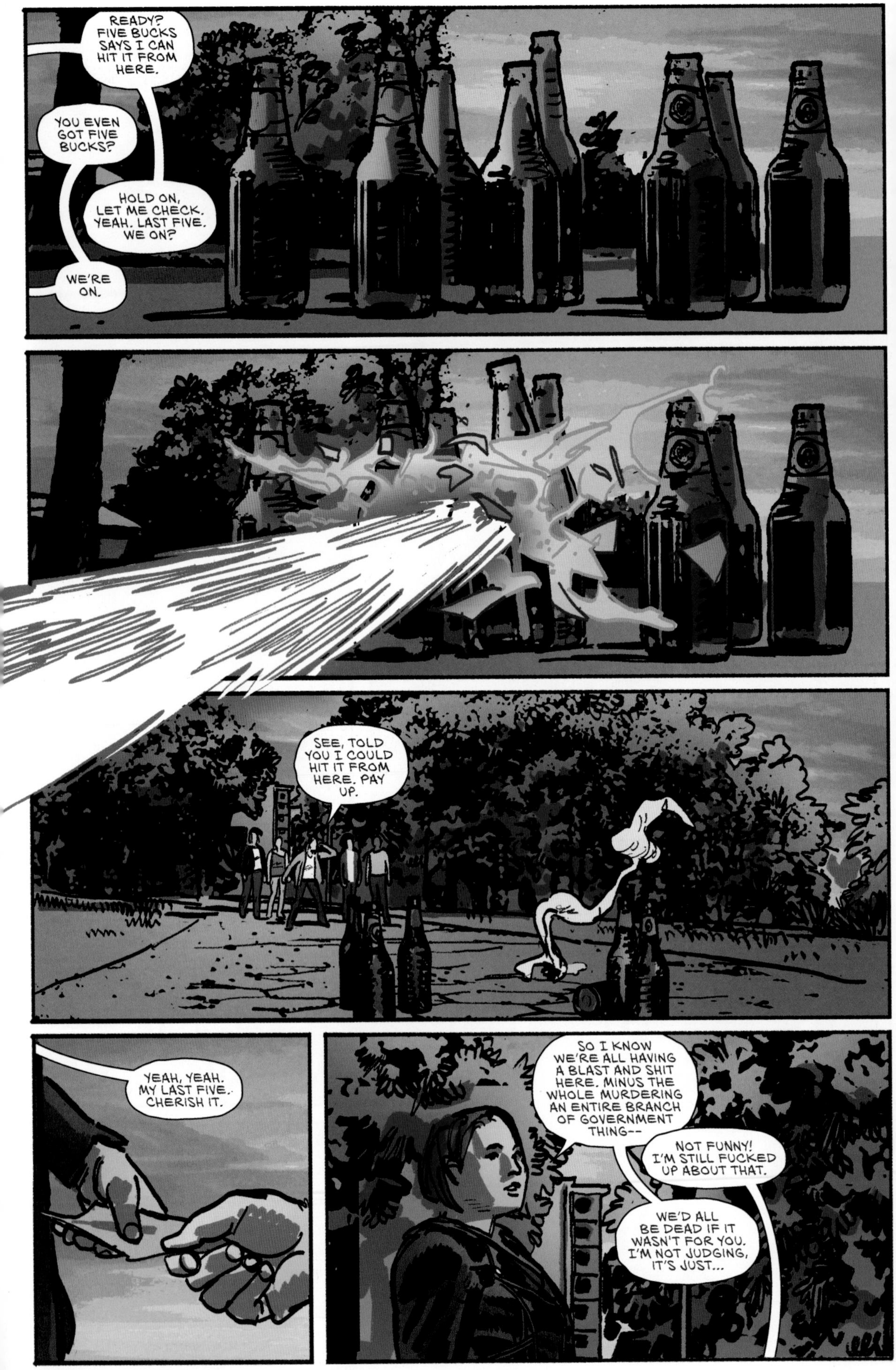
READY? FIVE BUCKS SAYS I CAN HIT IT FROM HERE.
YOU EVEN GOT FIVE BUCKS?
HOLD ON, LET ME CHECK. YEAH. LAST FIVE. WE ON?
WE'RE ON.
SEE, TOLD YOU I COULD HIT IT FROM HERE. PAY UP.
YEAH, YEAH. MY LAST FIVE. CHERISH IT.
SO I KNOW WE'RE ALL HAVING A BLAST AND SHIT HERE. MINUS THE WHOLE MURDERING AN ENTIRE BRANCH OF GOVERNMENT THING--
NOT FUNNY! I'M STILL FUCKED UP ABOUT THAT.
WE'D ALL BE DEAD IF IT WASN'T FOR YOU. I'M NOT JUDGING, IT'S JUST...

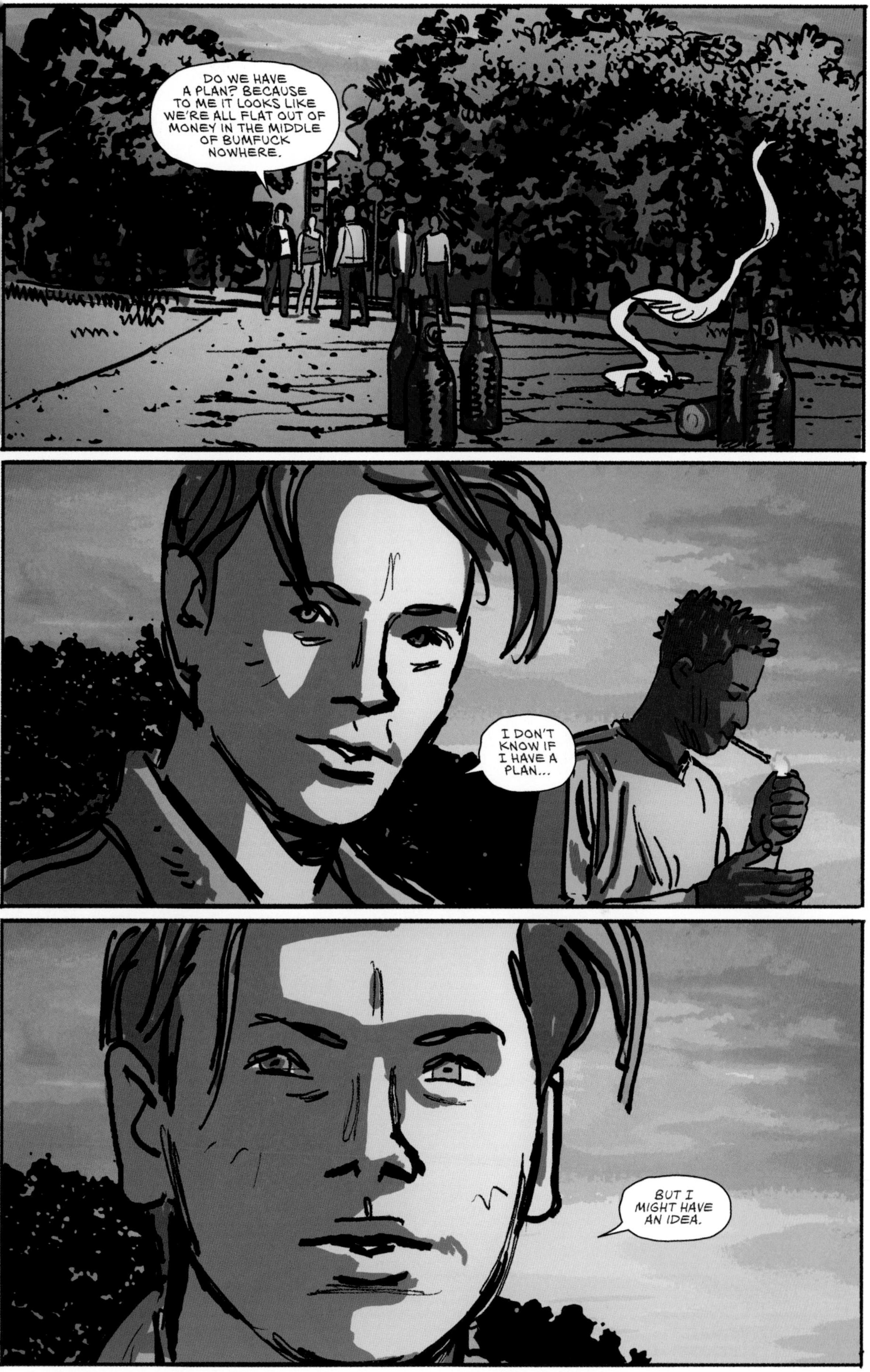
DO WE HAVE A PLAN? BECAUSE TO ME IT LOOKS LIKE WE'RE ALL FLAT OUT OF MONEY IN THE MIDDLE OF BUMFUCK NOWHERE.
I DON'T KNOW IF I HAVE A PLAN...
BUT I MIGHT HAVE AN IDEA.

AND SO:

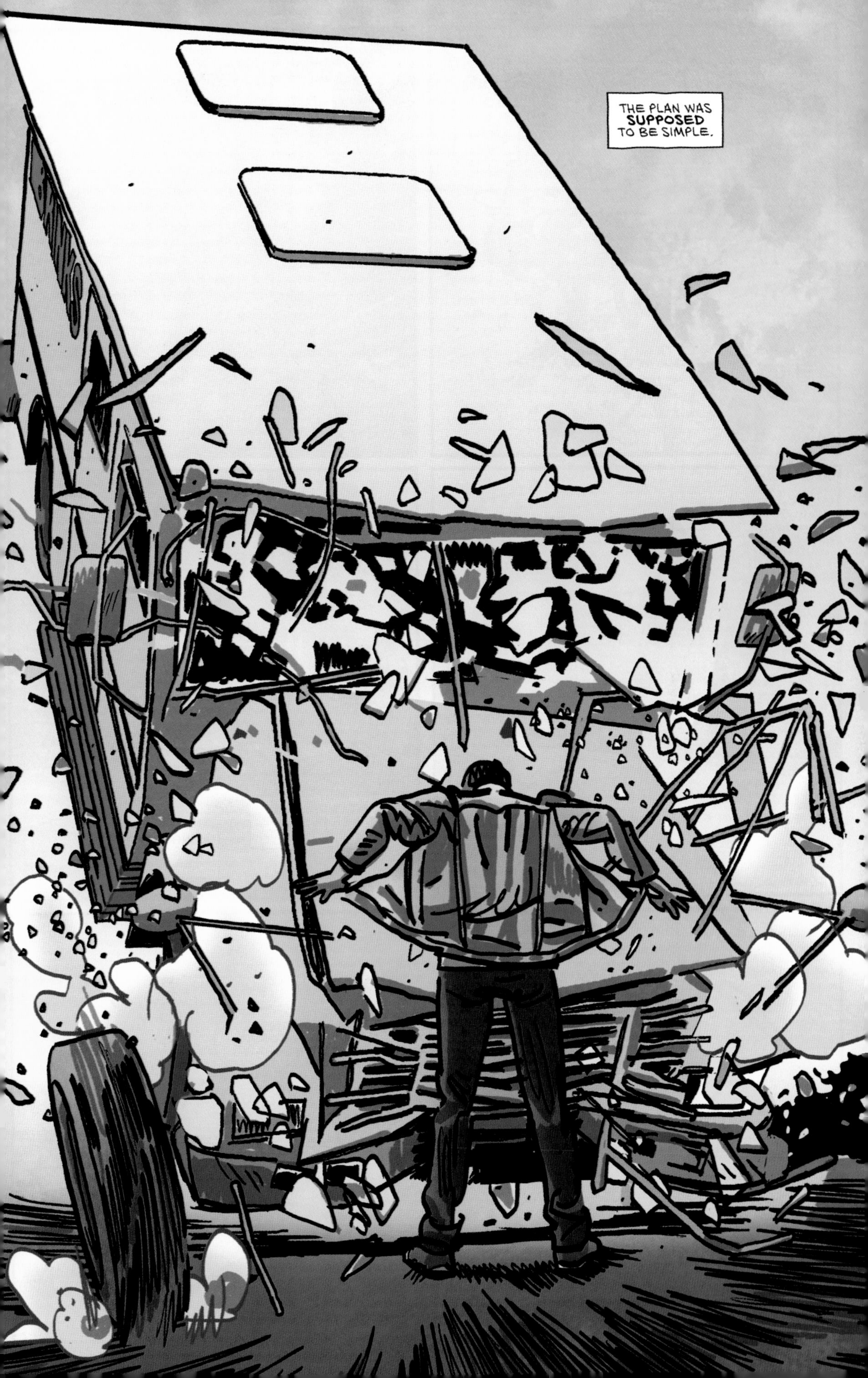
THE PLAN WAS **SUPPOSED** TO BE SIMPLE.

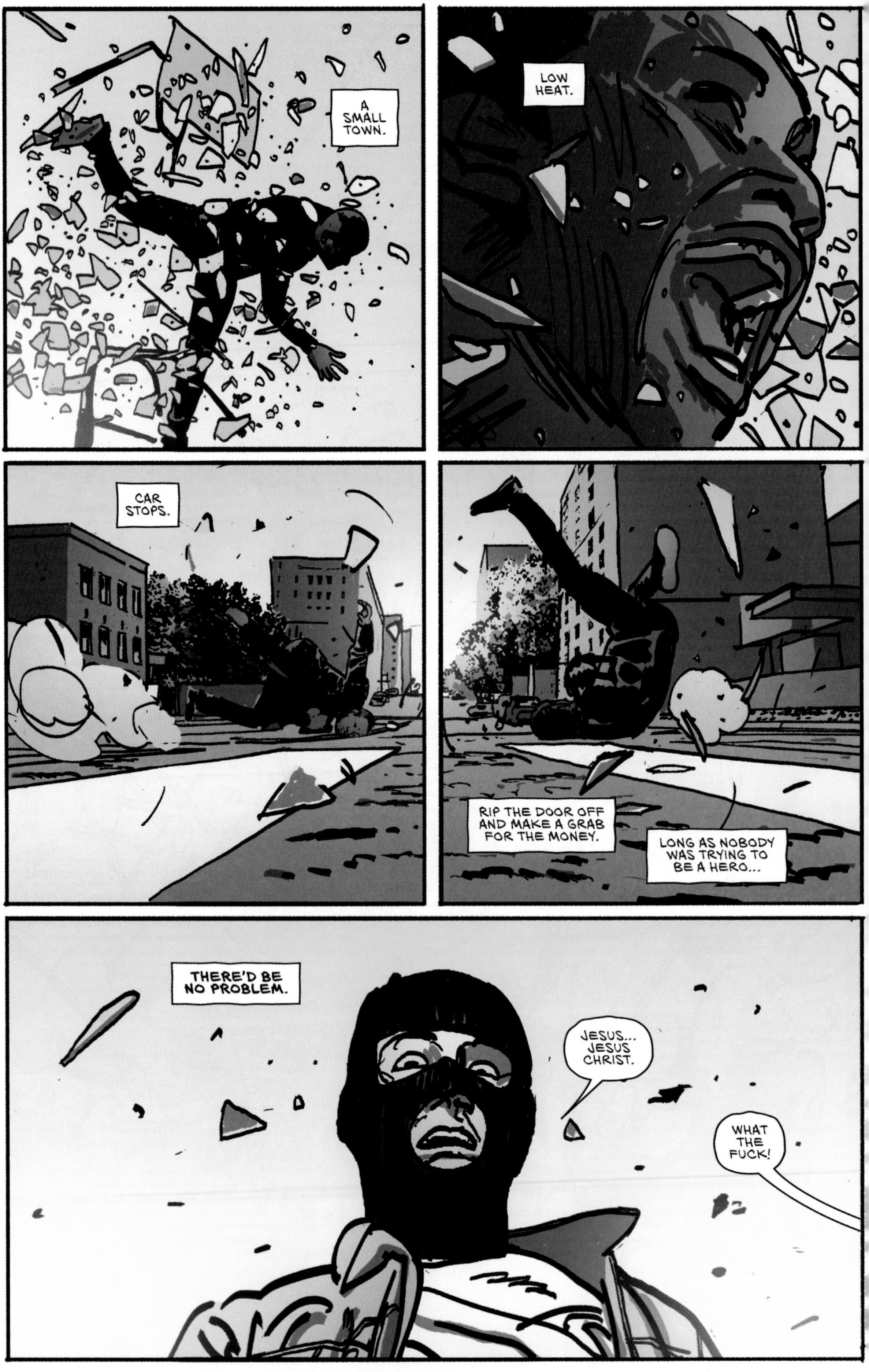
A SMALL TOWN.
LOW HEAT.
CAR STOPS.
RIP THE DOOR OFF AND MAKE A GRAB FOR THE MONEY.
LONG AS NOBODY WAS TRYING TO BE A HERO...
THERE'D BE NO PROBLEM.
JESUS... JESUS CHRIST.
WHAT THE FUCK!

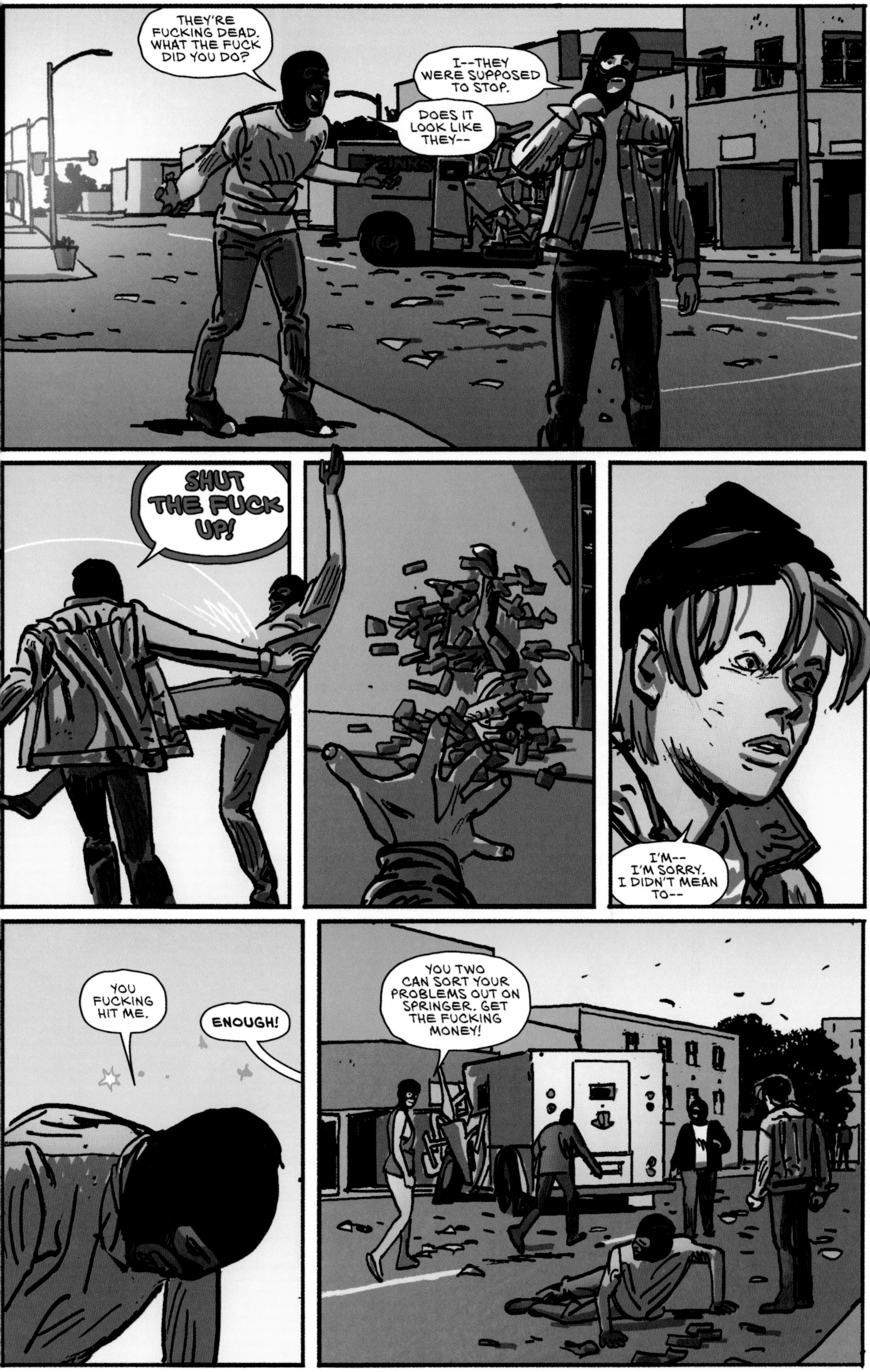
THEY'RE FUCKING DEAD. WHAT THE FUCK DID YOU DO?
I--THEY WERE SUPPOSED TO STOP.
DOES IT LOOK LIKE THEY--
SHUT THE FUCK UP!
I'M-- I'M SORRY. I DIDN'T MEAN TO--
YOU FUCKING HIT ME.
ENOUGH!
YOU TWO CAN SORT YOUR PROBLEMS OUT ON SPRINGER. GET THE FUCKING MONEY!

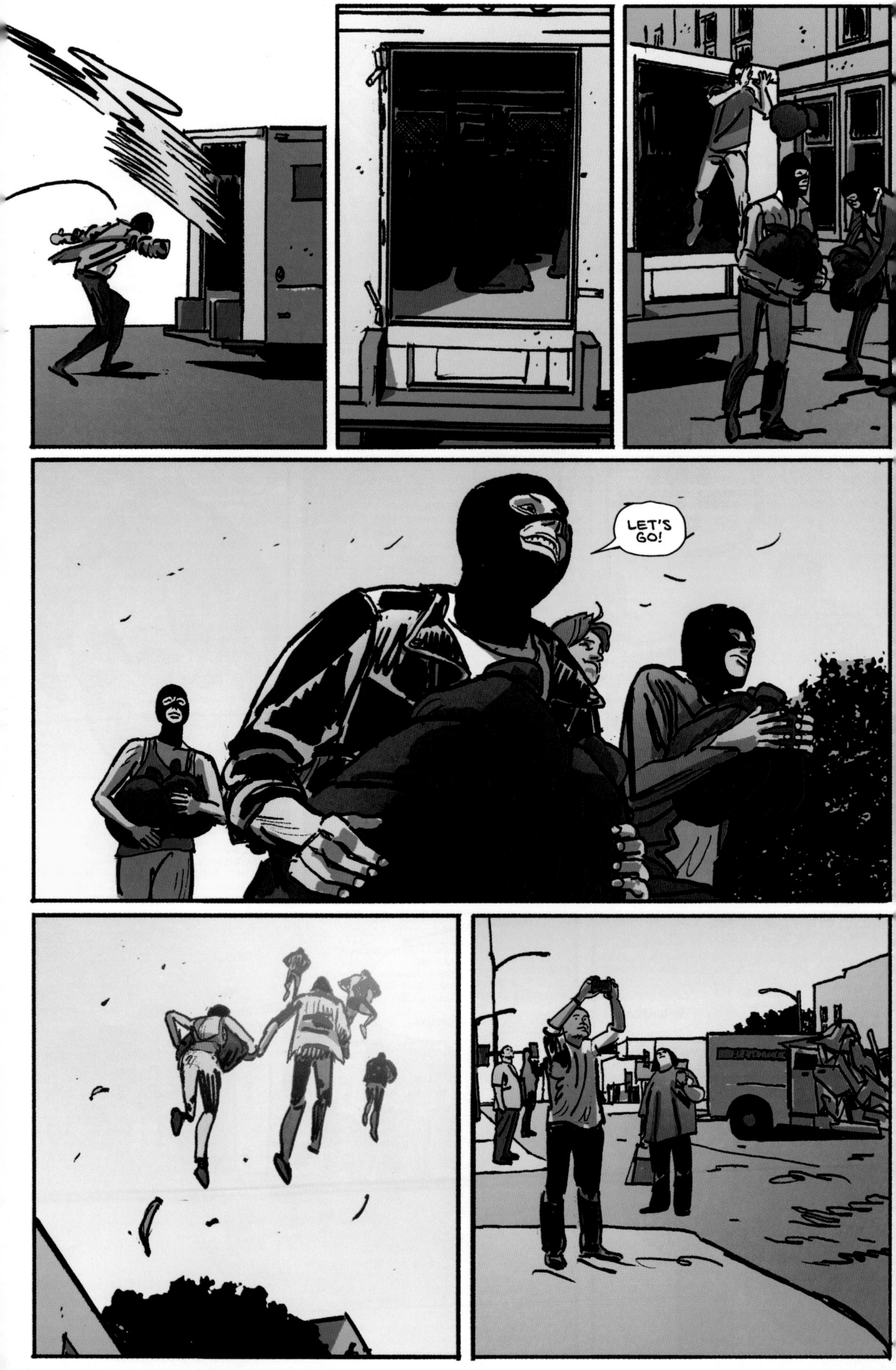
LET'S GO!

WE TOOK WHAT WE NEEDED AND BURIED THE REST IN THE
DESERT. WE MARKED THE SPOT, BUT I'D DOUBT WE'D EVER
BE ABLE TO FIND IT AGAIN. WE WERE SO SHOOK UP.

AFTER THAT WE DID PRETTY MUCH WHAT YOU'D
EXPECT OF A BUNCH OF KIDS WHO JUST MADE MORE
MONEY THAN THEY'D SEEN IN THEIR LIVES...

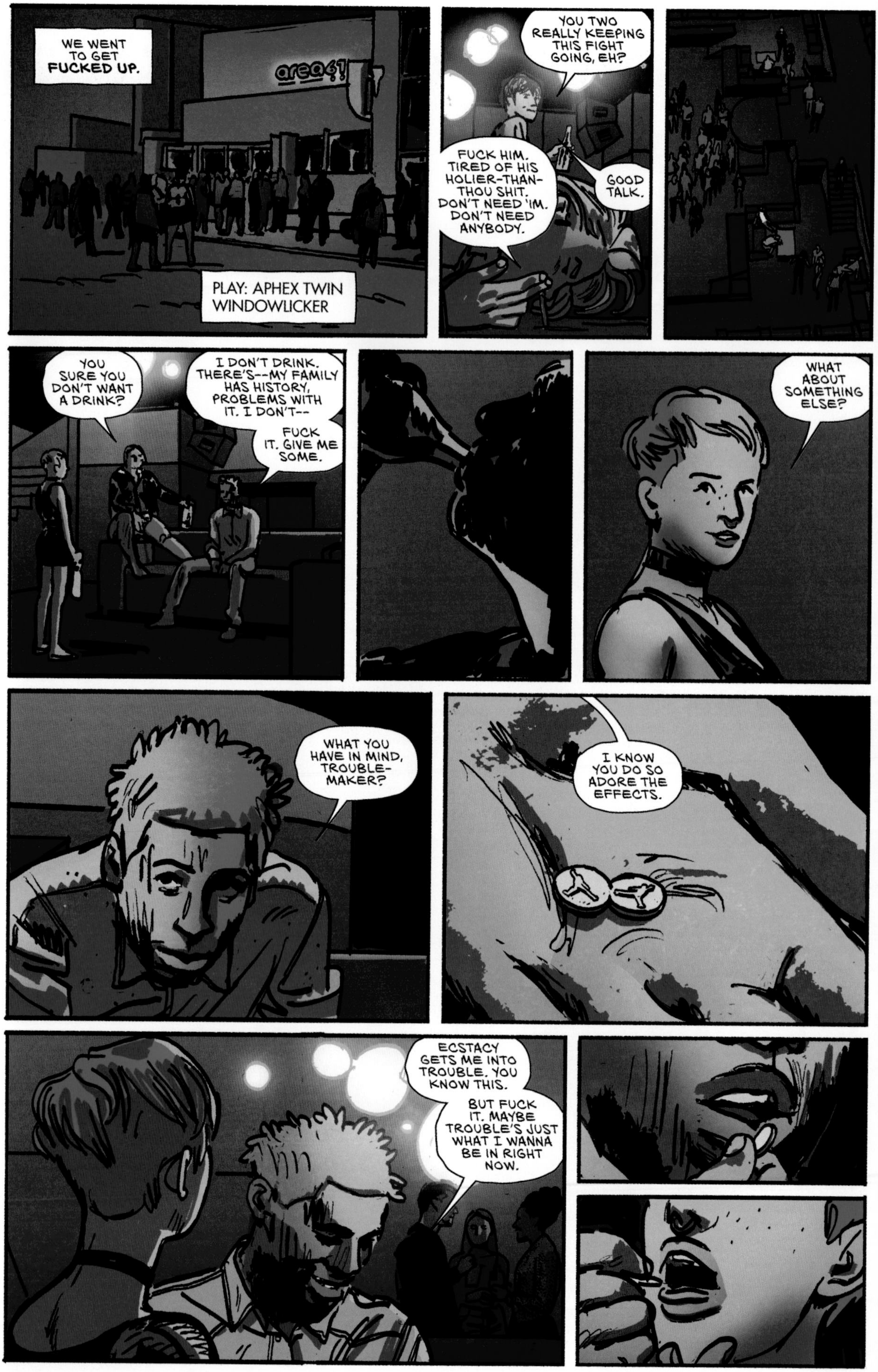
WE WENT TO GET FUCKED UP.
area41
PLAY: APHEX TWIN WINDOWLICKER
YOU TWO REALLY KEEPING THIS FIGHT GOING, EH?
FUCK HIM. TIRED OF HIS HOLIER-THAN-THOU SHIT. DON'T NEED 'IM. DON'T NEED ANYBODY.
GOOD TALK.
YOU SURE YOU DON'T WANT A DRINK?
I DON'T DRINK. THERE'S--MY FAMILY HAS HISTORY, PROBLEMS WITH IT. I DON'T--
FUCK IT. GIVE ME SOME.
WHAT ABOUT SOMETHING ELSE?
WHAT YOU HAVE IN MIND, TROUBLE-MAKER?
I KNOW YOU DO SO ADORE THE EFFECTS.
ECSTACY GETS ME INTO TROUBLE. YOU KNOW THIS.
BUT FUCK IT. MAYBE TROUBLE'S JUST WHAT I WANNA BE IN RIGHT NOW.

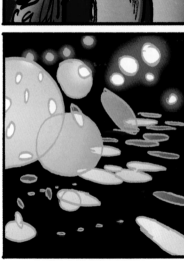

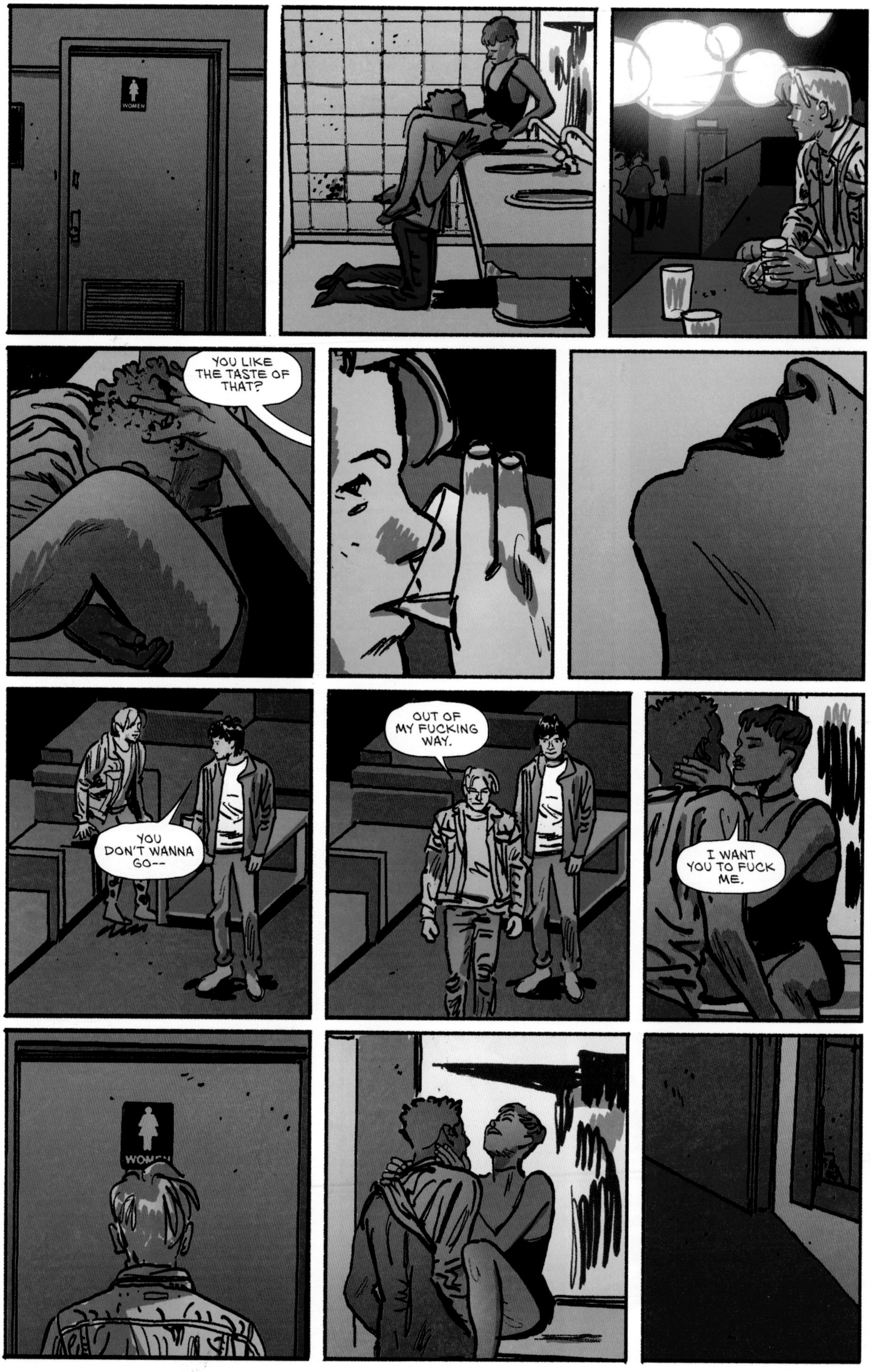
WOMEN
YOU LIKE THE TASTE OF THAT?
YOU DON'T WANNA GO--
OUT OF MY FUCKING WAY.
I WANT YOU TO FUCK ME.

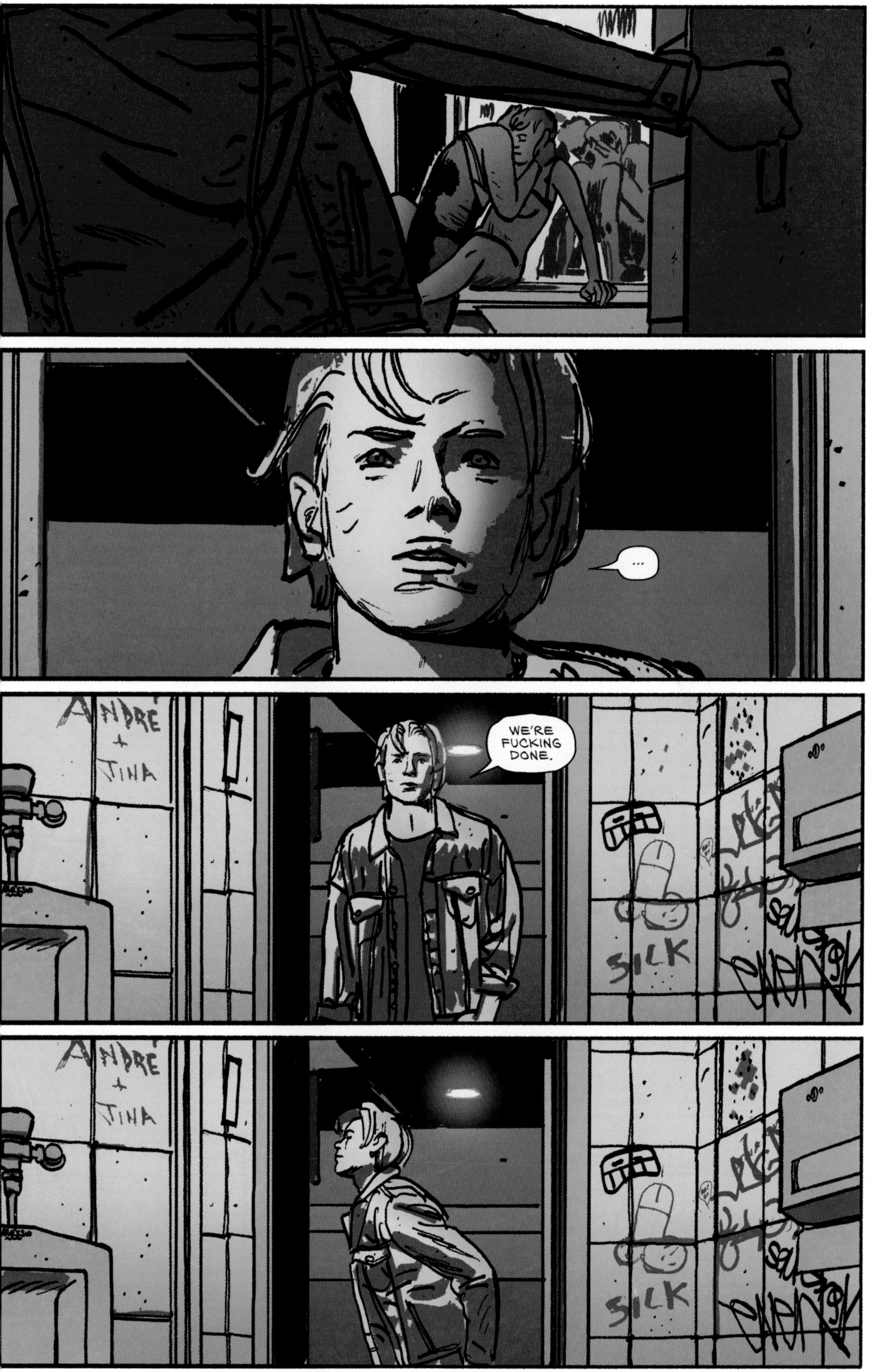
...
ANDRÉ + TINA
WE'RE FUCKING DONE.
SILK

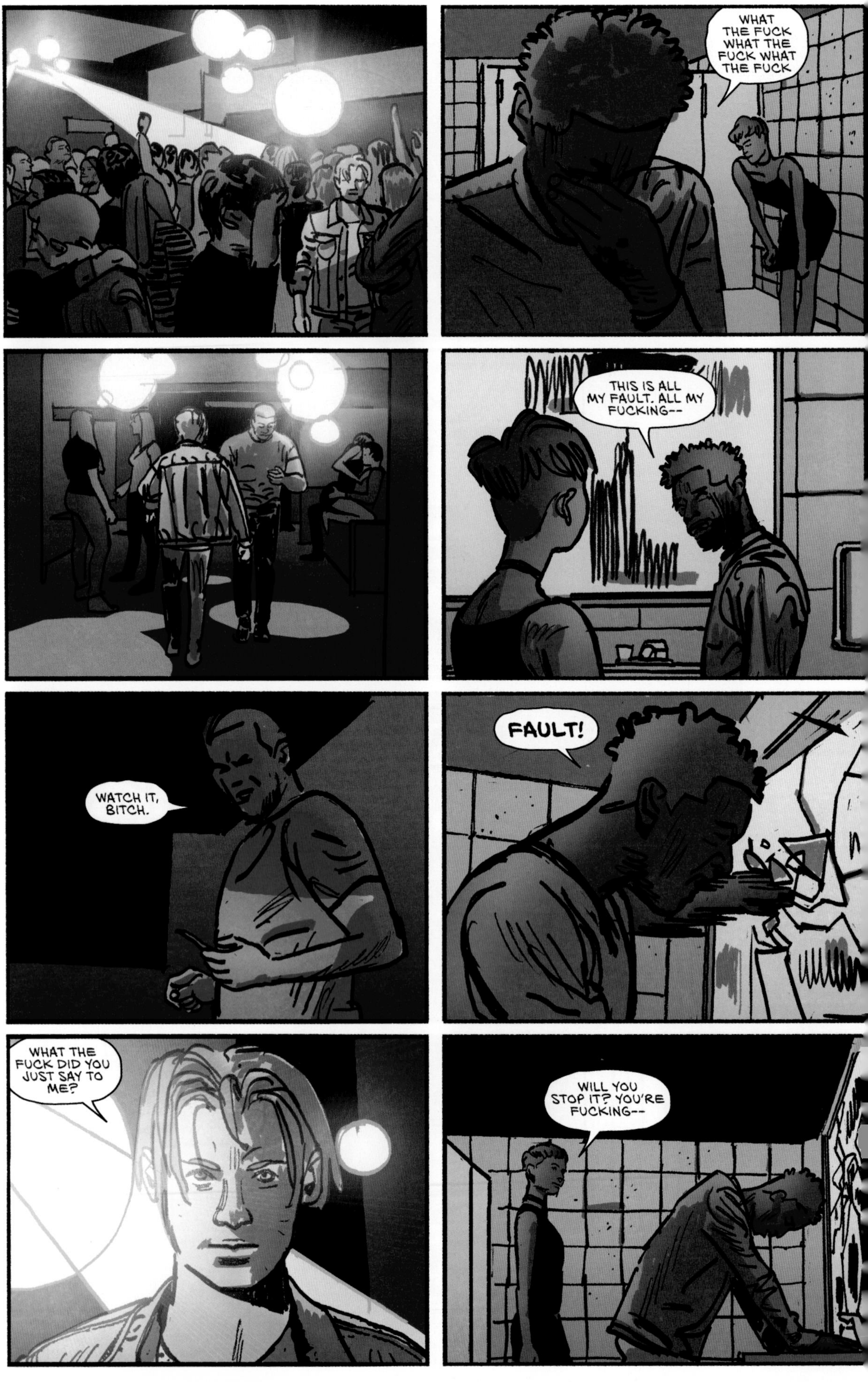
WHAT THE FUCK WHAT THE FUCK WHAT THE FUCK
THIS IS ALL MY FAULT. ALL MY FUCKING--
WATCH IT, BITCH.
FAULT!
WHAT THE FUCK DID YOU JUST SAY TO ME?
WILL YOU STOP IT? YOU'RE FUCKING--

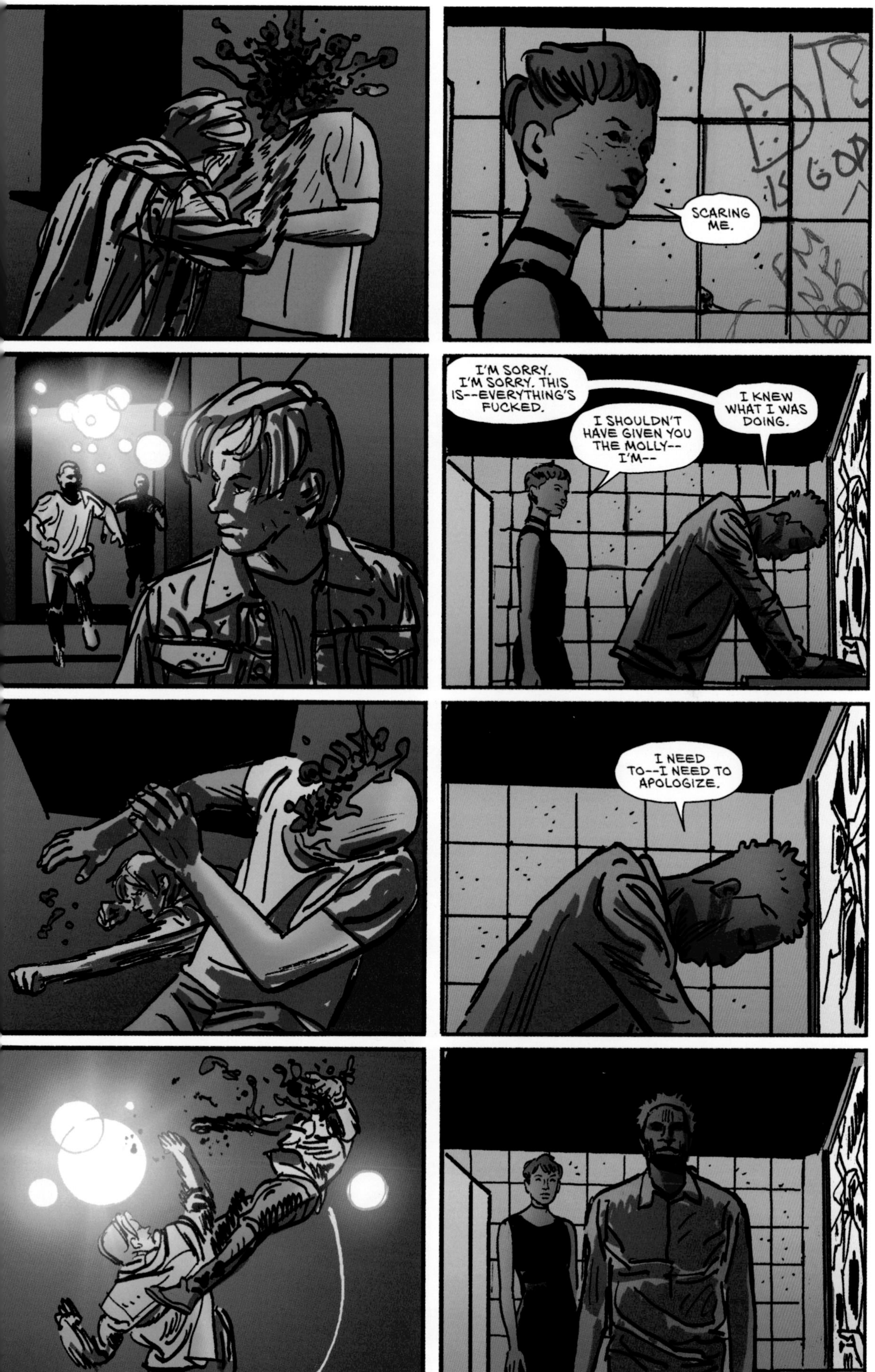
SCARING ME.
I'M SORRY. I'M SORRY. THIS IS--EVERYTHING'S FUCKED.
I SHOULDN'T HAVE GIVEN YOU THE MOLLY-- I'M--
I KNEW WHAT I WAS DOING.
I NEED TO--I NEED TO APOLOGIZE.

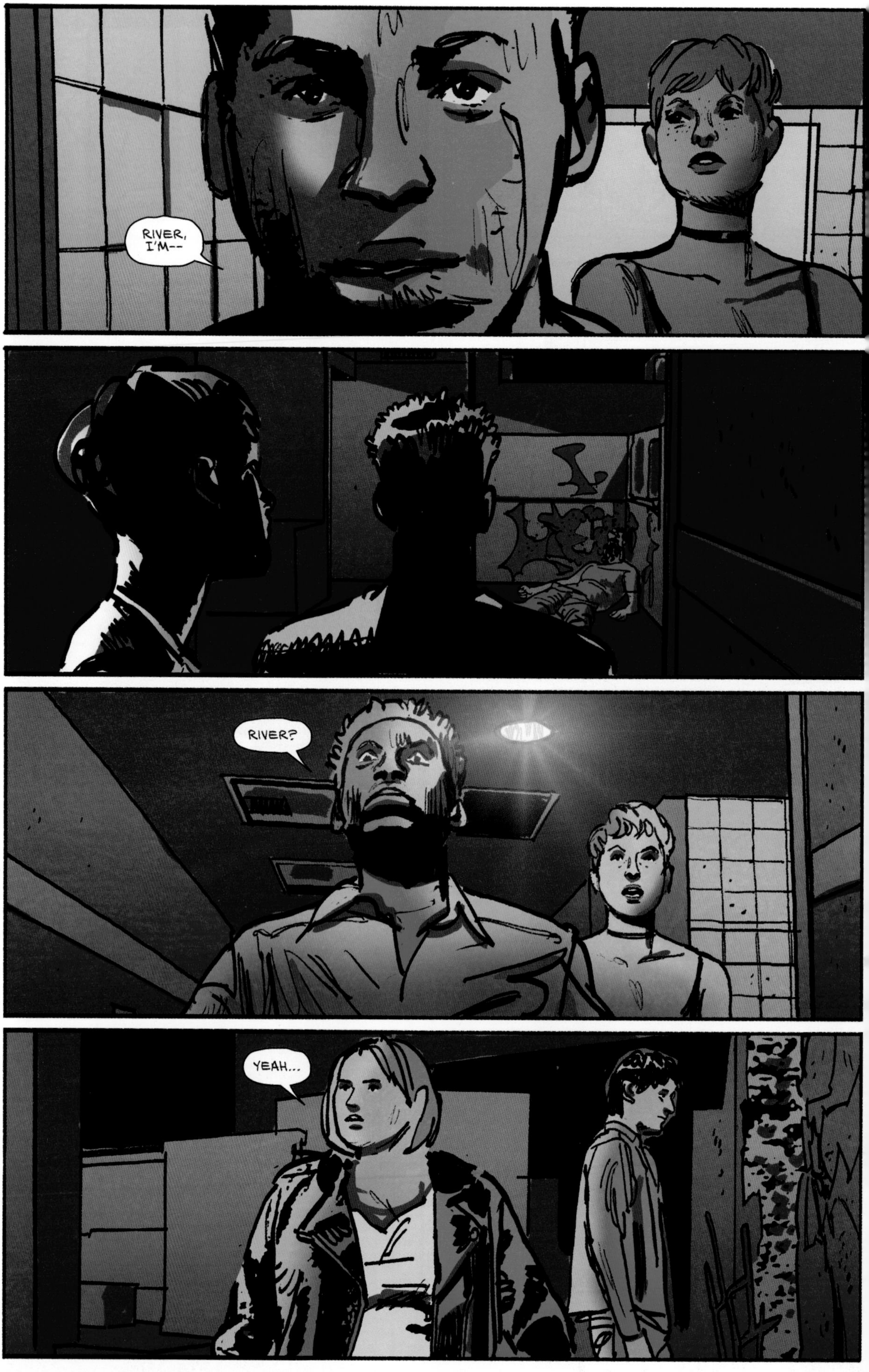
RIVER, I'M--
RIVER?
YEAH...

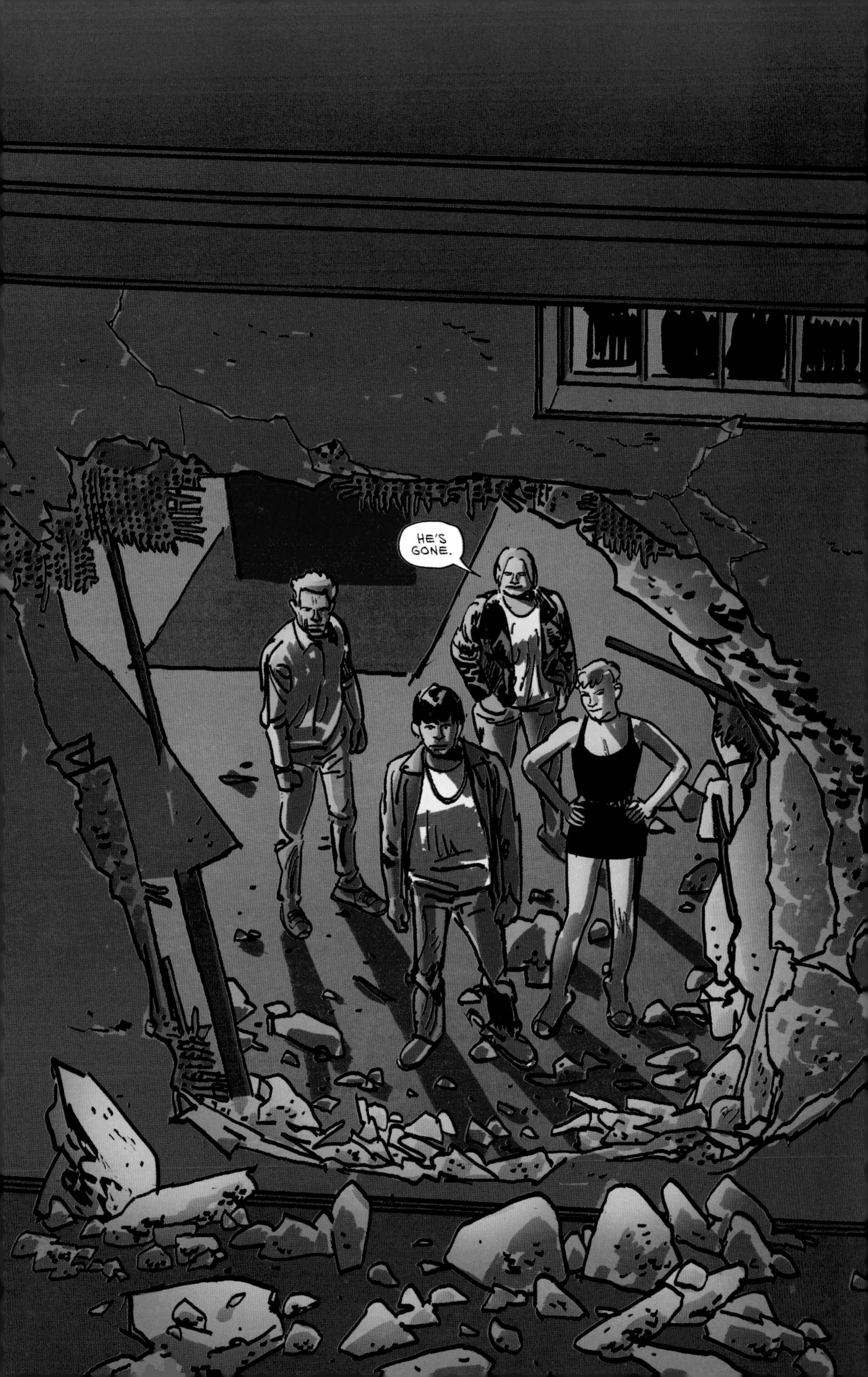
HE'S GONE.

Youth

Chapter Three

Baptism under Neon

"Marlon Brando used to go cha-cha dancing with us. He could dance his ass off. He was the most charming mother-fucker you ever met. He'd fuck anything. Anything! He'd fuck a mailbox."
– Quincy Jones

Youth

Youth

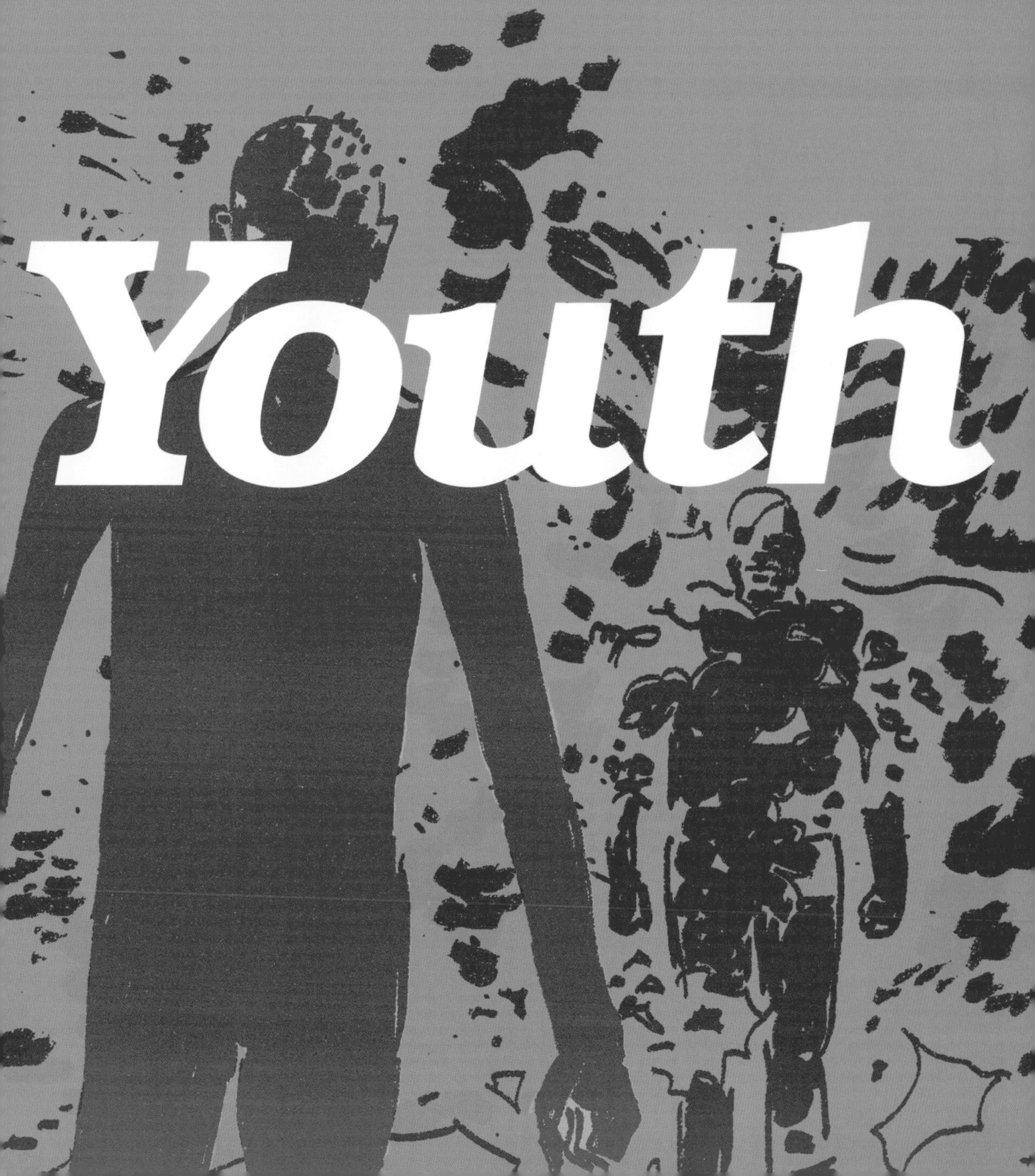

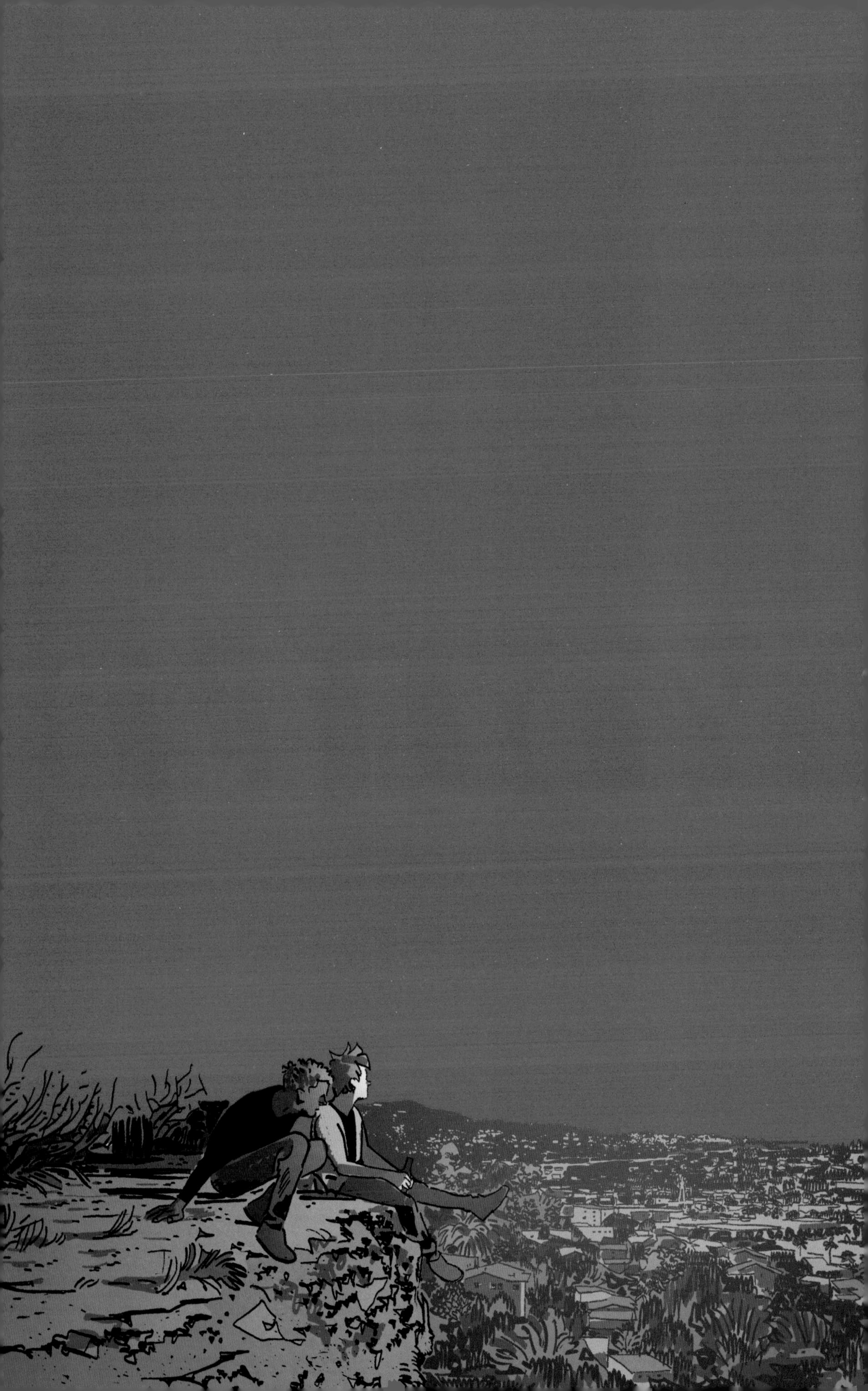

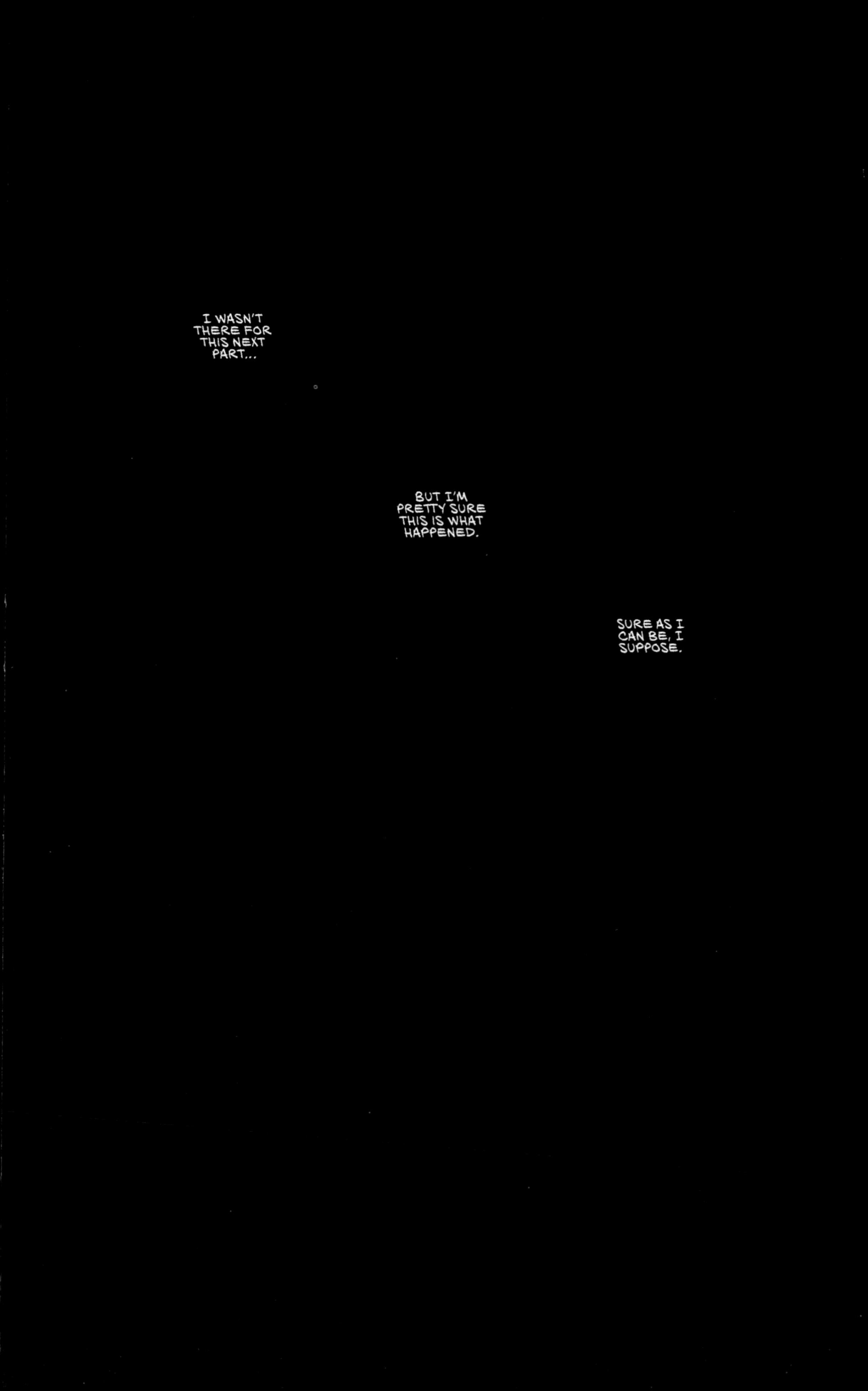
I WASN'T THERE FOR THIS NEXT PART...
BUT I'M PRETTY SURE THIS IS WHAT HAPPENED.
SURE AS I CAN BE, I SUPPOSE.

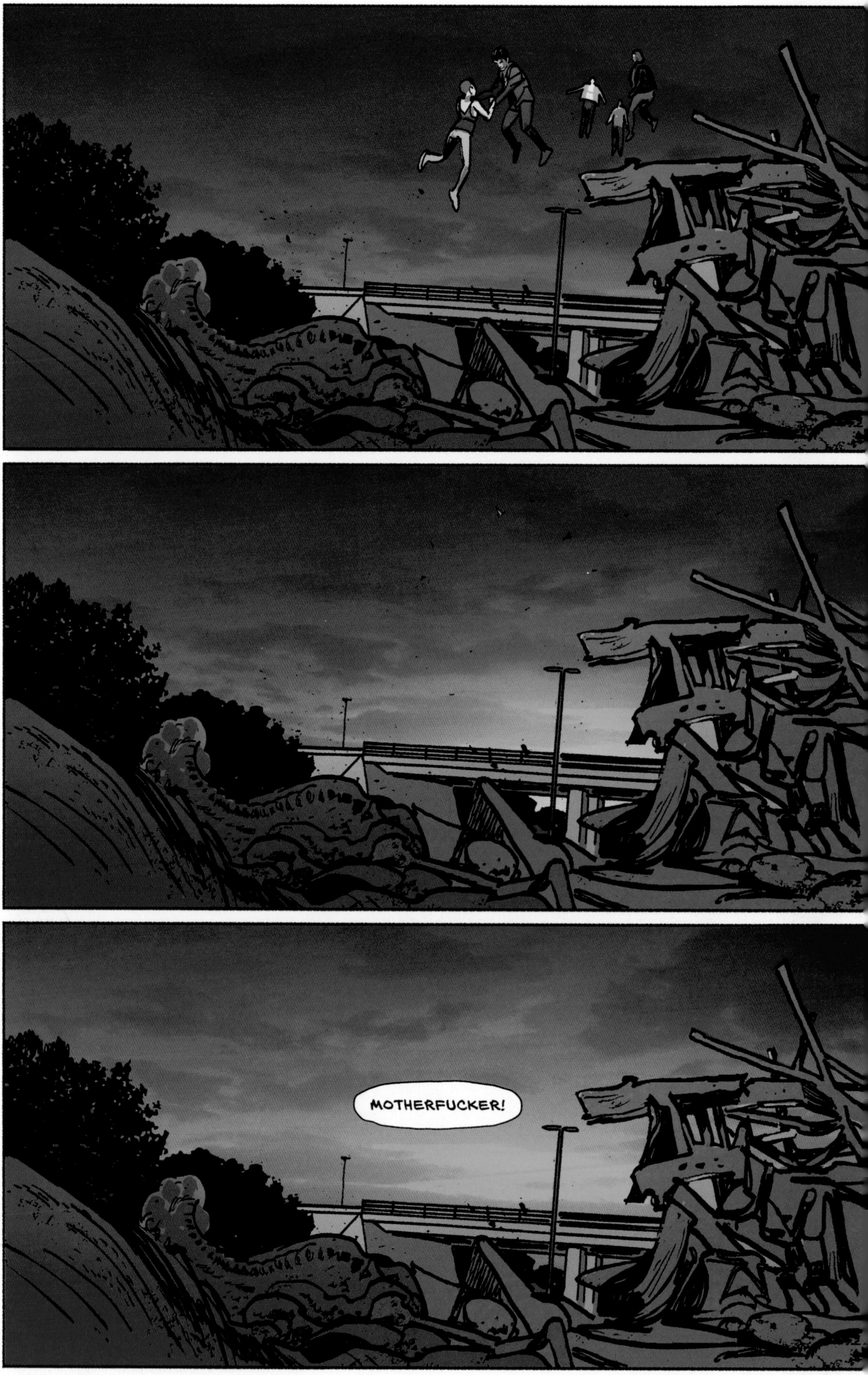
MOTHERFUCKER!

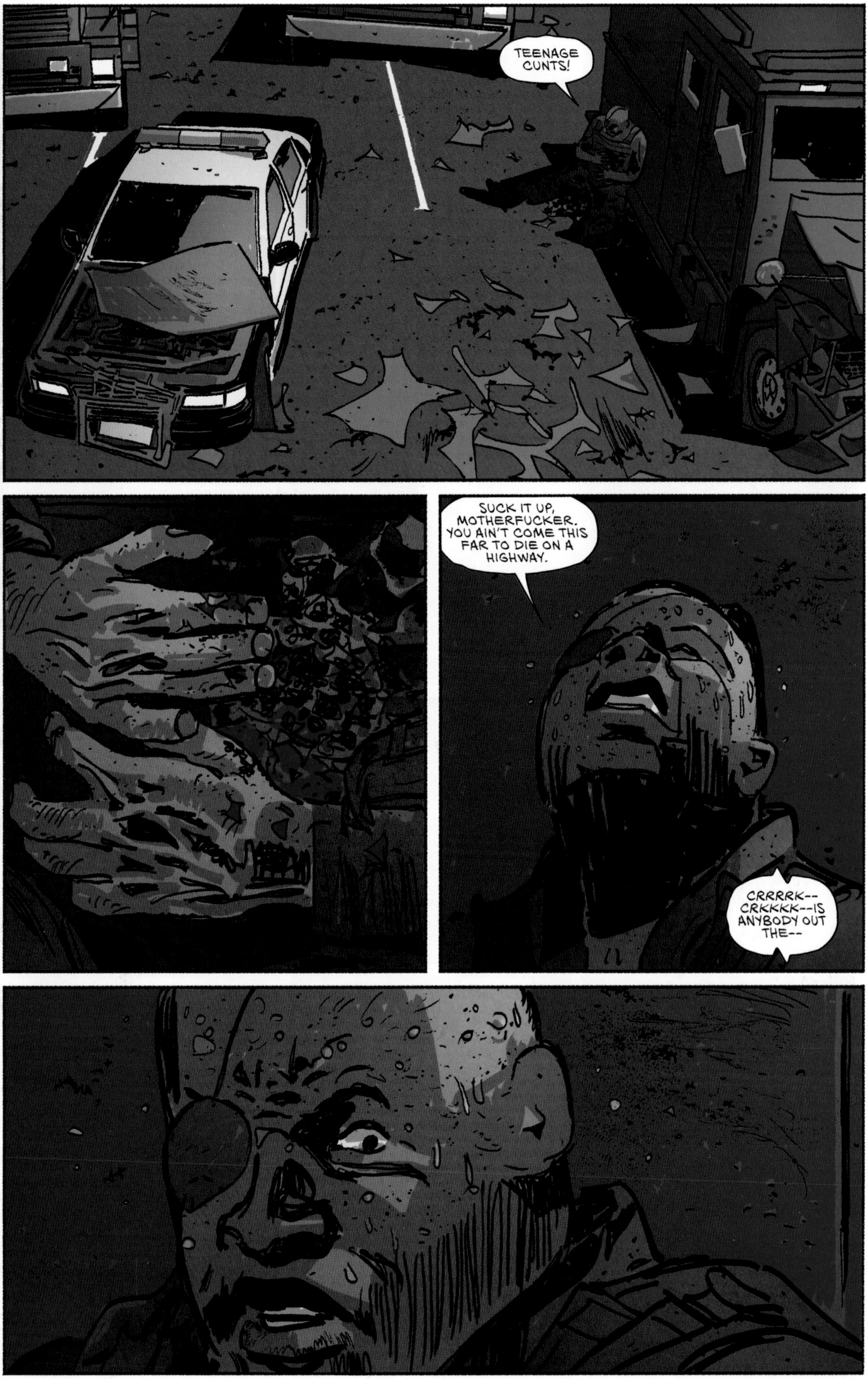
TEENAGE CUNTS!
SUCK IT UP, MOTHERFUCKER. YOU AIN'T COME THIS FAR TO DIE ON A HIGHWAY.
CRRRRK--CRKKKK--IS ANYBODY OUT THE--

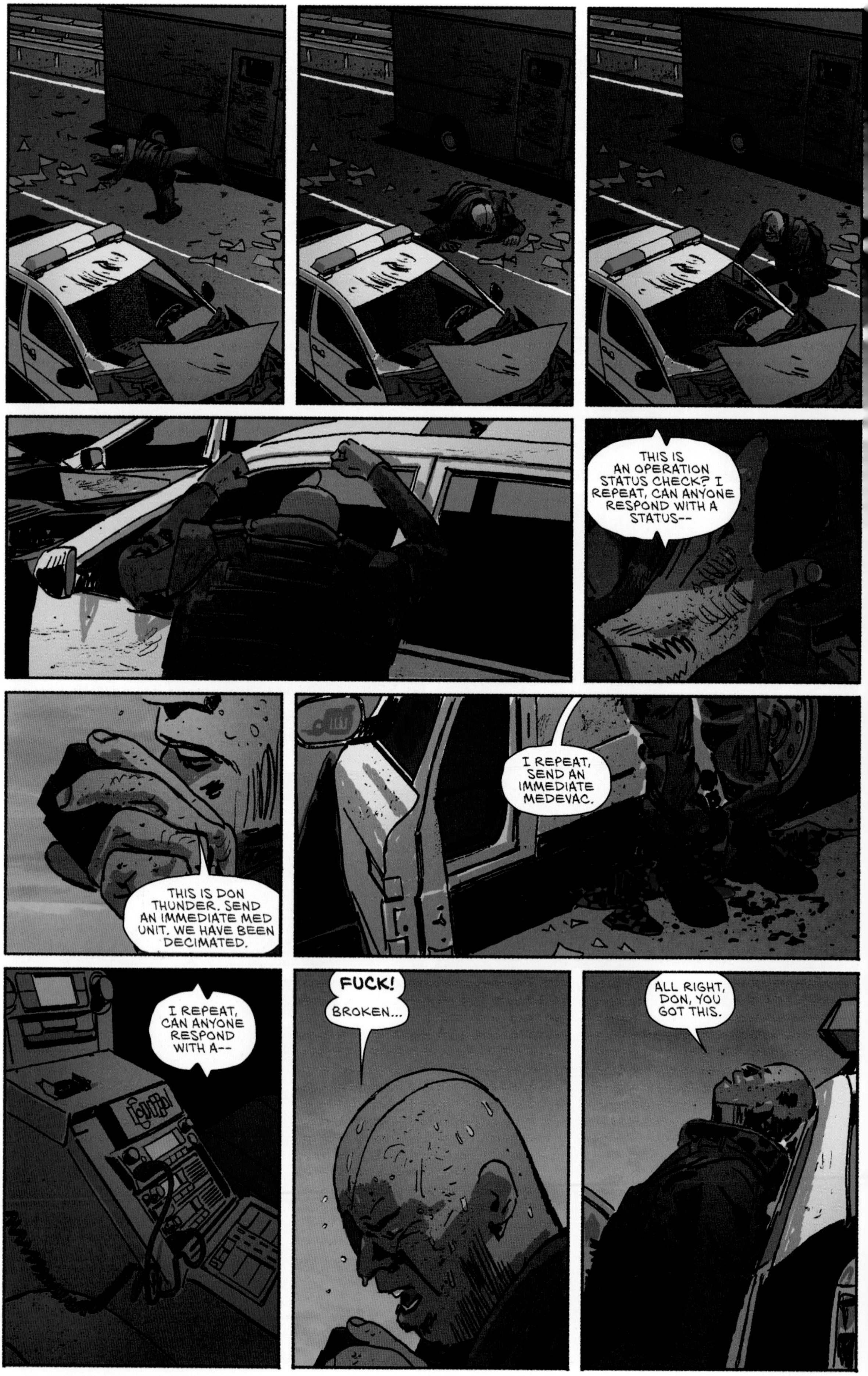
THIS IS AN OPERATION STATUS CHECK? I REPEAT, CAN ANYONE RESPOND WITH A STATUS--
THIS IS DON THUNDER. SEND AN IMMEDIATE MED UNIT. WE HAVE BEEN DECIMATED.
I REPEAT, SEND AN IMMEDIATE MEDEVAC.
I REPEAT, CAN ANYONE RESPOND WITH A--
FUCK!
BROKEN...
ALL RIGHT, DON, YOU GOT THIS.

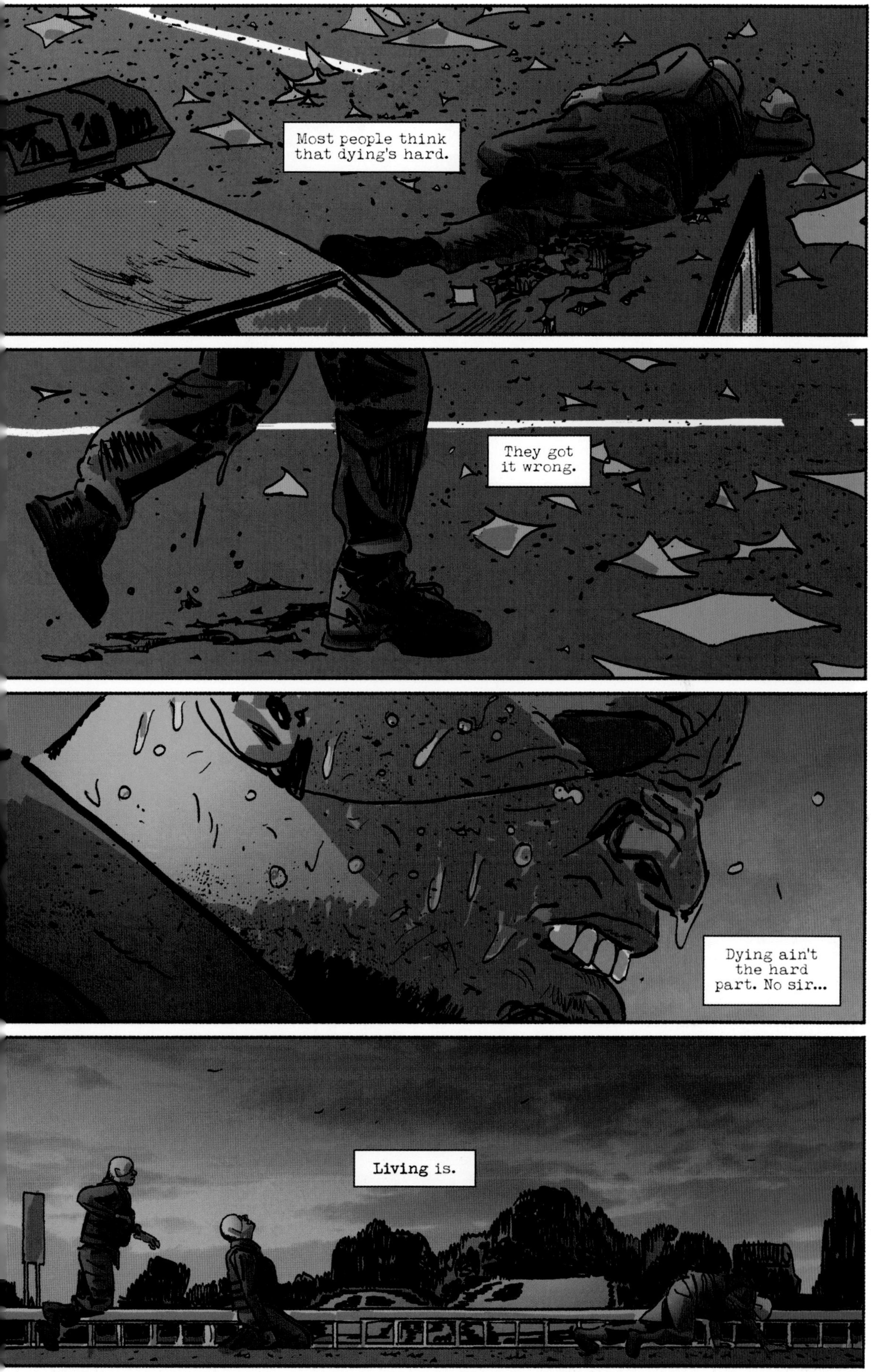
Most people think
that dying's hard.
They got
it wrong.
Dying ain't
the hard
part. No sir...
Living is.

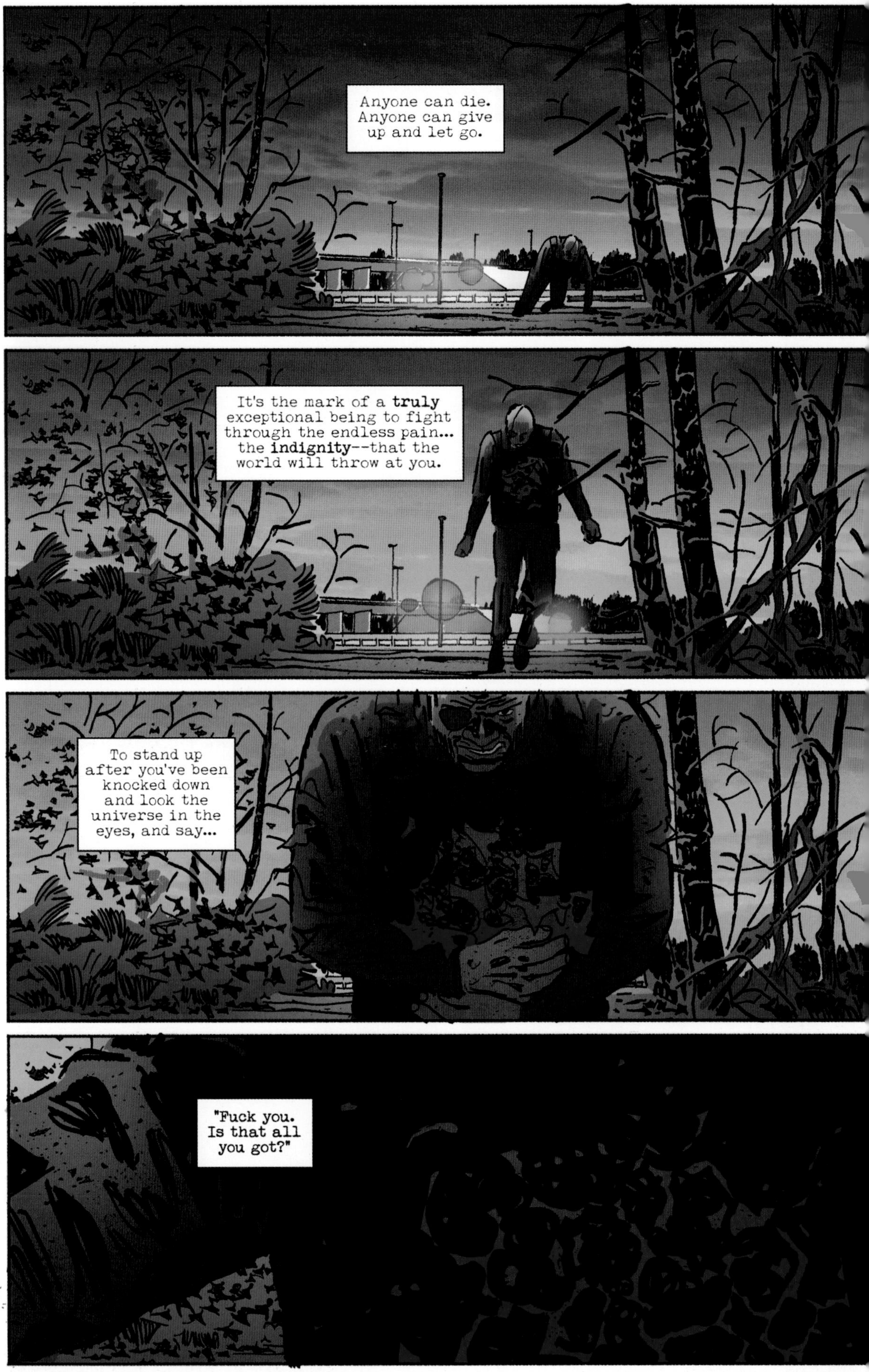
Anyone can die. Anyone can give up and let go.
It's the mark of a **truly** exceptional being to fight through the endless pain... the **indignity**--that the world will throw at you.
To stand up after you've been knocked down and look the universe in the eyes, and say...
"Fuck you. Is that all you got?"

This would be a fine
death...out here
among the trees.

But not a
warrior's
death.

Vietnam. The Gulf. All
the missions and wars **so
redacted** he doesn't know
what to call them. All
those **endless deserts** and
blood-drenched conflicts.

He didn't survive
all that to die here
now. Gut shot from
some **dumb teenager.
No. He can't die yet.**

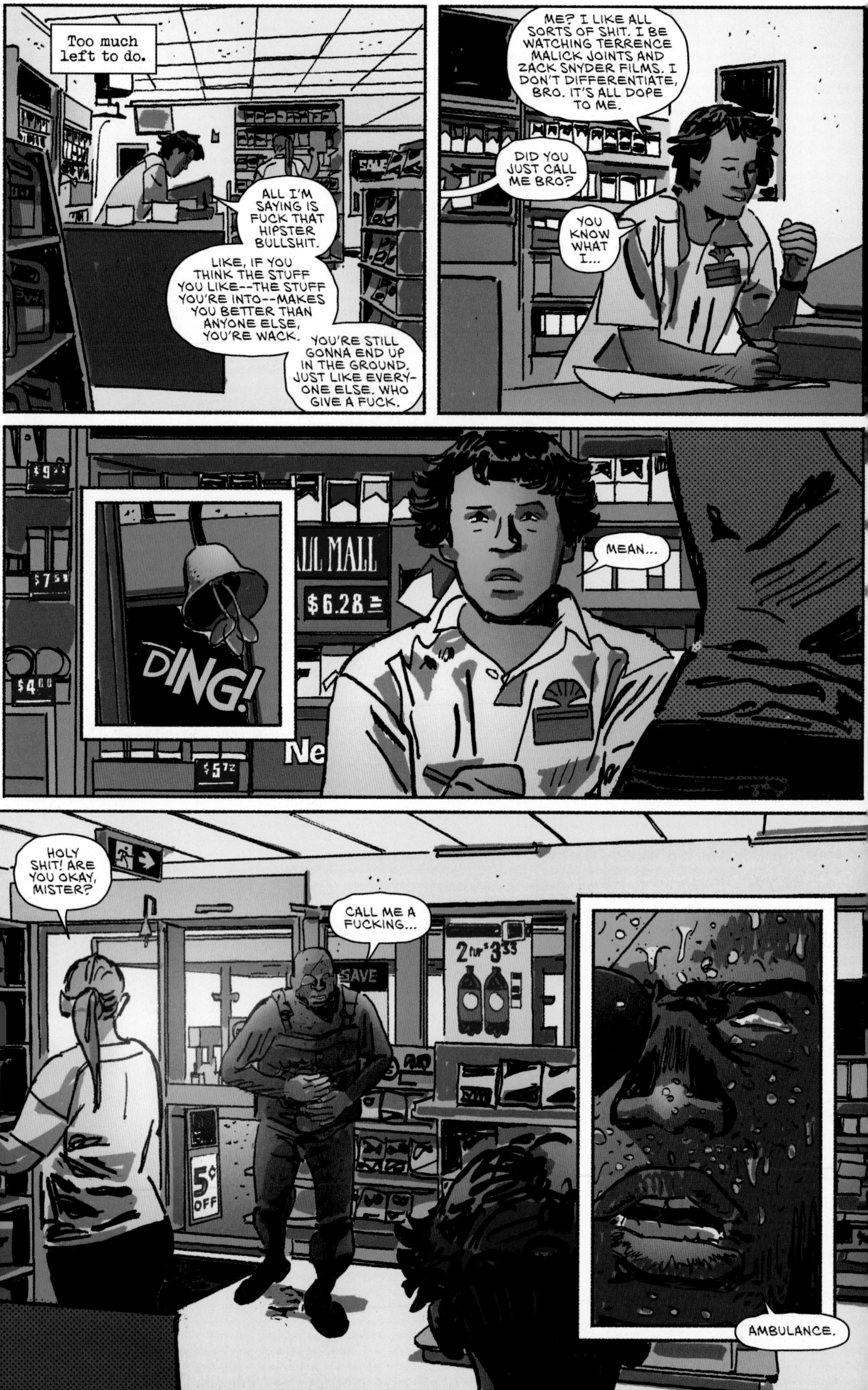
Too much left to do.
ALL I'M SAYING IS FUCK THAT HIPSTER BULLSHIT.
LIKE, IF YOU THINK THE STUFF YOU LIKE--THE STUFF YOU'RE INTO--MAKES YOU BETTER THAN ANYONE ELSE, YOU'RE WACK.
YOU'RE STILL GONNA END UP IN THE GROUND. JUST LIKE EVERY-ONE ELSE. WHO GIVE A FUCK.
ME? I LIKE ALL SORTS OF SHIT. I BE WATCHING TERRENCE MALICK JOINTS AND ZACK SNYDER FILMS. I DON'T DIFFERENTIATE, BRO. IT'S ALL DOPE TO ME.
DID YOU JUST CALL ME BRO?
YOU KNOW WHAT I...
DING!
MEAN...
$6.28
HOLY SHIT! ARE YOU OKAY, MISTER?
CALL ME A FUCKING...
SAVE
5¢ OFF
AMBULANCE.

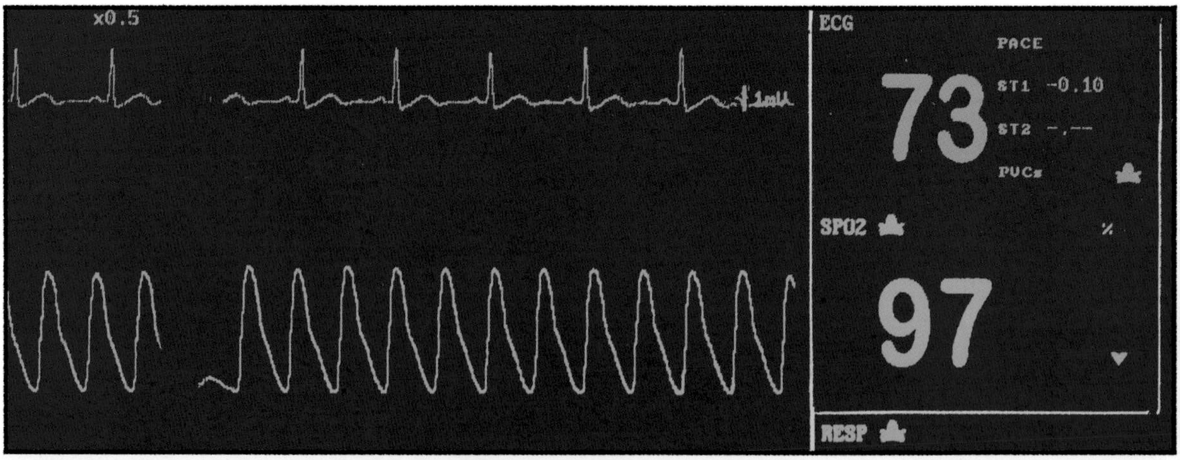
x0.5
1mV
ECG
PACE
73
ST1 -0.10
ST2 -.--
PVCs
SPO2
%
97
RESP

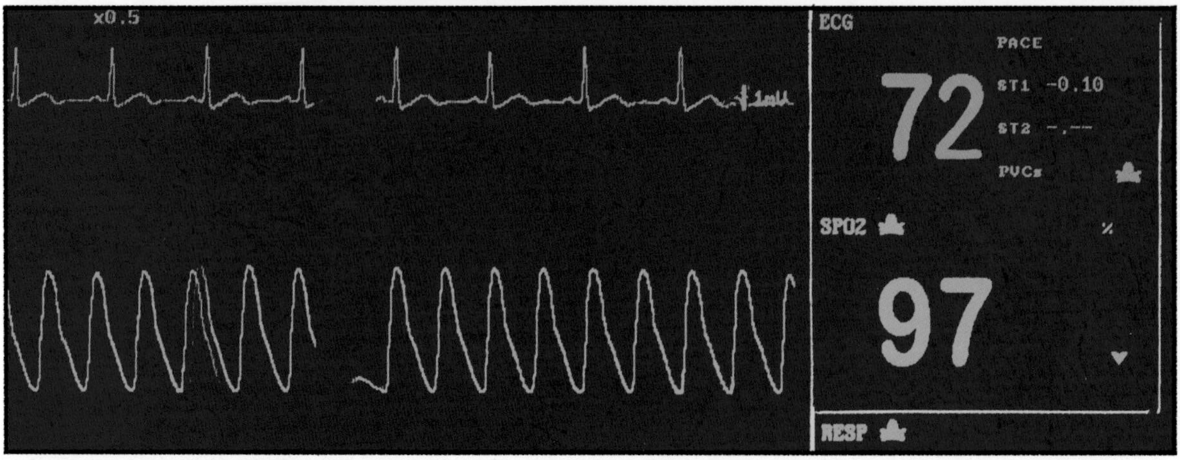
x0.5
1mV
ECG
PACE
72
ST1 -0.10
ST2 -.--
PVCs
SPO2
%
97
RESP

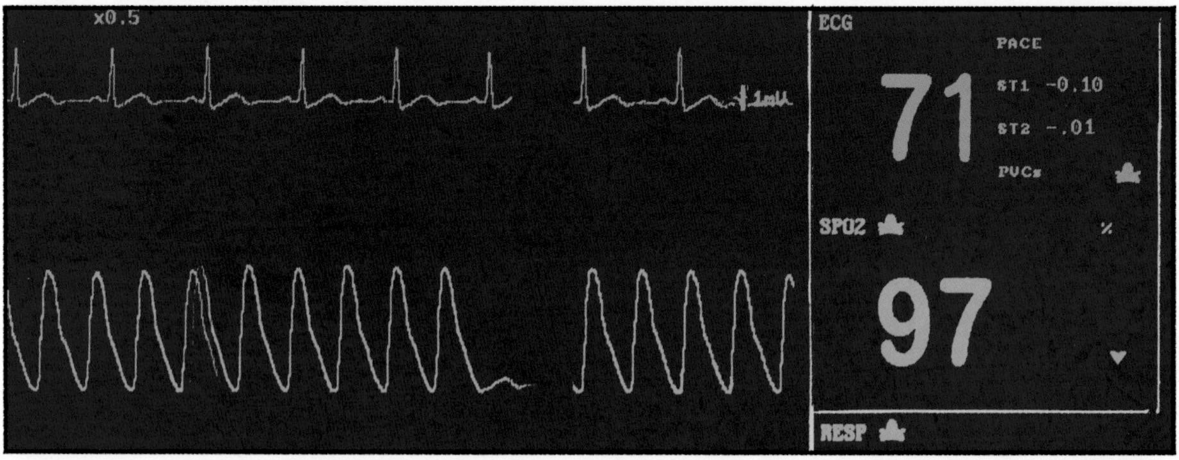
x0.5
1mV
ECG
PACE
71
ST1 -0.10
ST2 -.01
PVCs
SPO2
%
97
RESP

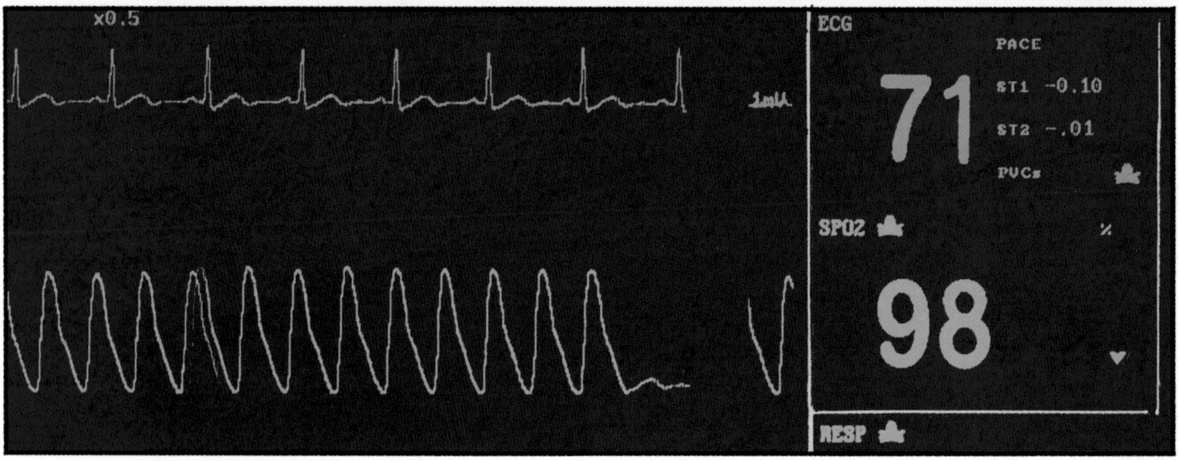
x0.5
1mV
ECG
PACE
71
ST1 -0.10
ST2 -.01
PVCs
SPO2
%
98
RESP

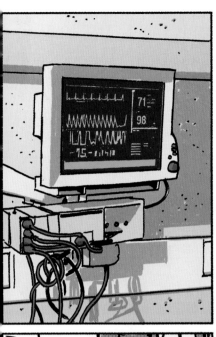

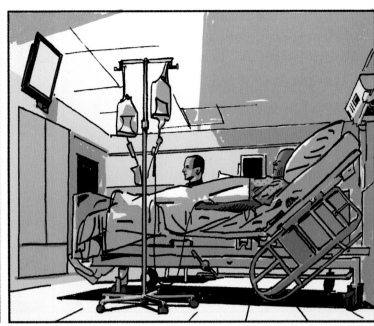

ARMORED TRUCK ROBBERY

BREATHTAKING FOOTAGE ALLEGEDLY TAKEN IN A LOCAL ROBBERY IS DRAWING CONVERSATION ONLINE.

IS THIS FOOTAGE ALTERED? EDITED? A VIRAL MARKETING STUNT FOR SOME SORT OF FILM? MORE AFTER THE BREAK...

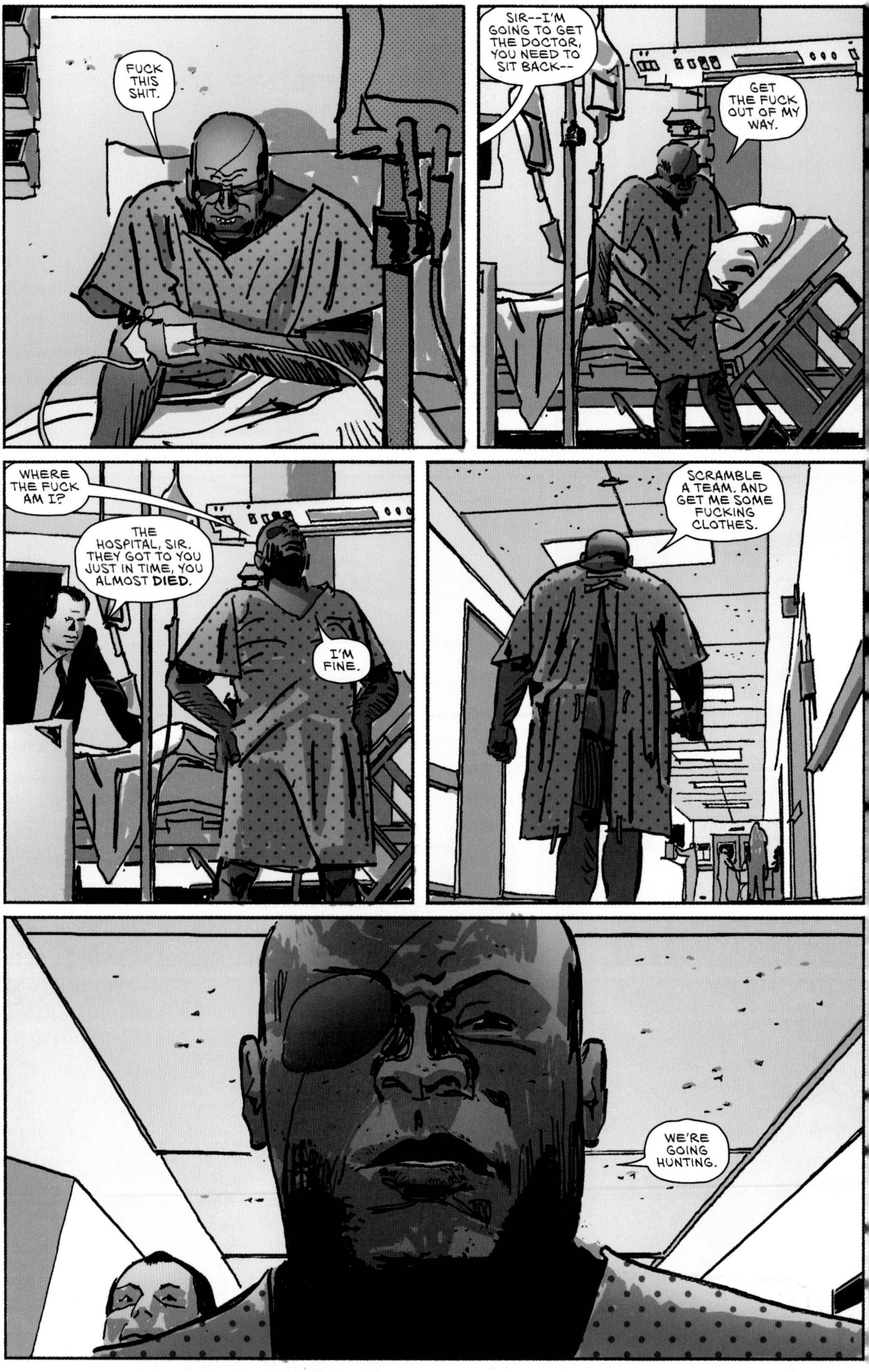
FUCK THIS SHIT.
SIR--I'M GOING TO GET THE DOCTOR, YOU NEED TO SIT BACK--
GET THE FUCK OUT OF MY WAY.
WHERE THE FUCK AM I?
THE HOSPITAL, SIR. THEY GOT TO YOU JUST IN TIME, YOU ALMOST DIED.
I'M FINE.
SCRAMBLE A TEAM. AND GET ME SOME FUCKING CLOTHES.
WE'RE GOING HUNTING.

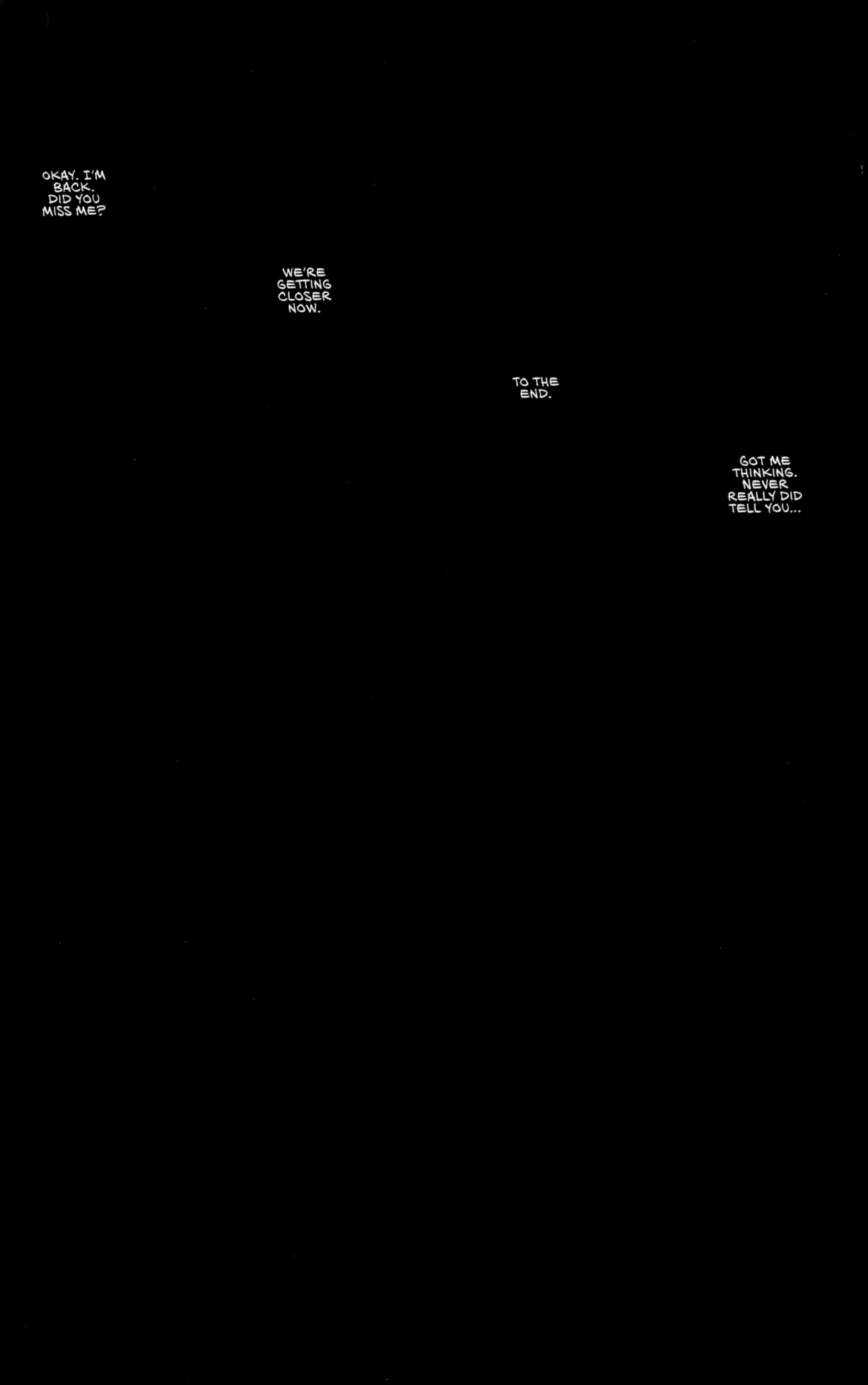
OKAY. I'M BACK. DID YOU MISS ME?
WE'RE GETTING CLOSER NOW.
TO THE END.
GOT ME THINKING. NEVER REALLY DID TELL YOU...

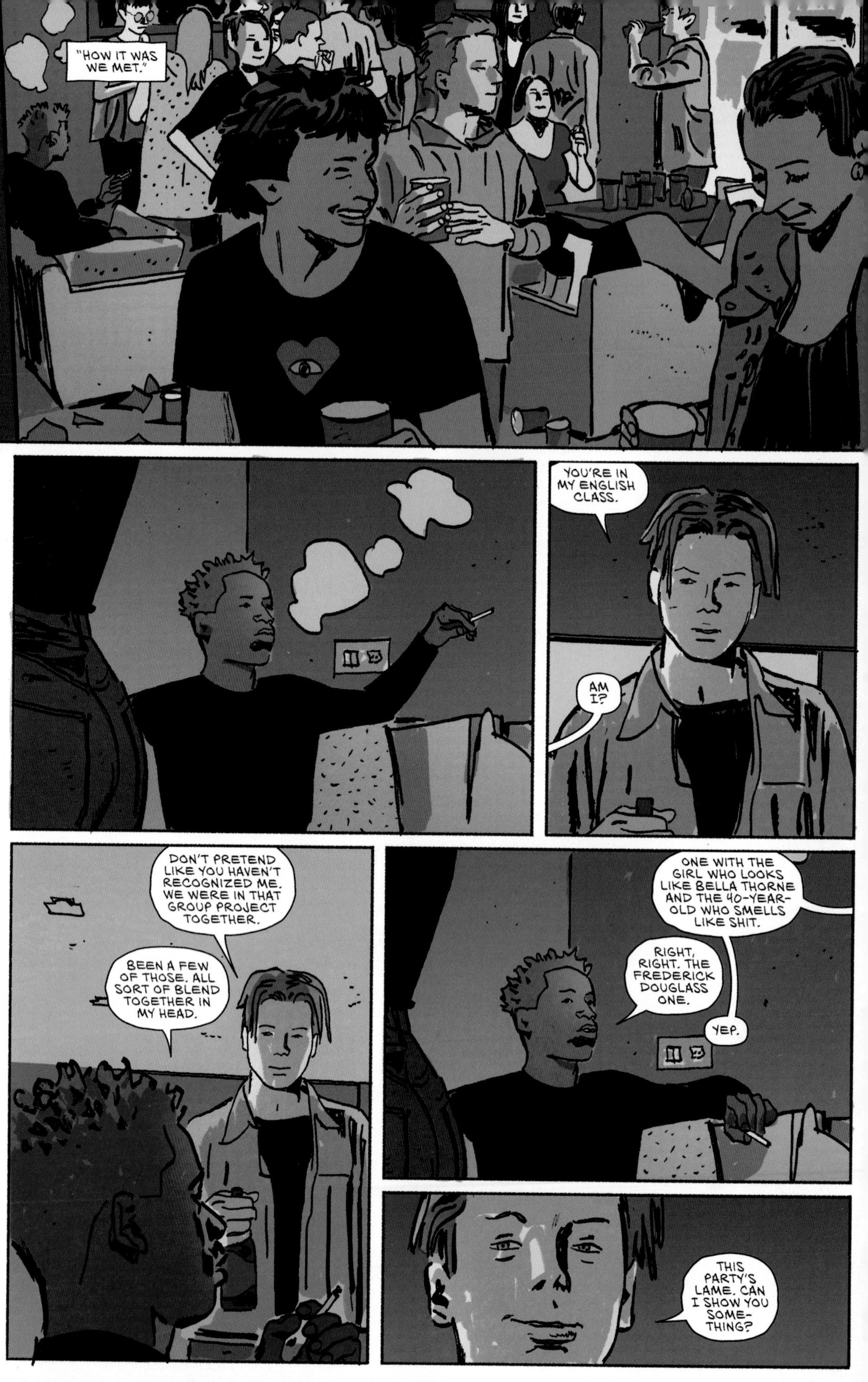
"HOW IT WAS WE MET."
YOU'RE IN MY ENGLISH CLASS.
AM I?
DON'T PRETEND LIKE YOU HAVEN'T RECOGNIZED ME. WE WERE IN THAT GROUP PROJECT TOGETHER.
BEEN A FEW OF THOSE. ALL SORT OF BLEND TOGETHER IN MY HEAD.
ONE WITH THE GIRL WHO LOOKS LIKE BELLA THORNE AND THE 40-YEAR-OLD WHO SMELLS LIKE SHIT.
RIGHT, RIGHT. THE FREDERICK DOUGLASS ONE.
YEP.
THIS PARTY'S LAME. CAN I SHOW YOU SOME-THING?

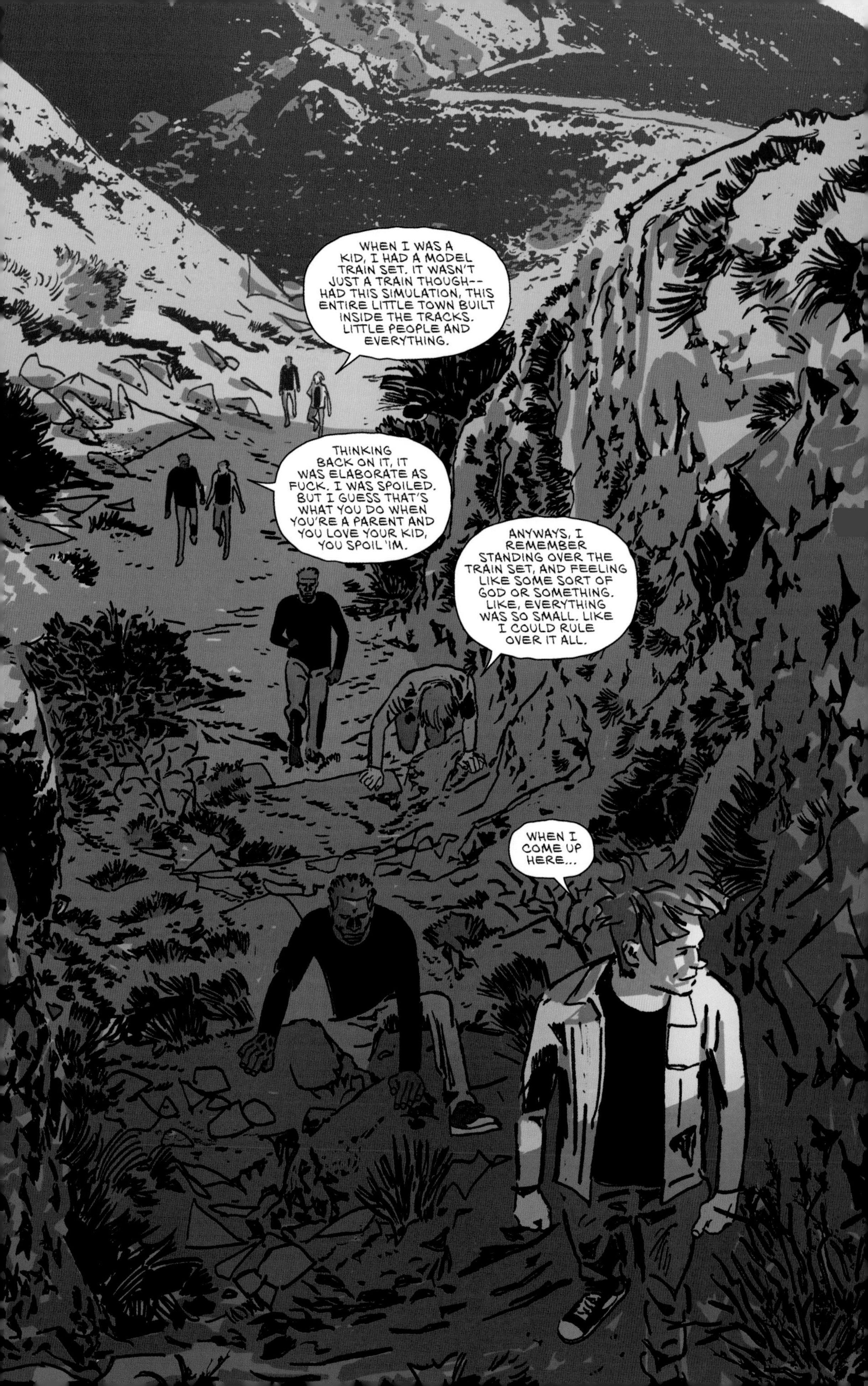
WHEN I WAS A KID, I HAD A MODEL TRAIN SET. IT WASN'T JUST A TRAIN THOUGH-- HAD THIS SIMULATION, THIS ENTIRE LITTLE TOWN BUILT INSIDE THE TRACKS. LITTLE PEOPLE AND EVERYTHING.
THINKING BACK ON IT, IT WAS ELABORATE AS FUCK. I WAS SPOILED. BUT I GUESS THAT'S WHAT YOU DO WHEN YOU'RE A PARENT AND YOU LOVE YOUR KID, YOU SPOIL 'IM.
ANYWAYS, I REMEMBER STANDING OVER THE TRAIN SET, AND FEELING LIKE SOME SORT OF GOD OR SOMETHING. LIKE, EVERYTHING WAS SO SMALL. LIKE I COULD RULE OVER IT ALL.
WHEN I COME UP HERE...

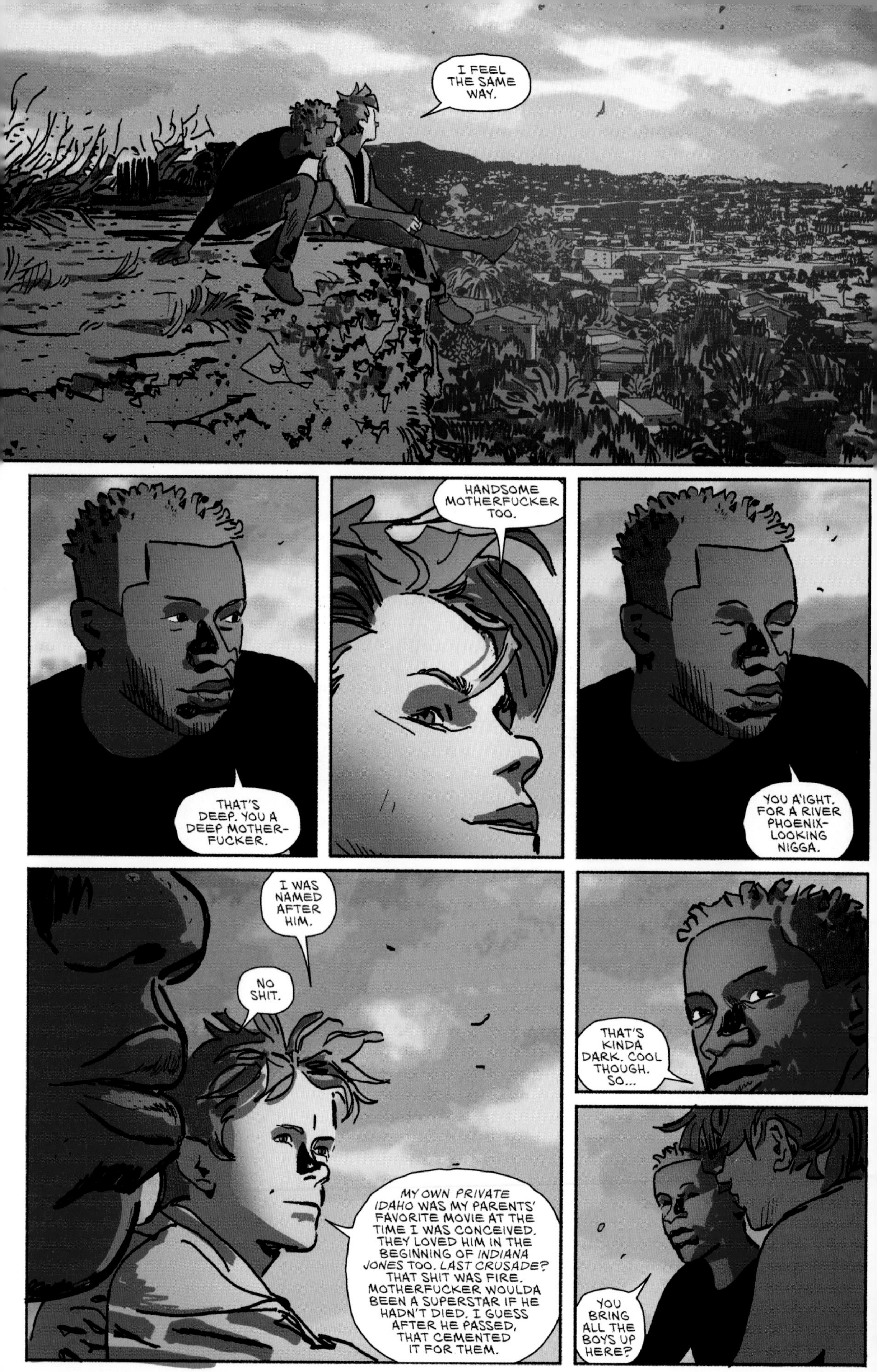
I FEEL THE SAME WAY.
THAT'S DEEP. YOU A DEEP MOTHER-FUCKER.
HANDSOME MOTHERFUCKER TOO.
YOU A'IGHT. FOR A RIVER PHOENIX-LOOKING NIGGA.
I WAS NAMED AFTER HIM.
NO SHIT.
MY OWN PRIVATE IDAHO WAS MY PARENTS' FAVORITE MOVIE AT THE TIME I WAS CONCEIVED. THEY LOVED HIM IN THE BEGINNING OF INDIANA JONES TOO. LAST CRUSADE? THAT SHIT WAS FIRE. MOTHERFUCKER WOULDA BEEN A SUPERSTAR IF HE HADN'T DIED. I GUESS AFTER HE PASSED, THAT CEMENTED IT FOR THEM.
THAT'S KINDA DARK. COOL THOUGH. SO...
YOU BRING ALL THE BOYS UP HERE?

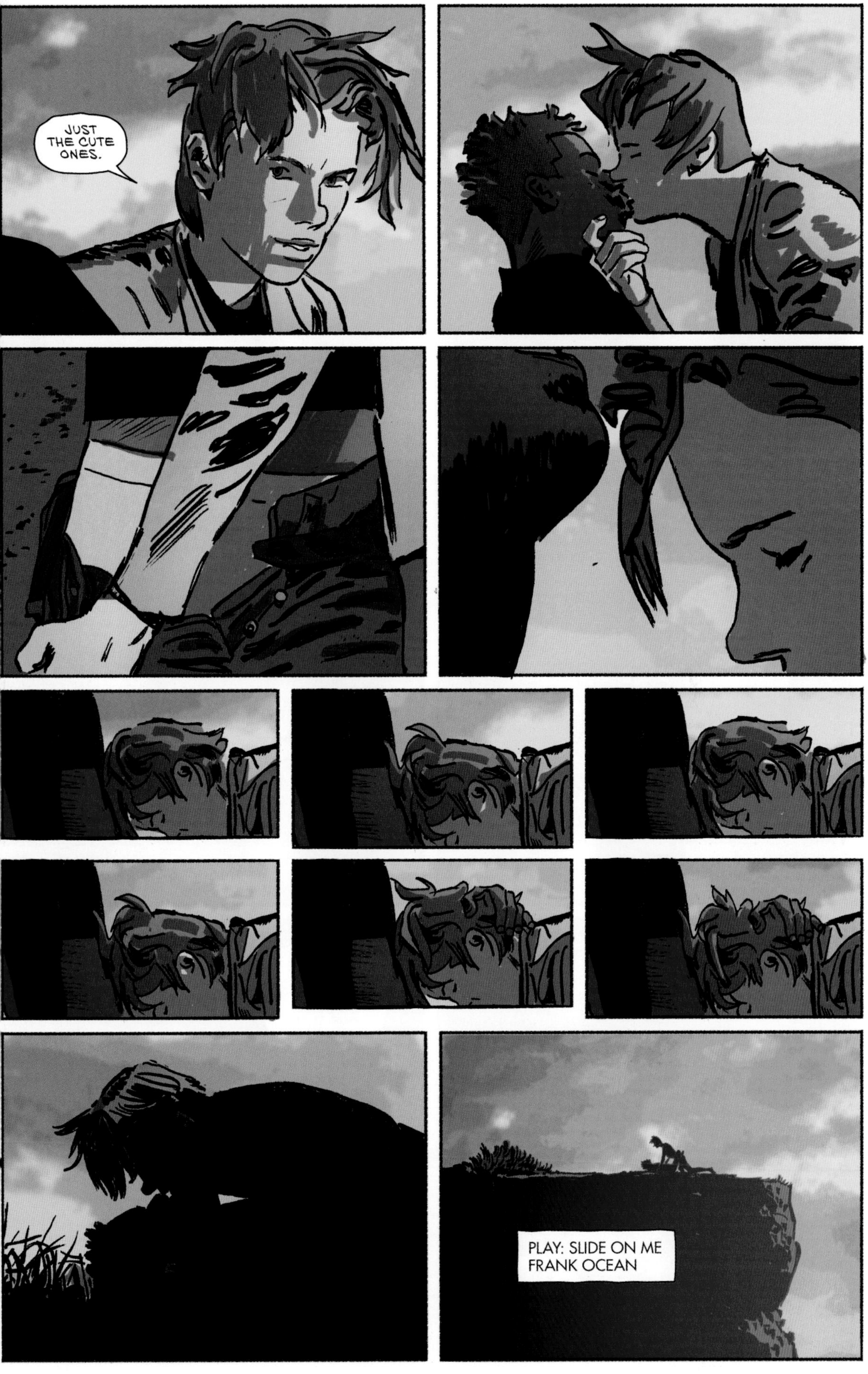
JUST THE CUTE ONES.
PLAY: SLIDE ON ME
FRANK OCEAN

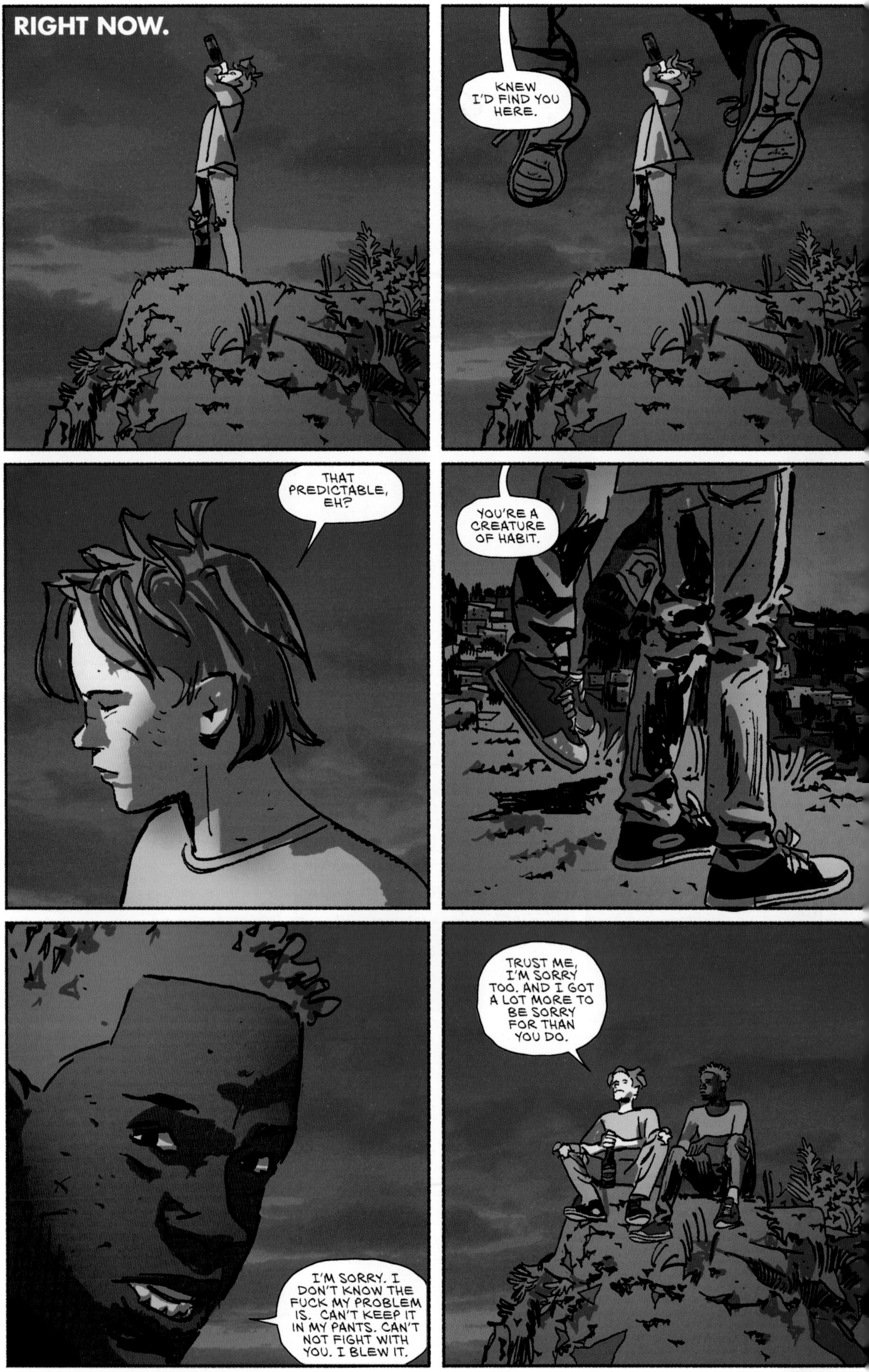
RIGHT NOW.
KNEW I'D FIND YOU HERE.
THAT PREDICTABLE, EH?
YOU'RE A CREATURE OF HABIT.
I'M SORRY. I DON'T KNOW THE FUCK MY PROBLEM IS. CAN'T KEEP IT IN MY PANTS. CAN'T NOT FIGHT WITH YOU. I BLEW IT.
TRUST ME, I'M SORRY TOO. AND I GOT A LOT MORE TO BE SORRY FOR THAN YOU DO.

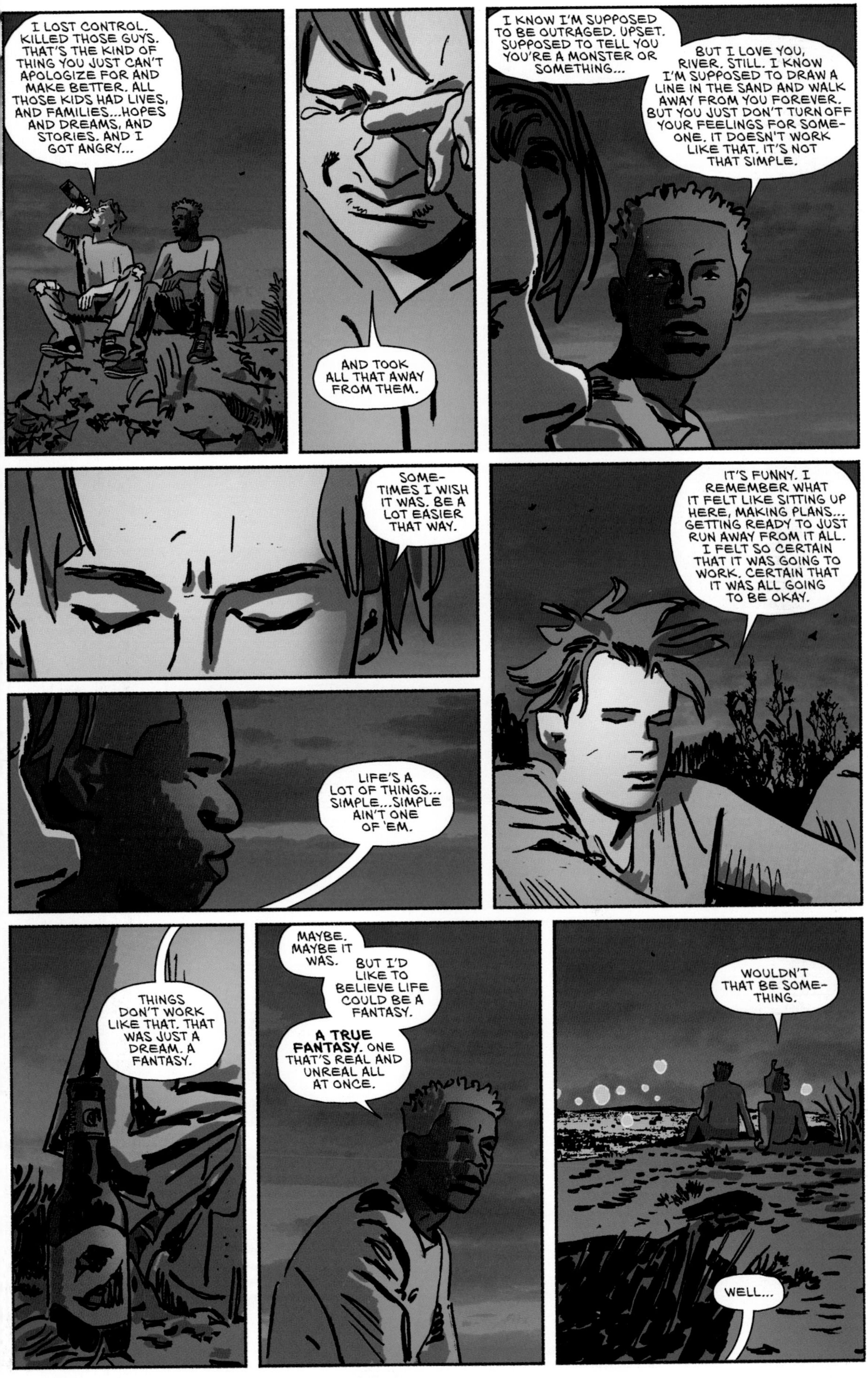
I LOST CONTROL. KILLED THOSE GUYS. THAT'S THE KIND OF THING YOU JUST CAN'T APOLOGIZE FOR AND MAKE BETTER. ALL THOSE KIDS HAD LIVES, AND FAMILIES...HOPES AND DREAMS, AND STORIES. AND I GOT ANGRY...
AND TOOK ALL THAT AWAY FROM THEM.
I KNOW I'M SUPPOSED TO BE OUTRAGED. UPSET. SUPPOSED TO TELL YOU YOU'RE A MONSTER OR SOMETHING...
BUT I LOVE YOU, RIVER. STILL. I KNOW I'M SUPPOSED TO DRAW A LINE IN THE SAND AND WALK AWAY FROM YOU FOREVER. BUT YOU JUST DON'T TURN OFF YOUR FEELINGS FOR SOME-ONE. IT DOESN'T WORK LIKE THAT. IT'S NOT THAT SIMPLE.
SOME-TIMES I WISH IT WAS. BE A LOT EASIER THAT WAY.
LIFE'S A LOT OF THINGS... SIMPLE...SIMPLE AIN'T ONE OF 'EM.
IT'S FUNNY. I REMEMBER WHAT IT FELT LIKE SITTING UP HERE, MAKING PLANS... GETTING READY TO JUST RUN AWAY FROM IT ALL. I FELT SO CERTAIN THAT IT WAS GOING TO WORK. CERTAIN THAT IT WAS ALL GOING TO BE OKAY.
THINGS DON'T WORK LIKE THAT. THAT WAS JUST A DREAM. A FANTASY.
MAYBE. MAYBE IT WAS.
BUT I'D LIKE TO BELIEVE LIFE COULD BE A FANTASY.
A TRUE FANTASY. ONE THAT'S REAL AND UNREAL ALL AT ONCE.
WOULDN'T THAT BE SOME-THING.
WELL...

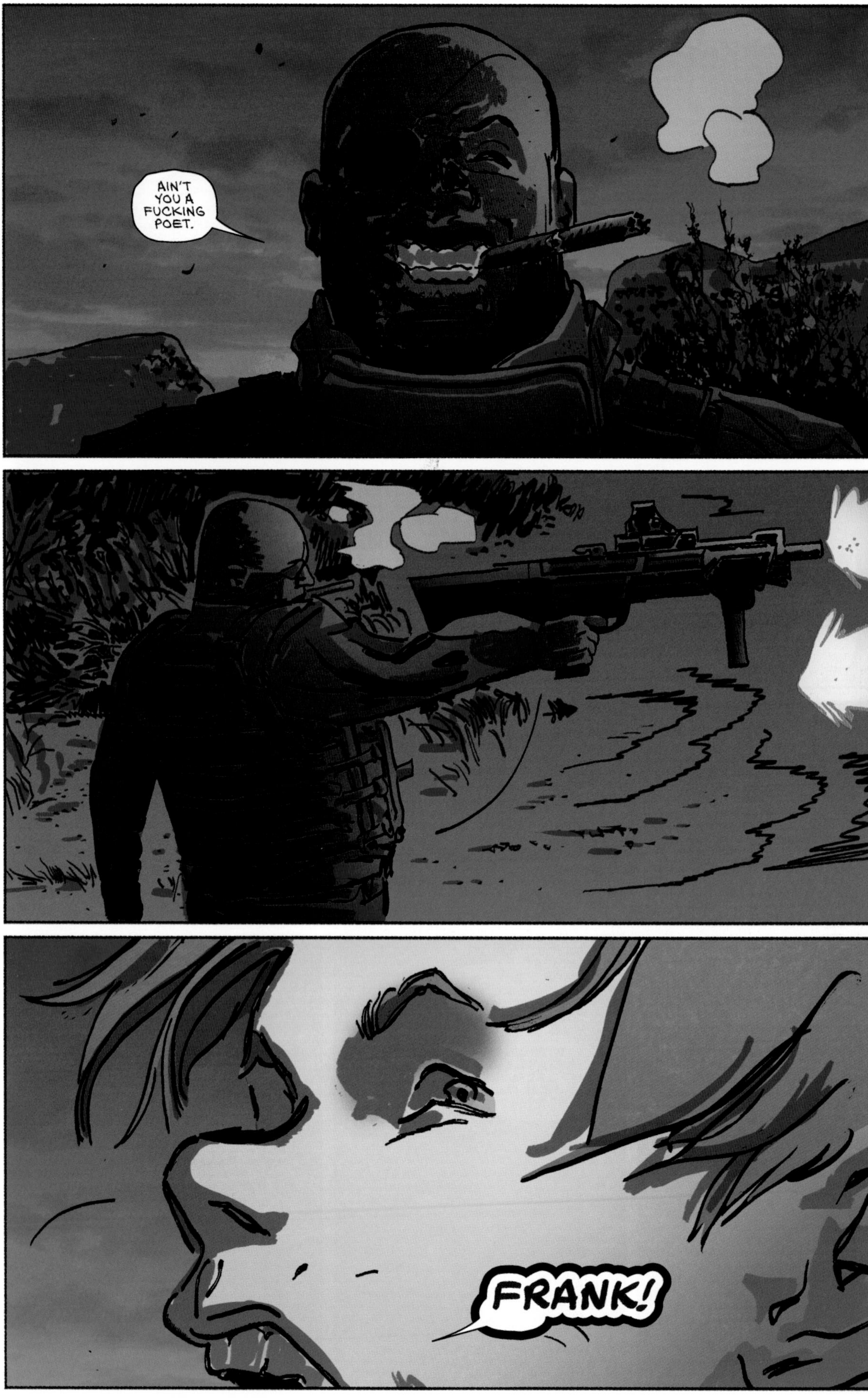
AIN'T YOU A FUCKING POET.
FRANK!

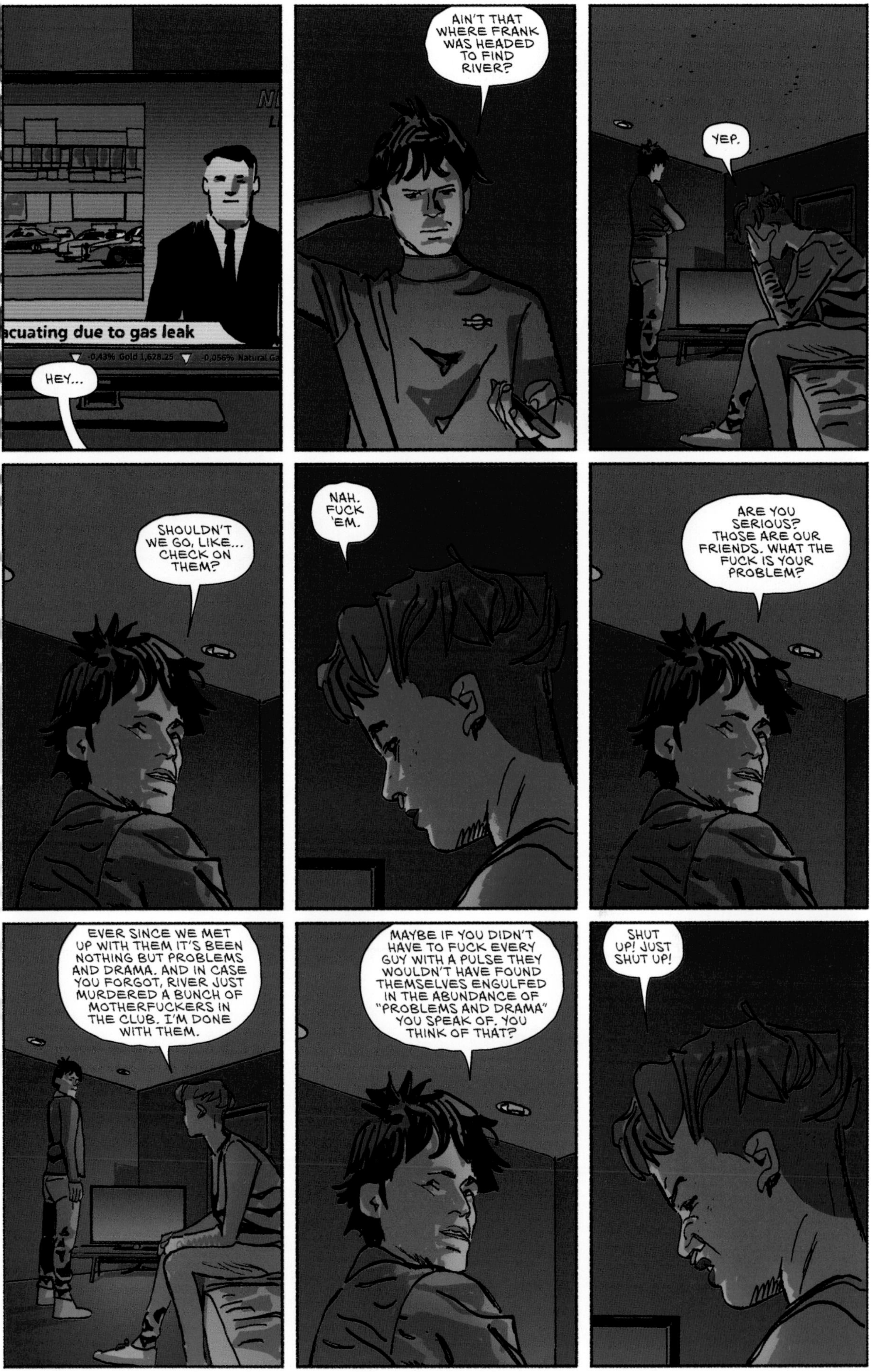
acuating due to gas leak
-0,43% Gold 1,628.25 -0,056% Natural Ga
HEY...
AIN'T THAT WHERE FRANK WAS HEADED TO FIND RIVER?
YEP.
SHOULDN'T WE GO, LIKE... CHECK ON THEM?
NAH. FUCK 'EM.
ARE YOU SERIOUS? THOSE ARE OUR FRIENDS. WHAT THE FUCK IS YOUR PROBLEM?
EVER SINCE WE MET UP WITH THEM IT'S BEEN NOTHING BUT PROBLEMS AND DRAMA. AND IN CASE YOU FORGOT, RIVER JUST MURDERED A BUNCH OF MOTHERFUCKERS IN THE CLUB. I'M DONE WITH THEM.
MAYBE IF YOU DIDN'T HAVE TO FUCK EVERY GUY WITH A PULSE THEY WOULDN'T HAVE FOUND THEMSELVES ENGULFED IN THE ABUNDANCE OF "PROBLEMS AND DRAMA" YOU SPEAK OF. YOU THINK OF THAT?
SHUT UP! JUST SHUT UP!

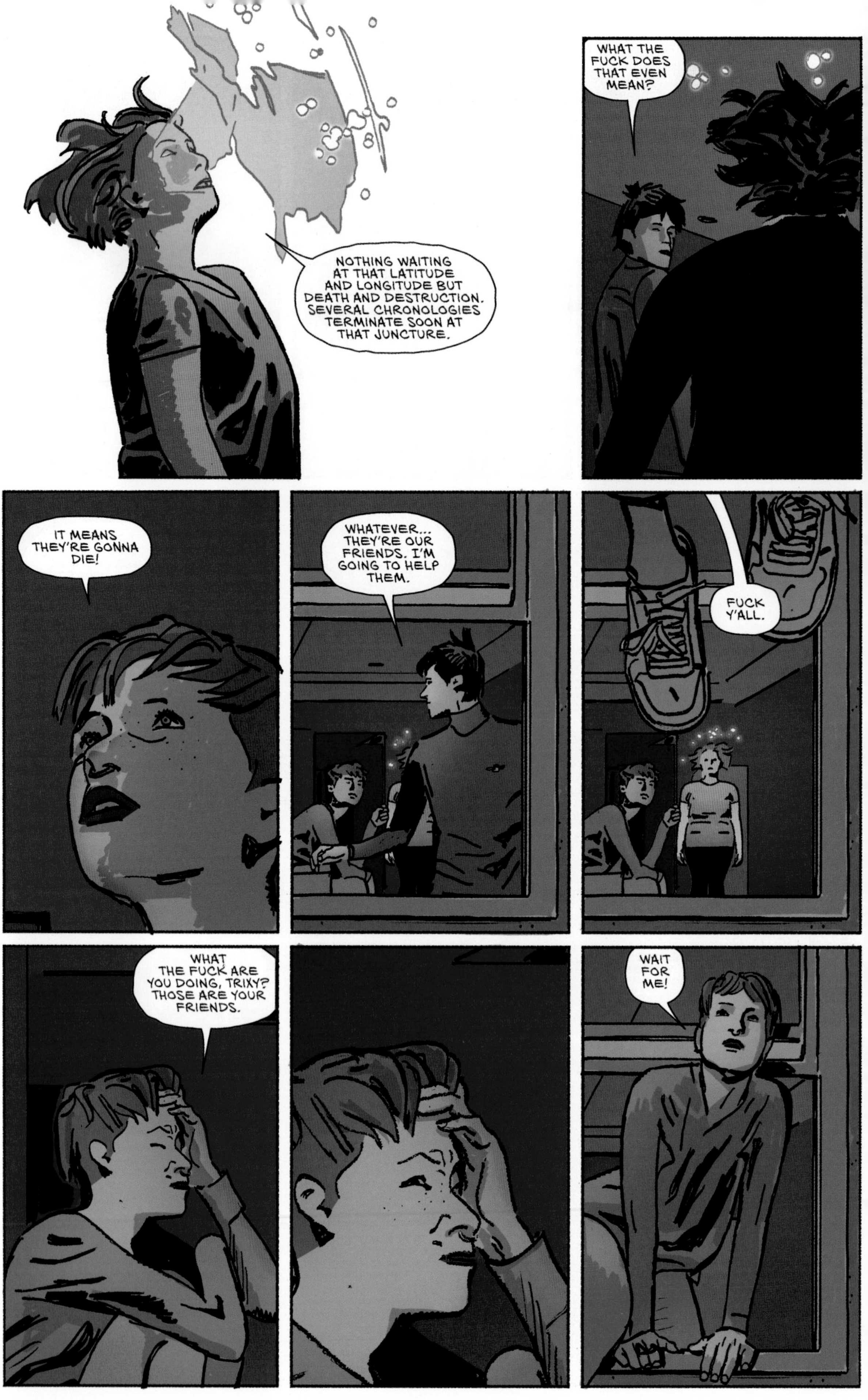
NOTHING WAITING AT THAT LATITUDE AND LONGITUDE BUT DEATH AND DESTRUCTION. SEVERAL CHRONOLOGIES TERMINATE SOON AT THAT JUNCTURE.
WHAT THE FUCK DOES THAT EVEN MEAN?
IT MEANS THEY'RE GONNA DIE!
WHATEVER... THEY'RE OUR FRIENDS. I'M GOING TO HELP THEM.
FUCK Y'ALL.
WHAT THE FUCK ARE YOU DOING, TRIXY? THOSE ARE YOUR FRIENDS.
WAIT FOR ME!

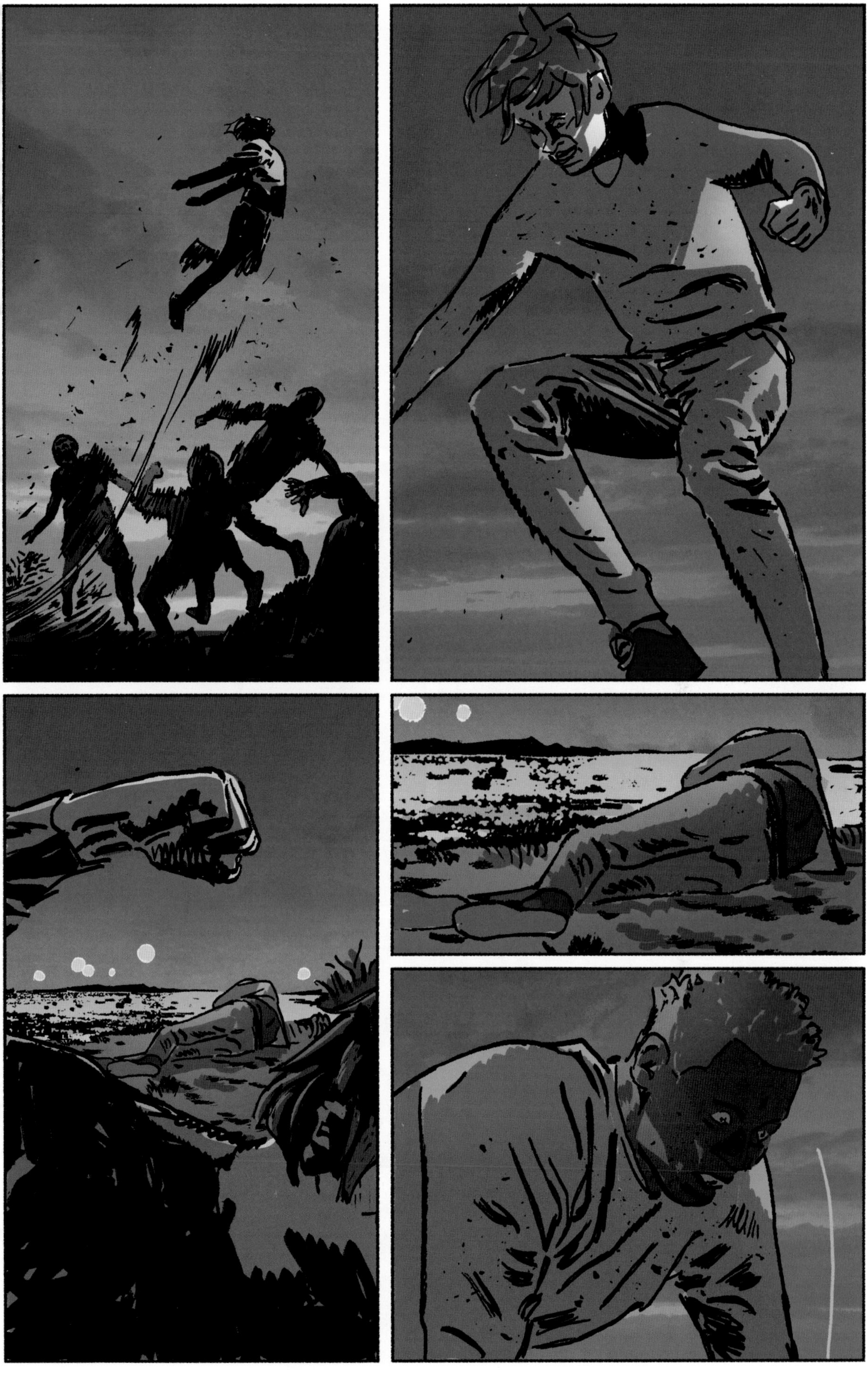

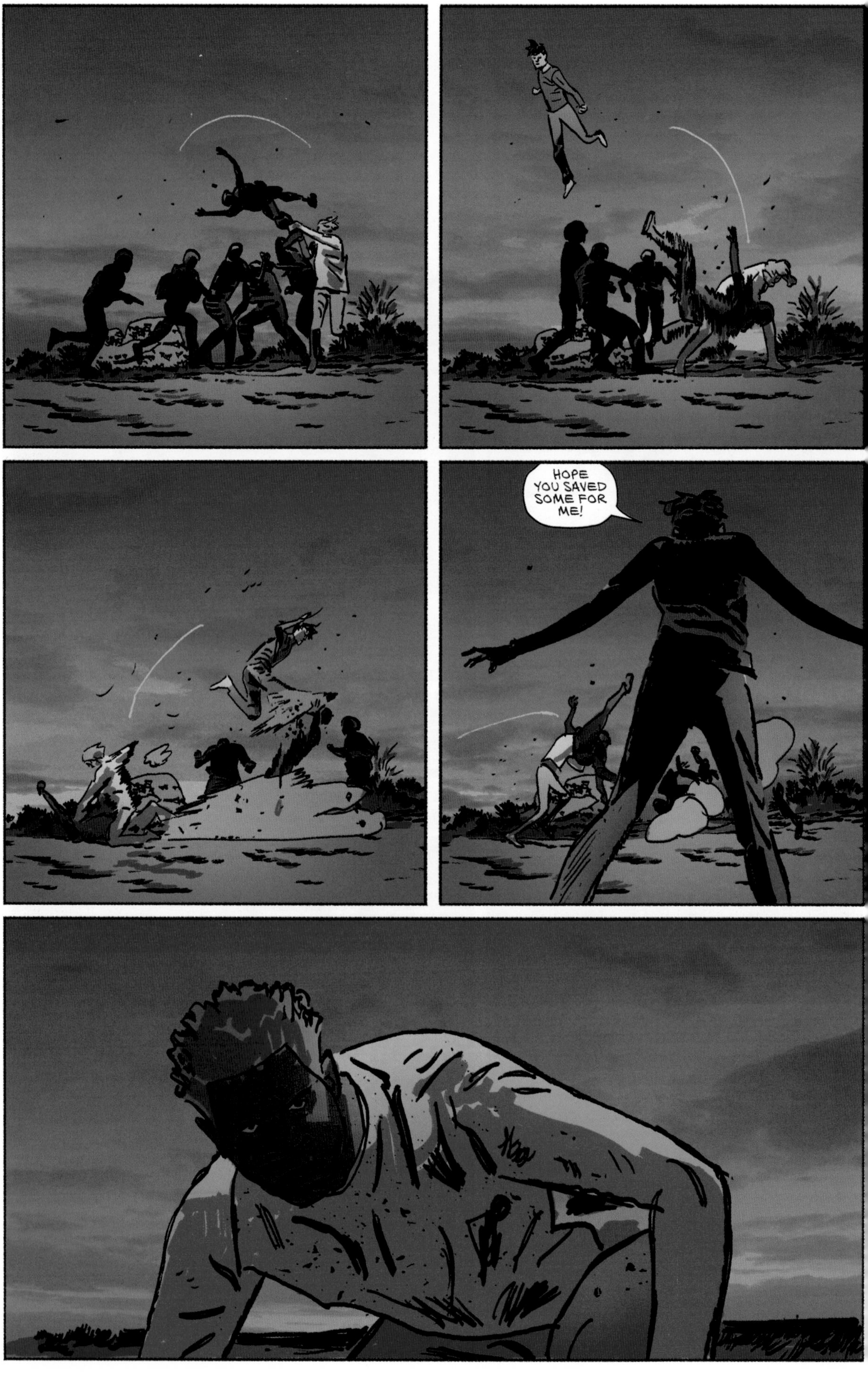
HOPE YOU SAVED SOME FOR ME!

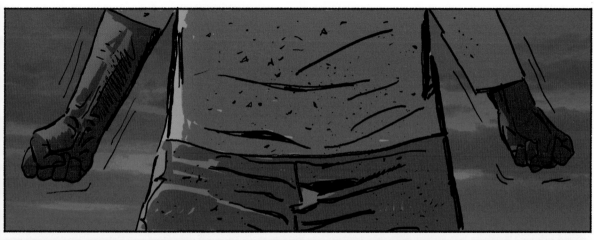

ANTICLIMACTIC.
I KNOW.

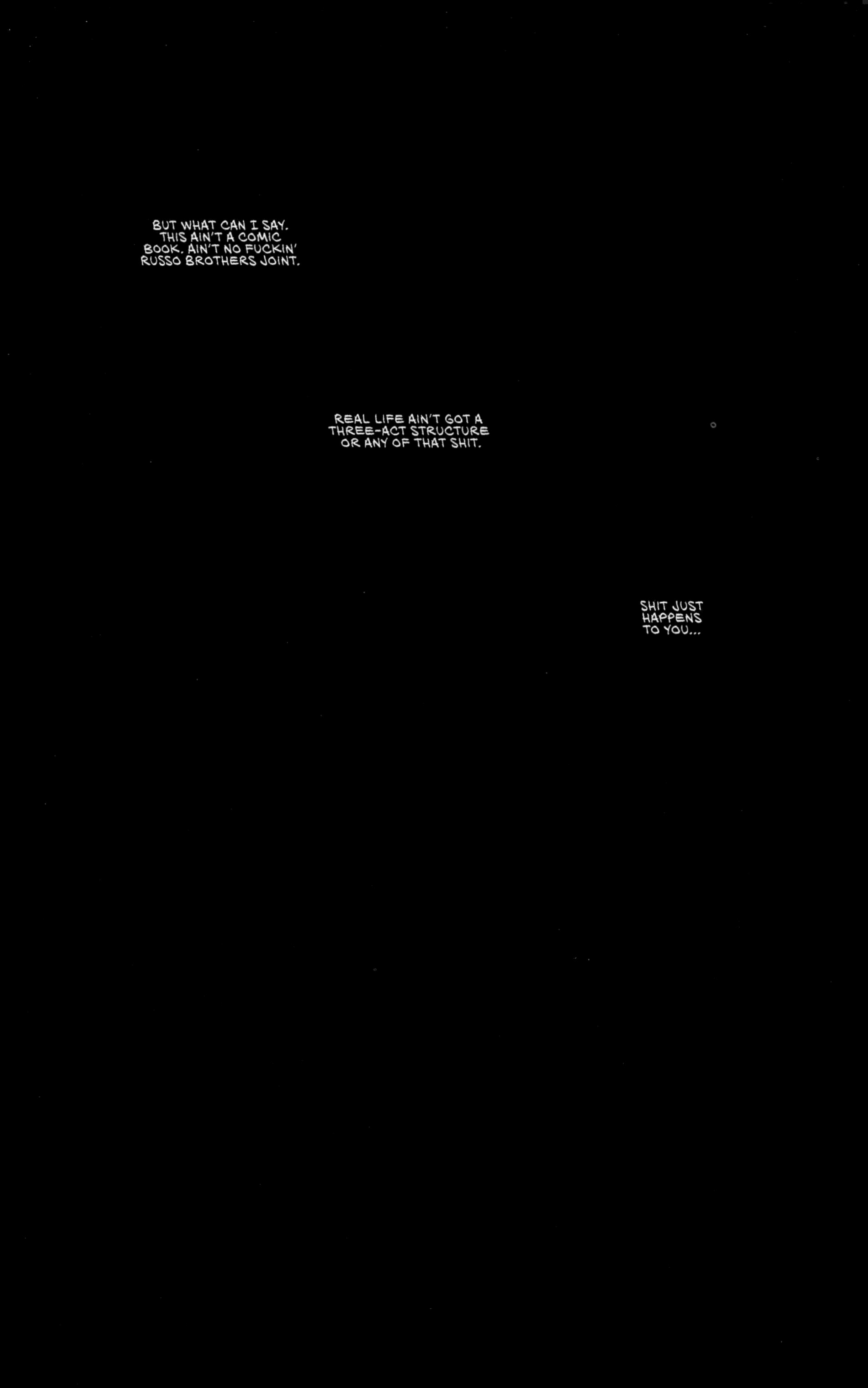
BUT WHAT CAN I SAY. THIS AIN'T A COMIC BOOK. AIN'T NO FUCKIN' RUSSO BROTHERS JOINT.
REAL LIFE AIN'T GOT A THREE-ACT STRUCTURE OR ANY OF THAT SHIT.
SHIT JUST HAPPENS TO YOU...

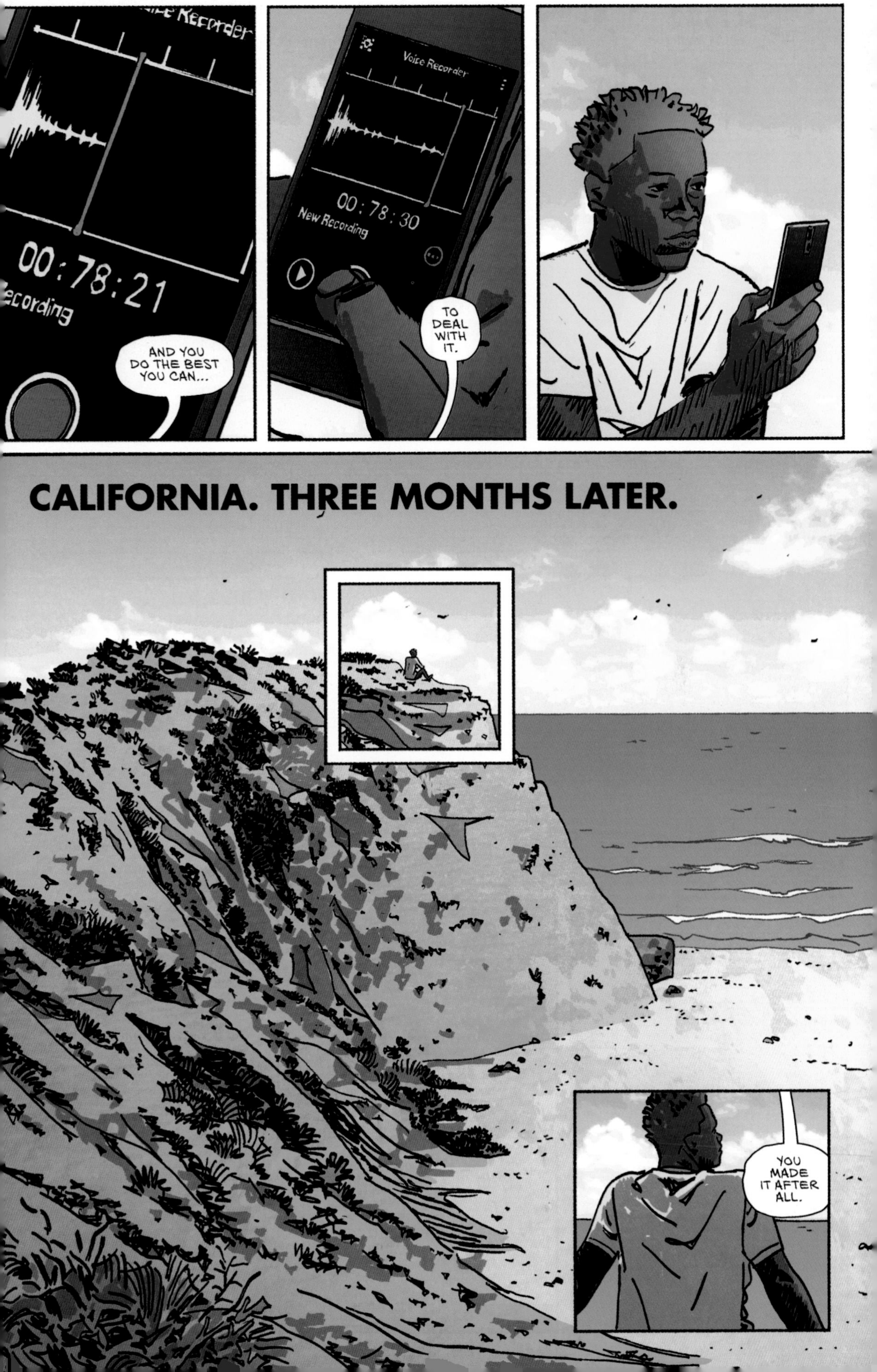
Voice Recorder
00:78:21
Recording
AND YOU DO THE BEST YOU CAN...
Voice Recorder
00:78:30
New Recording
TO DEAL WITH IT.
CALIFORNIA. THREE MONTHS LATER.
YOU MADE IT AFTER ALL.

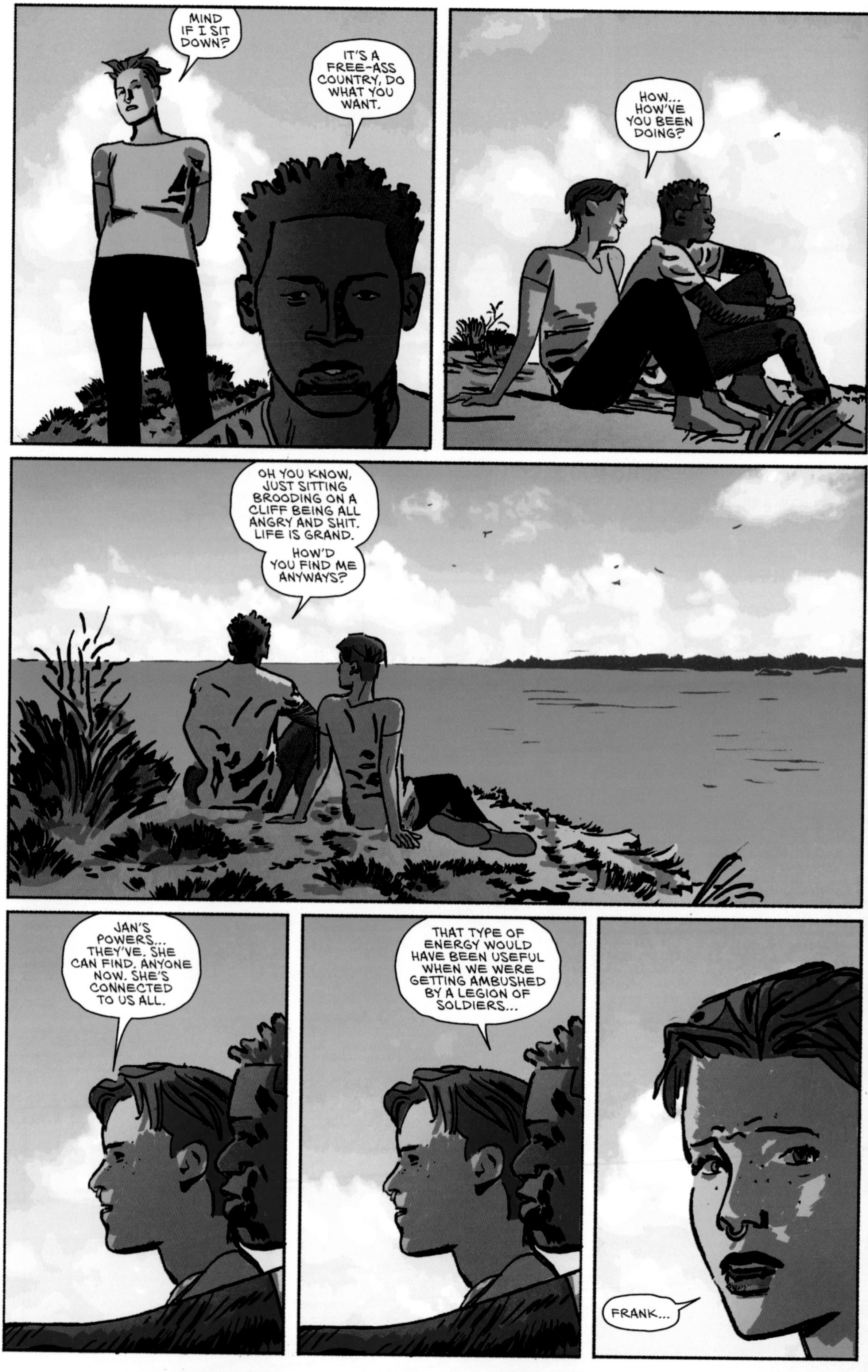
MIND IF I SIT DOWN?
IT'S A FREE-ASS COUNTRY, DO WHAT YOU WANT.
HOW... HOW'VE YOU BEEN DOING?
OH YOU KNOW, JUST SITTING BROODING ON A CLIFF BEING ALL ANGRY AND SHIT. LIFE IS GRAND.
HOW'D YOU FIND ME ANYWAYS?
JAN'S POWERS... THEY'VE. SHE CAN FIND. ANYONE NOW. SHE'S CONNECTED TO US ALL.
THAT TYPE OF ENERGY WOULD HAVE BEEN USEFUL WHEN WE WERE GETTING AMBUSHED BY A LEGION OF SOLDIERS...
FRANK...

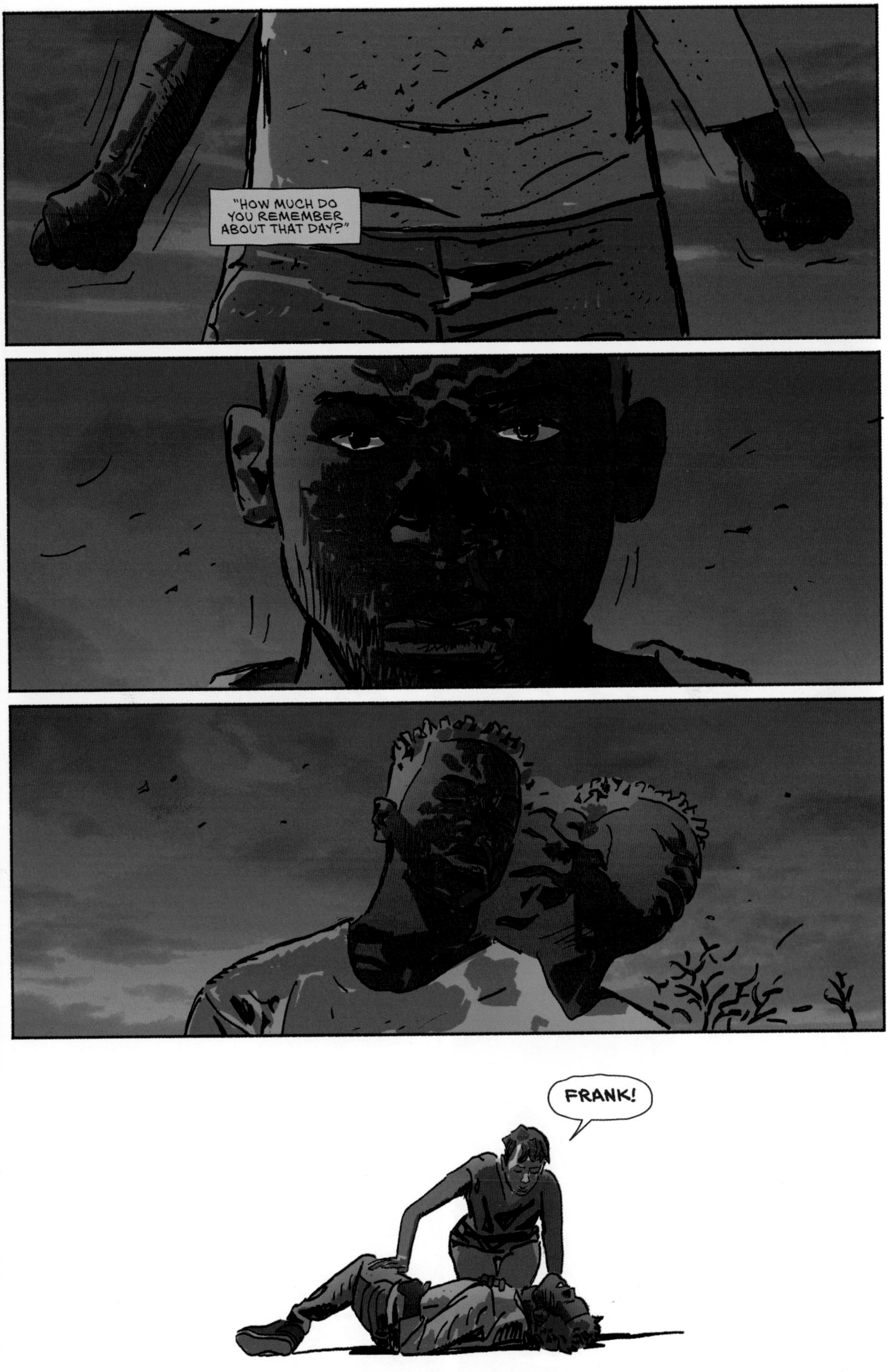
"HOW MUCH DO YOU REMEMBER ABOUT THAT DAY?"
FRANK!

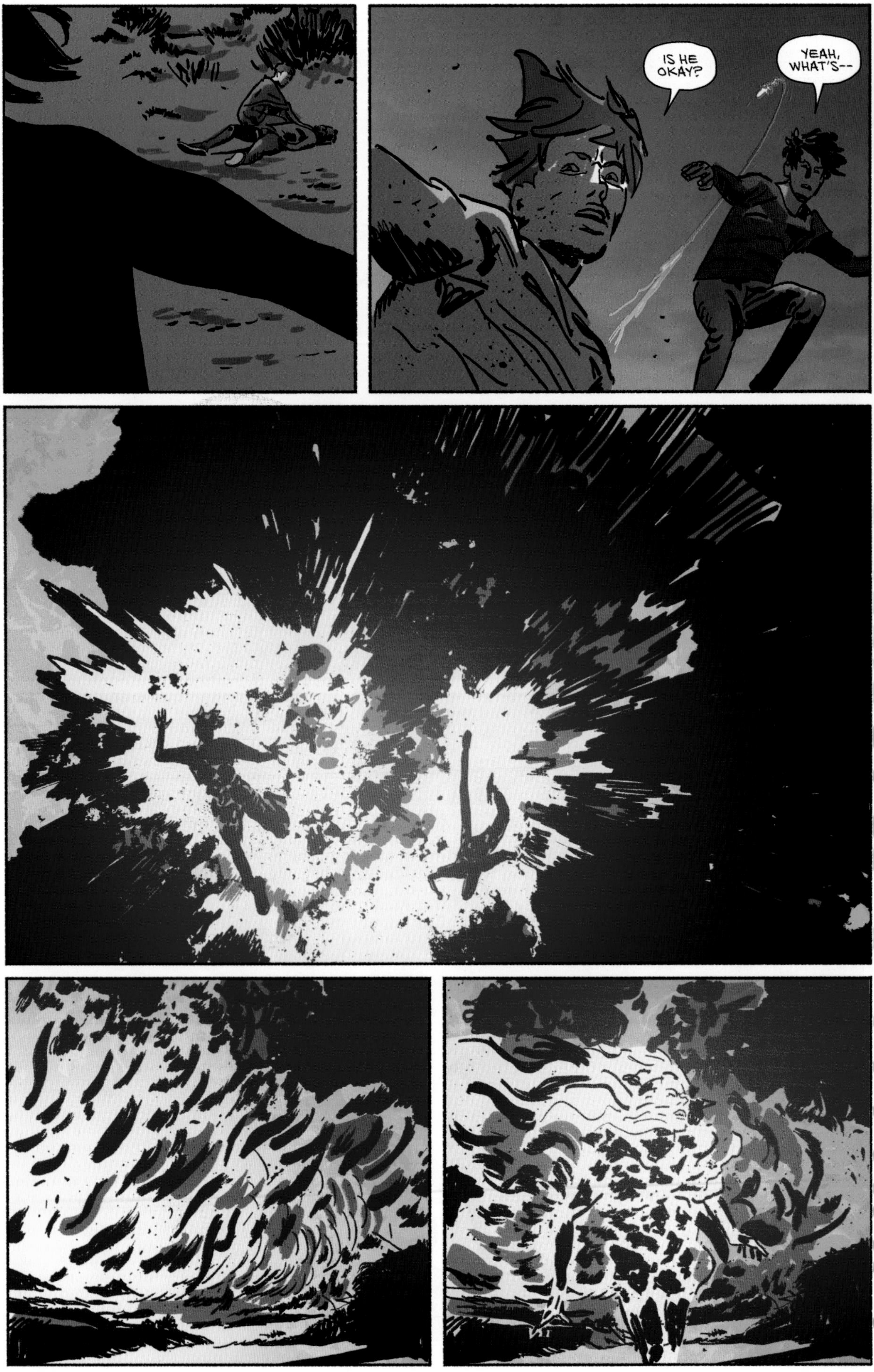
IS HE OKAY?
YEAH, WHAT'S--

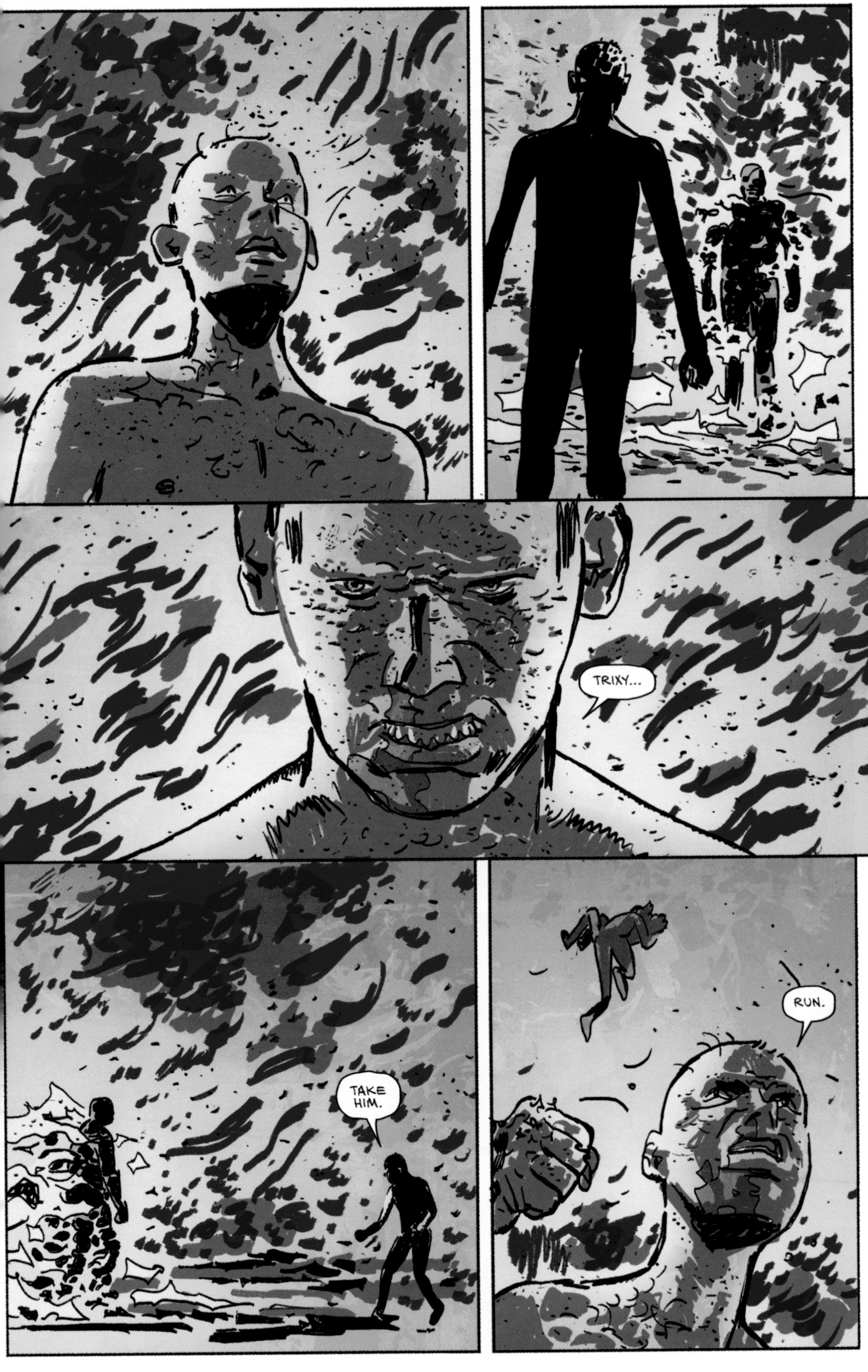
TRIXY...
TAKE HIM.
RUN.

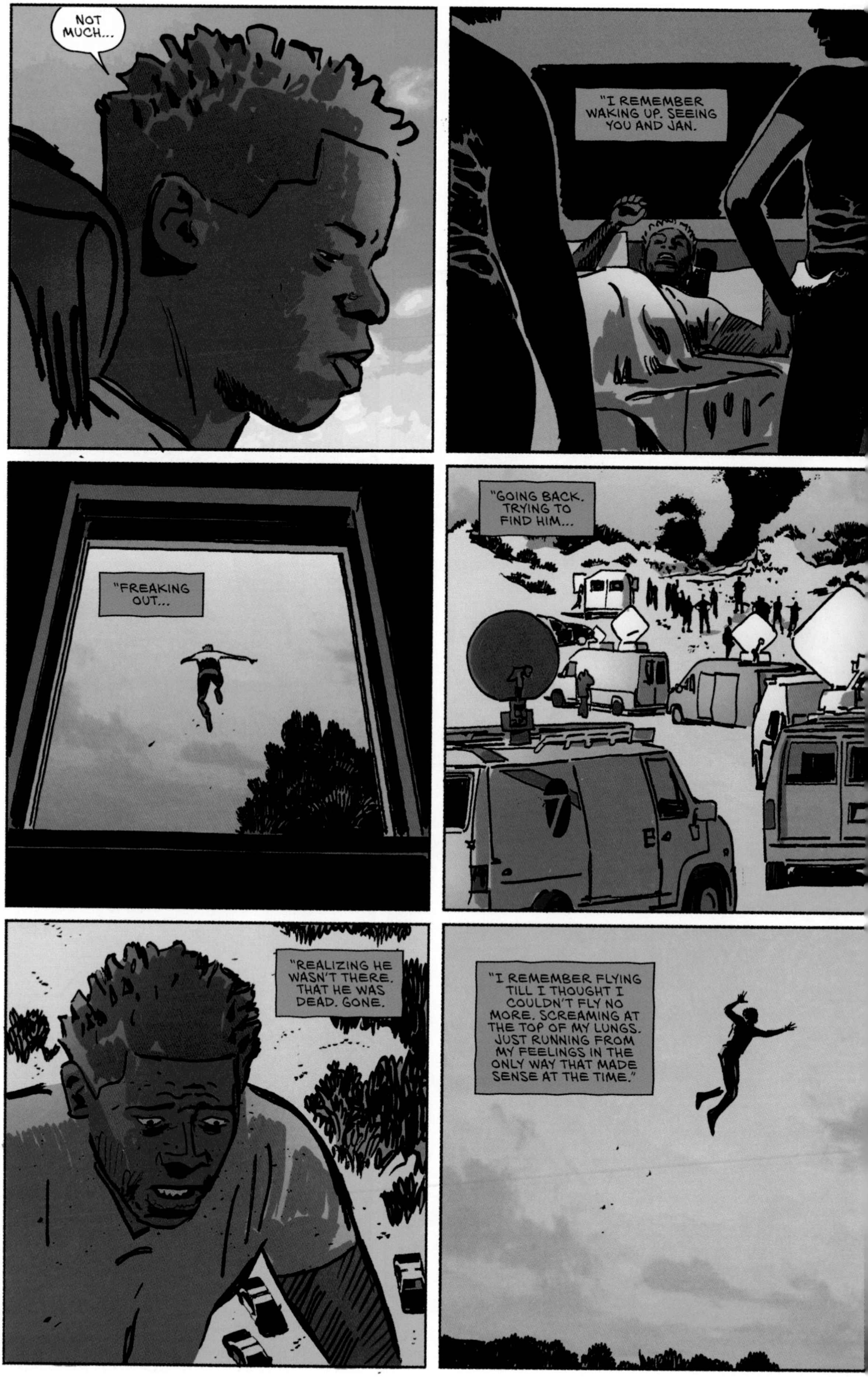
NOT MUCH...
"I REMEMBER WAKING UP. SEEING YOU AND JAN.
"FREAKING OUT...
"GOING BACK. TRYING TO FIND HIM...
"REALIZING HE WASN'T THERE. THAT HE WAS DEAD. GONE.
"I REMEMBER FLYING TILL I THOUGHT I COULDN'T FLY NO MORE. SCREAMING AT THE TOP OF MY LUNGS. JUST RUNNING FROM MY FEELINGS IN THE ONLY WAY THAT MADE SENSE AT THE TIME."

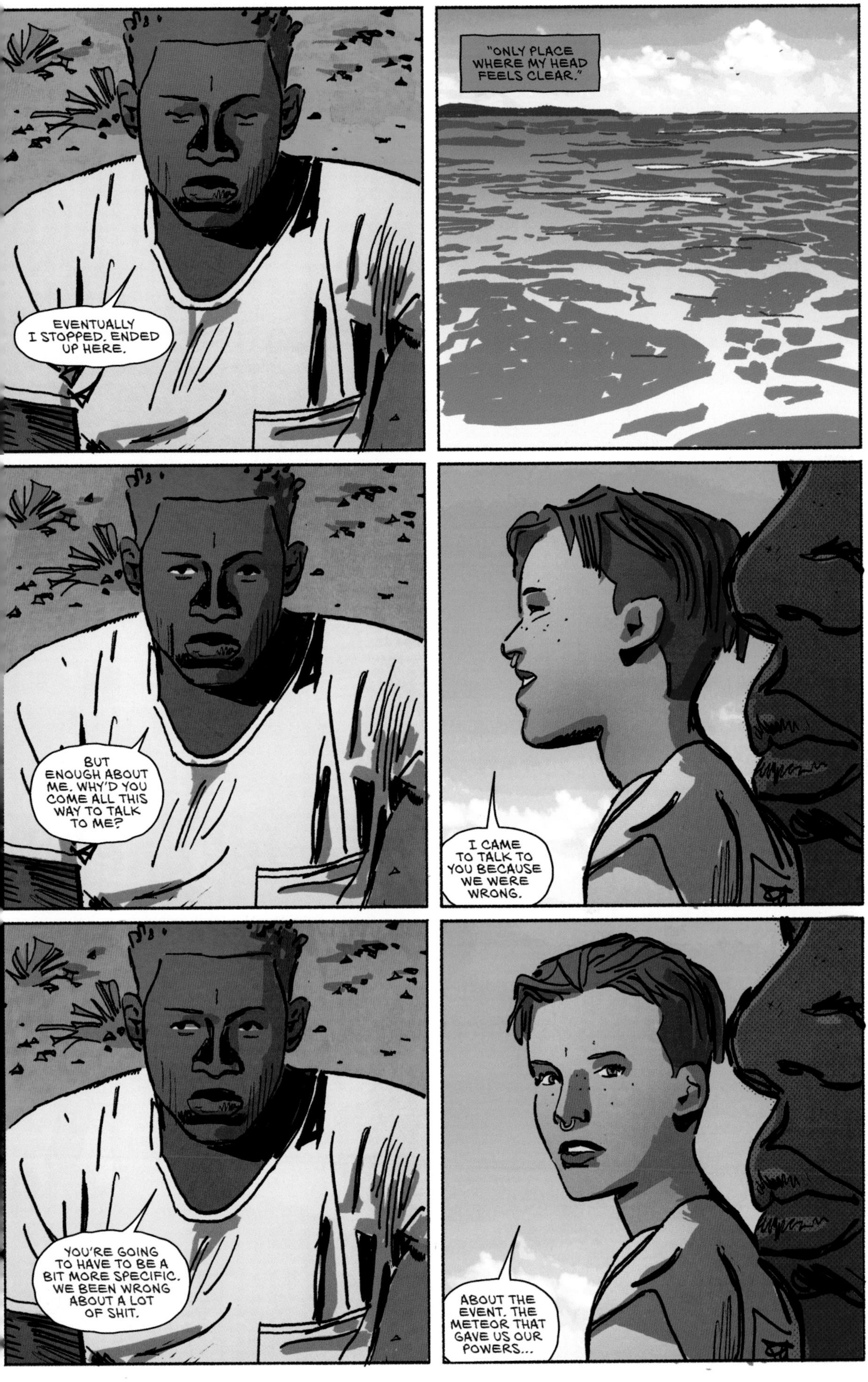
EVENTUALLY I STOPPED. ENDED UP HERE.
"ONLY PLACE WHERE MY HEAD FEELS CLEAR."
BUT ENOUGH ABOUT ME. WHY'D YOU COME ALL THIS WAY TO TALK TO ME?
I CAME TO TALK TO YOU BECAUSE WE WERE WRONG.
YOU'RE GOING TO HAVE TO BE A BIT MORE SPECIFIC. WE BEEN WRONG ABOUT A LOT OF SHIT.
ABOUT THE EVENT. THE METEOR THAT GAVE US OUR POWERS...

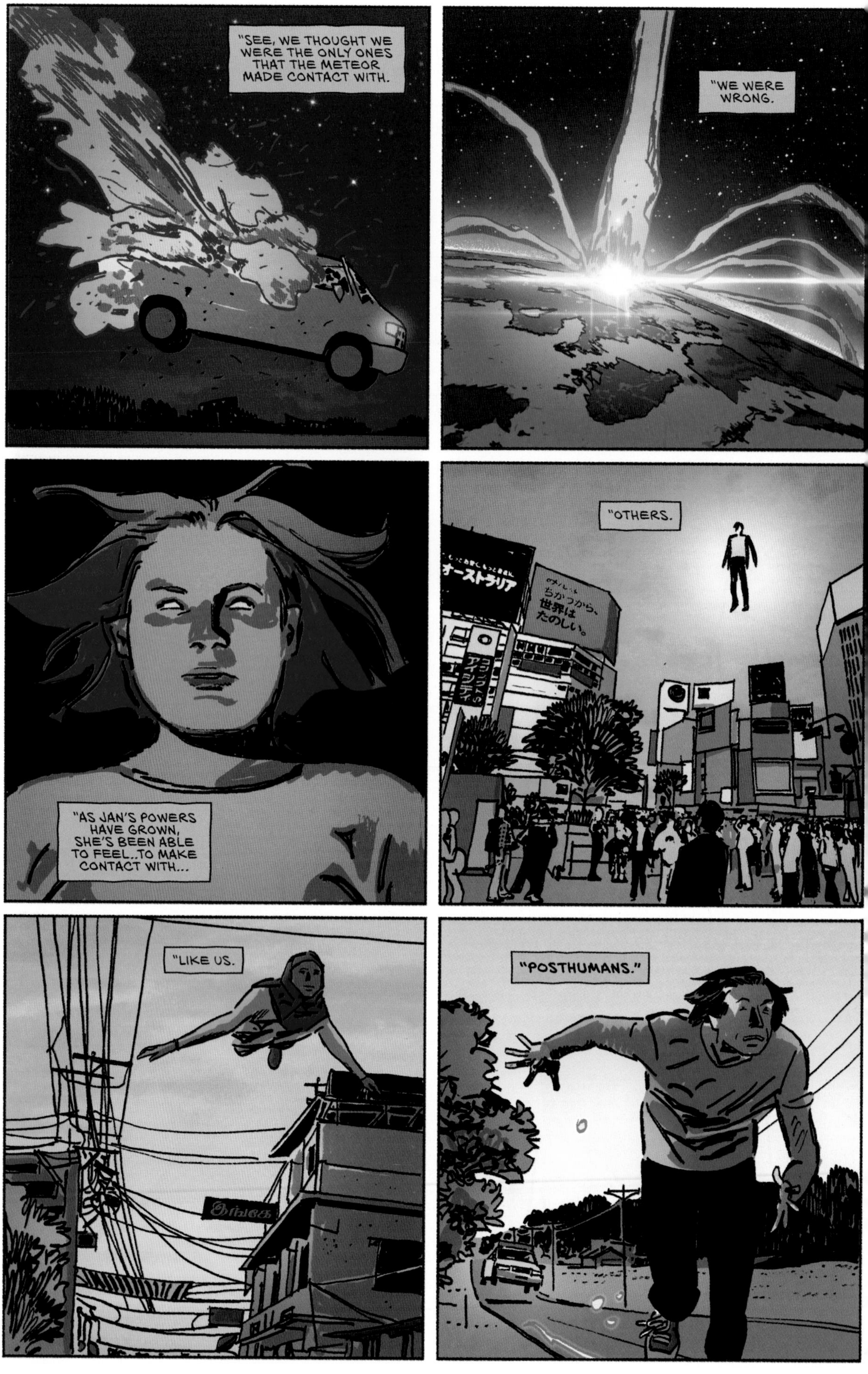
"SEE, WE THOUGHT WE WERE THE ONLY ONES THAT THE METEOR MADE CONTACT WITH.
"WE WERE WRONG.
"AS JAN'S POWERS HAVE GROWN, SHE'S BEEN ABLE TO FEEL...TO MAKE CONTACT WITH...
"OTHERS.
オーストラリア
"LIKE US.
"POSTHUMANS."

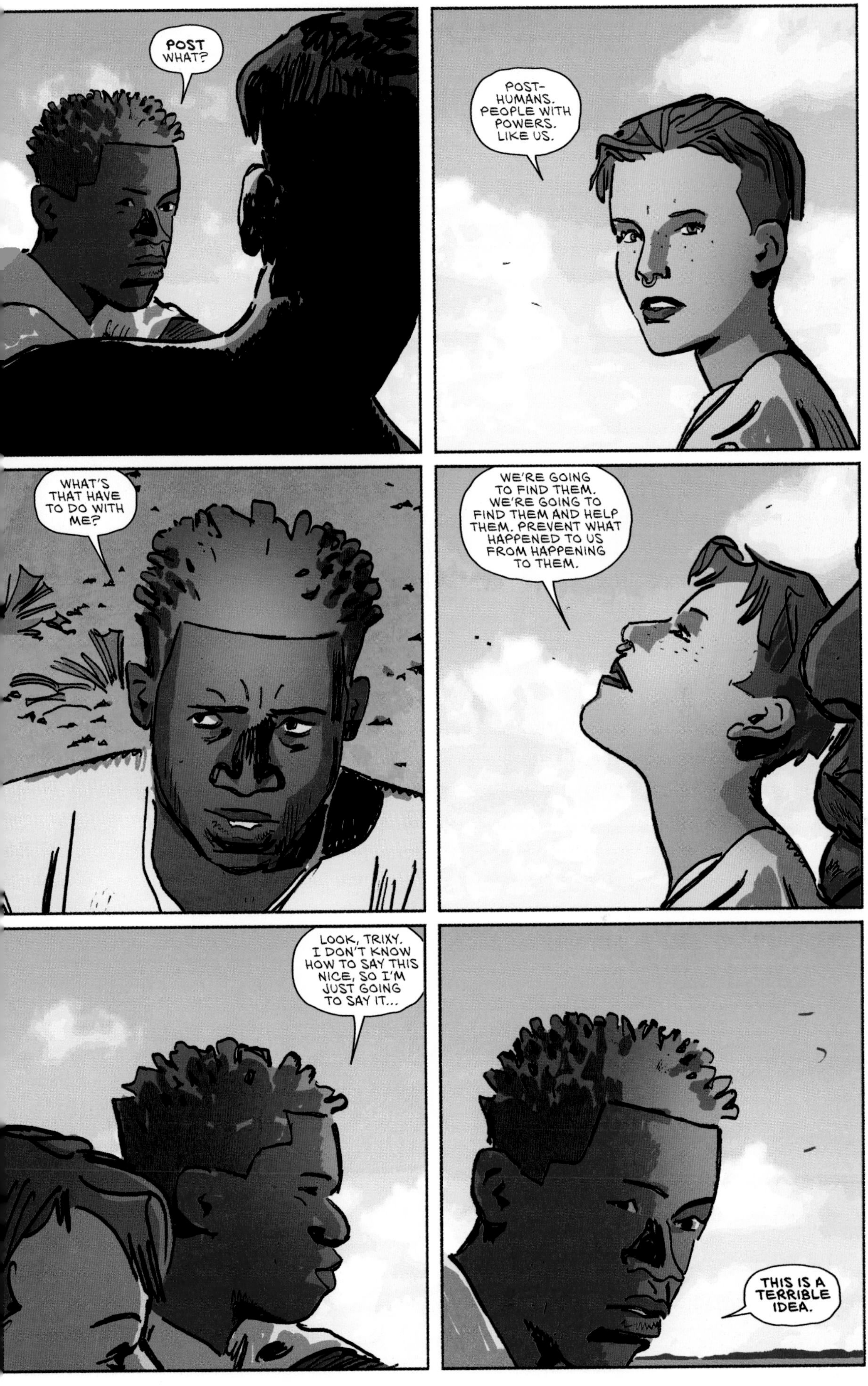
POST WHAT?
POST-HUMANS. PEOPLE WITH POWERS. LIKE US.
WHAT'S THAT HAVE TO DO WITH ME?
WE'RE GOING TO FIND THEM. WE'RE GOING TO FIND THEM AND HELP THEM. PREVENT WHAT HAPPENED TO US FROM HAPPENING TO THEM.
LOOK, TRIXY. I DON'T KNOW HOW TO SAY THIS NICE, SO I'M JUST GOING TO SAY IT...
THIS IS A TERRIBLE IDEA.

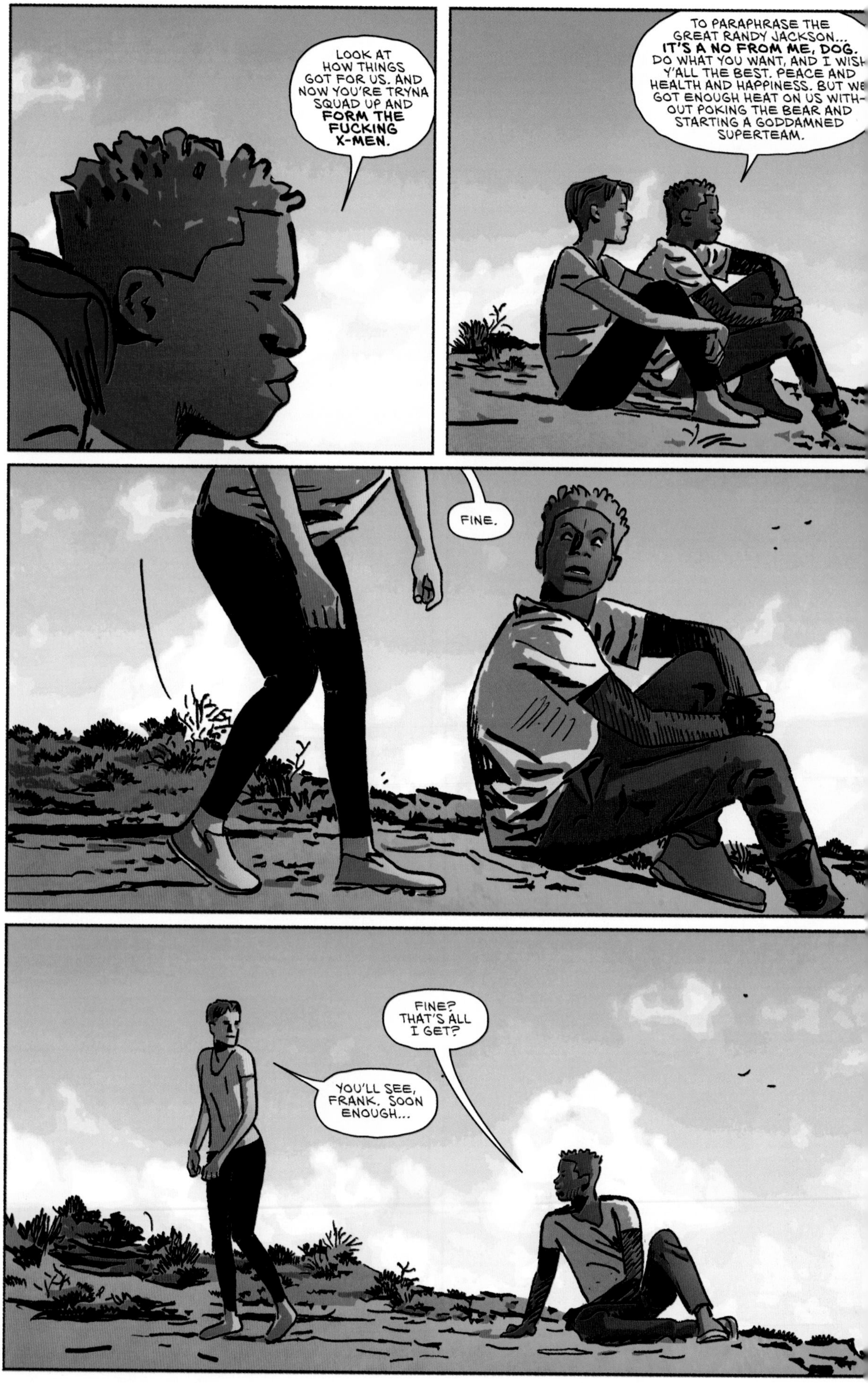
LOOK AT HOW THINGS GOT FOR US. AND NOW YOU'RE TRYNA SQUAD UP AND **FORM THE FUCKING X-MEN.**
TO PARAPHRASE THE GREAT RANDY JACKSON... **IT'S A NO FROM ME, DOG.** DO WHAT YOU WANT, AND I WISH Y'ALL THE BEST. PEACE AND HEALTH AND HAPPINESS. BUT WE GOT ENOUGH HEAT ON US WITHOUT POKING THE BEAR AND STARTING A GODDAMNED SUPERTEAM.
FINE.
FINE? THAT'S ALL I GET?
YOU'LL SEE, FRANK. SOON ENOUGH...

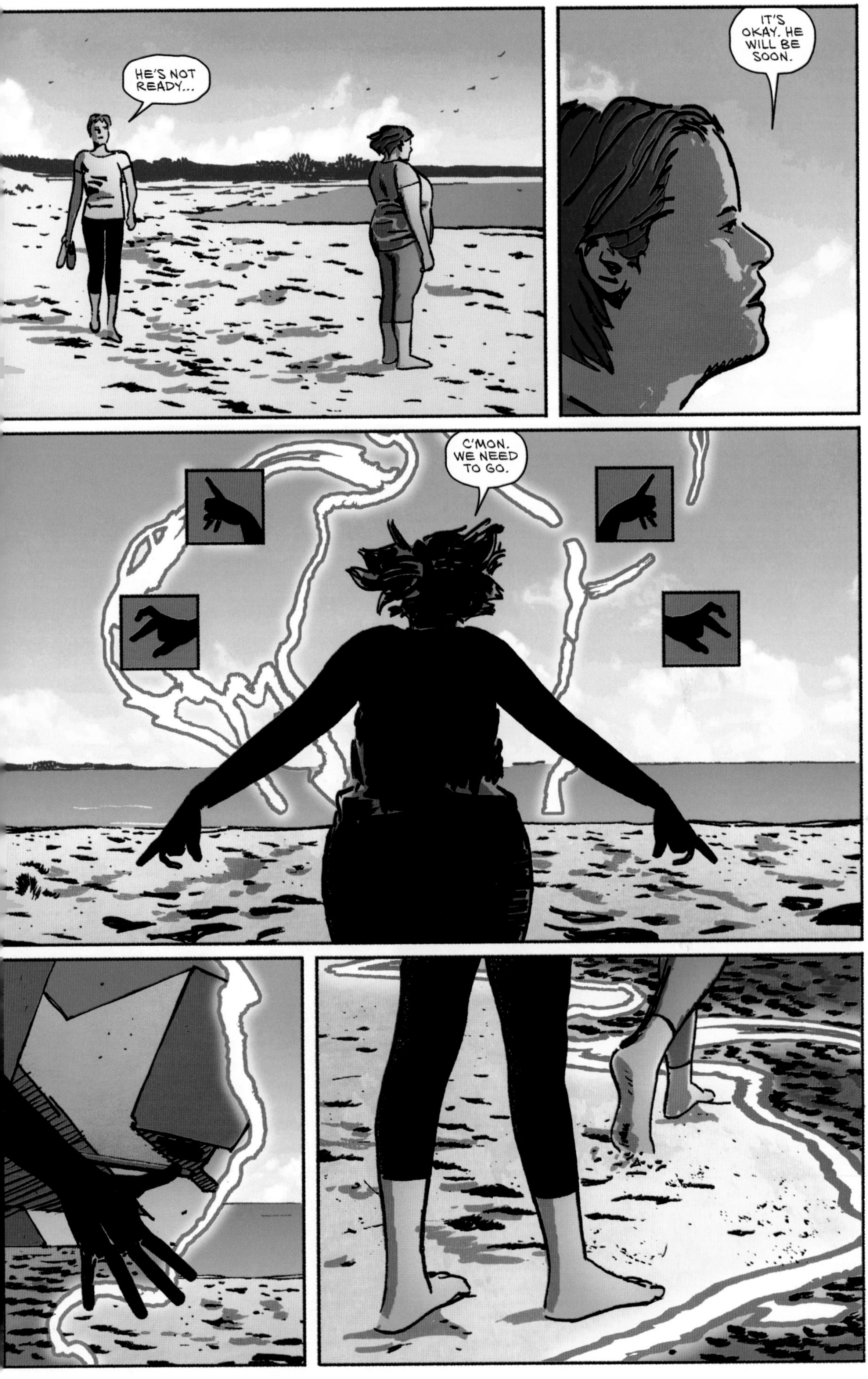
HE'S NOT READY...
IT'S OKAY. HE WILL BE SOON.
C'MON. WE NEED TO GO.

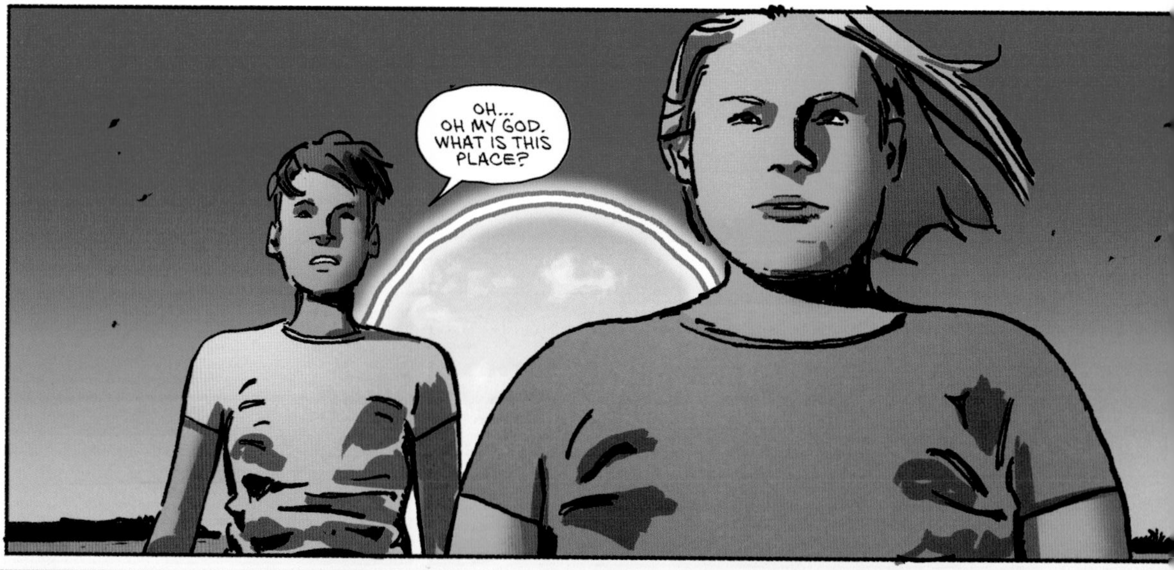
OH... OH MY GOD. WHAT IS THIS PLACE?

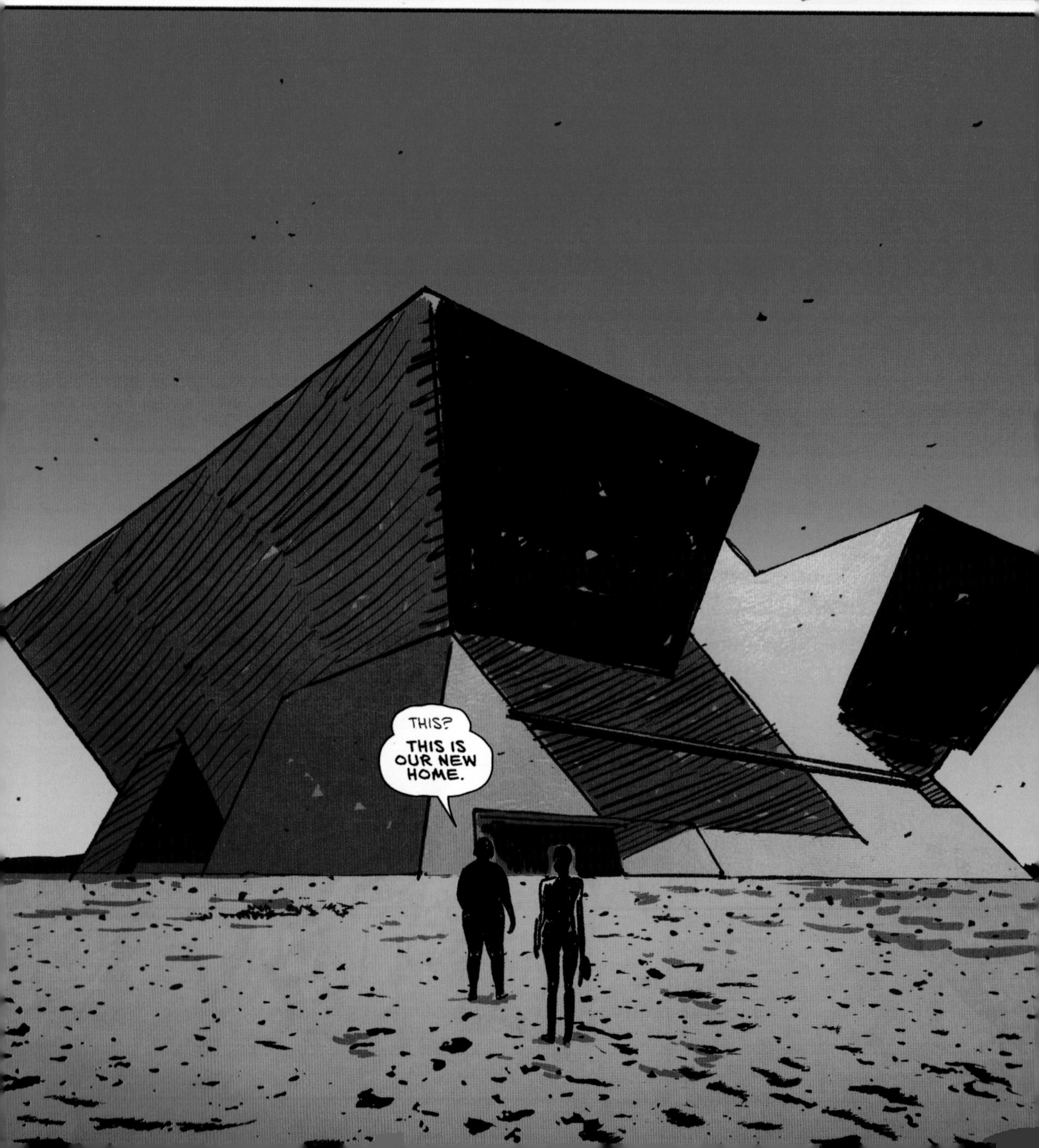
THIS? THIS IS OUR NEW HOME.

Youth

Chapter Four

True Fantasy

"Run to the rescue with love,
and peace will follow."
– River Phoenix

BLACK HAMMER
Jeff Lemire and Dean Ormston
BLACK HAMMER LIBRARY EDITION: VOLUME ONE
ISBN 978-1-50671-073-0 | $49.99
BLACK HAMMER LIBRARY EDITION: VOLUME TWO
ISBN 978-1-50671-185-0 | $49.99
VOLUME 1: SECRET ORIGINS
ISBN 978-1-61655-786-7 | $14.99
VOLUME 2: THE EVENT
ISBN 978-1-50670-198-1 | $19.99
VOLUME 3: AGE OF DOOM, PART I
ISBN 978-1-50670-389-3 | $19.99
VOLUME 4: AGE OF DOOM, PART II
ISBN 978-1-50670-816-4 | $19.99

QUANTUM AGE: FROM THE WORLD OF BLACK HAMMER
Jeff Lemire and Wilfredo Torres
ISBN 978-1-50670-841-6 | $19.99

SHERLOCK FRANKENSTEIN & THE LEGION OF EVIL: FROM THE WORLD OF BLACK HAMMER
Jeff Lemire and David Rubín
ISBN 978-1-50670-526-2 | $17.99

EMPOWERED VOLUME 1
Adam Warren
ISBN 978-1-59307-672-6 | $17.99

THE PAYBACKS COLLECTION
Donny Cates, Eliot Rahal and Geof Shaw
ISBN 978-1-50670-482-1 | $24.99

THE BLACK BEETLE
Francesco Francavilla
KARA BOCEK
ISBN 978-1-50670-537-8 | $12.99

THE COMPLETE ANGEL CATBIRD
Margaret Atwood and Johnnie Christmas
ISBN 978-1-50670-456-2 | $24.99

HELLBOY OMNIBUS
Mike Mignola and others
VOLUME 1: SEED OF DESTRUCTION
ISBN 978-1-50670-666-5 | $24.99
VOLUME 2: STRANGE PLACES
ISBN 978-1-50670-667-2 | $24.99
VOLUME 3: THE WILD HUNT
ISBN 978-1-50670-668-9 | $24.99
HELLBOY IN HELL
ISBN 978-1-50670-749-5 | $24.99

ORIGINAL VISIONS—THRILLING TALES!

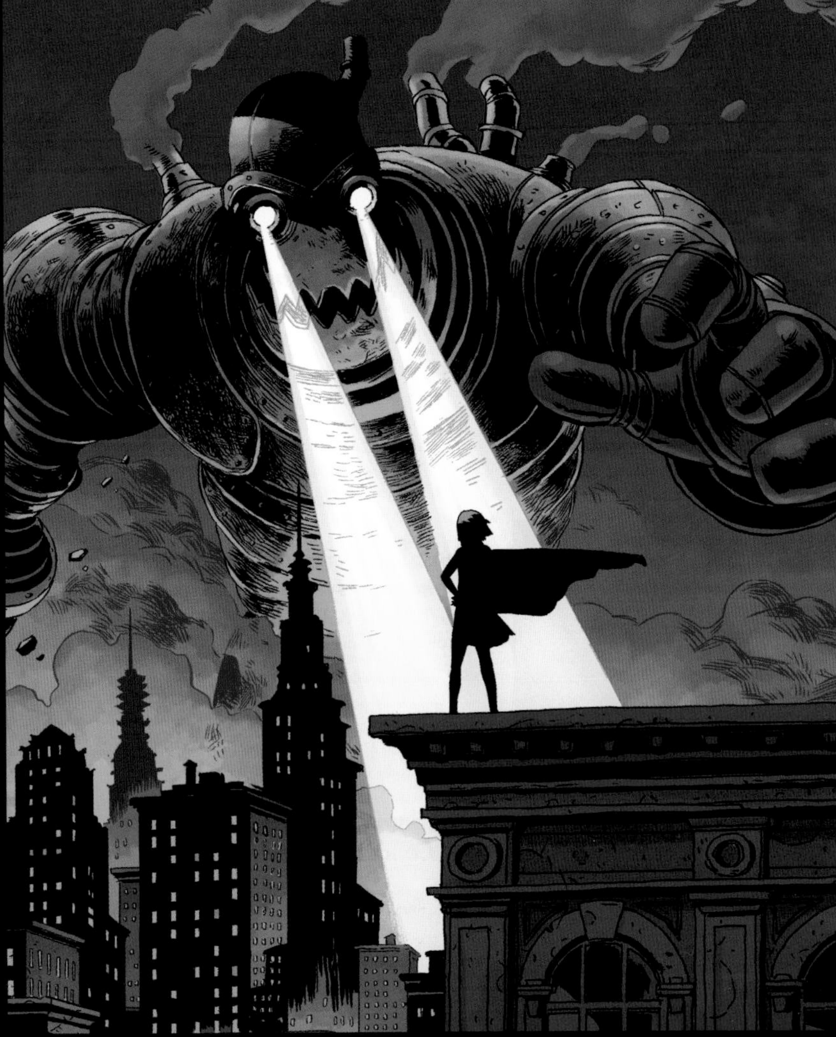

"These superheroes ain't no boy scouts in spandex. They're a high-octane blend of the damaged, quixotic heroes of pulp and detective fiction and the do-gooders in capes from the Golden and Silver Ages."
—Duane Swierczynski

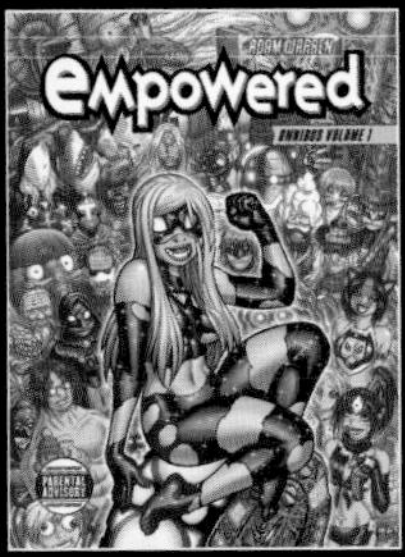
empowered
OMNIBUS VOLUME 1

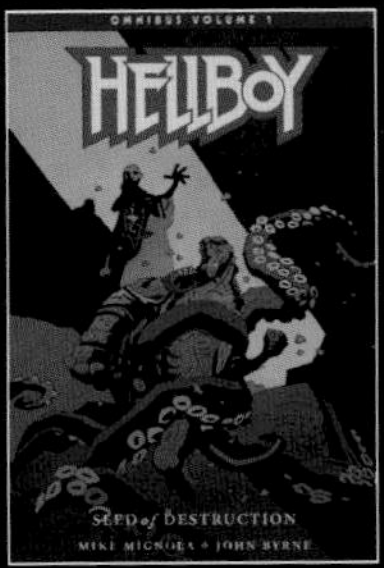
OMNIBUS VOLUME 1
HELLBOY
SEED of DESTRUCTION
MIKE MIGNOLA • JOHN BYRNE

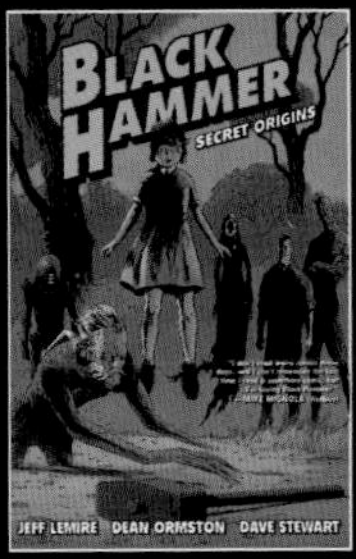
BLACK HAMMER
SECRET ORIGINS
JEFF LEMIRE DEAN ORMSTON DAVE STEWART

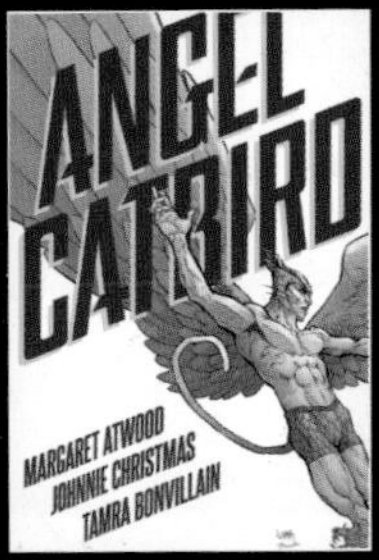
ANGEL CATBIRD
MARGARET ATWOOD
JOHNNIE CHRISTMAS
TAMRA BONVILLAIN

AVAILABLE AT YOUR LOCAL COMICS SHOP OR BOOKSTORE
To find a comics shop in your area, visit comicshoplocator.com. For more information or to order direct, visit DarkHorse.com

THE ULTIMATE **MONSTER** COLLECTOR'S EDITIONS!

OVER-SIZED, HARDCOVER, GILT-EDGED COLLECTION'S OF DARK HORSE'S EARLIEST SERIES!

TERMINATOR
THE ORIGINAL COMICS SERIES
TEMPEST AND ONE SHOT

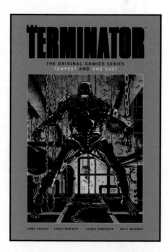

The Terminator: The Original Comics Series Tempest and One Shot

written by John Arcudi and James Robinson,
illustrated by Chris Warner and Matt Wagner

ISBN 978-1-50670-550-7

30TH ANNIVERSARY
ALIENS
THE ORIGINAL COMICS SERIES
MARK VERHEIDEN
MARK A. NELSON

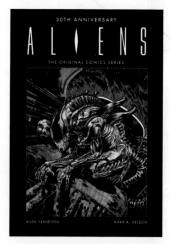

Aliens 30th Anniversary: The Original Comics Series

written by Mark Verheiden,
illustrated by Mark A. Nelson

ISBN 978-1-50670-078-6

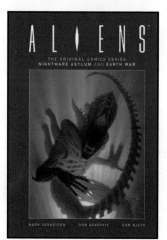

ALIENS
THE ORIGINAL COMICS SERIES
NIGHTMARE ASYLUM AND EARTH WAR
MARK VERHEIDEN
DEN BEAUVAIS
SAM KIETH

Aliens: The Original Comics Series Nightmare Asylum and Earth War

written by Mark Verheiden,
illustrated by Denis Beauvais and Sam Kieth

ISBN 978-1-50670-356-5

30TH ANNIVERSARY
PREDATOR
THE ORIGINAL COMICS SERIES
CONCRETE JUNGLE AND OTHER STORIES
MARK VERHEIDEN
CHRIS WARNER
RON RANDALL

Predator: The Original Comics Series Concrete Jungle and Other Stories

written by Mark Verheiden,
illustrated by Chris Warner and Ron Randall

ISBN 978-1-50670-342-8

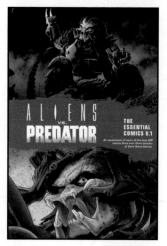

ALIENS VS. PREDATOR
THE ESSENTIAL COMICS V.1

Aliens vs Predator: The Essential Comics Volume 1

Written by Randy Stradley,
illustrated by Chris Warner, Phill Norwood,
Mike Manley, and Rick Leonardi

ISBN 978-1-50671-567-4

30TH ANNIVERSARY
ALIENS VS. PREDATOR
THE ORIGINAL COMICS SERIES
RANDY STRADLEY
PHILL NORWOOD
CHRIS WARNER

Aliens vs Predator: The Original Comics Series 30th Anniversary Edition

written by Randy Stradley,
illustrated by Chris Warner and Phill Norwood

ISBN 978-1-50671-568-1

DARKHORSE.COM | AVAILABLE AT YOUR LOCAL COMICS SHOP OR BOOKSTORE

To find a comics shop in your area, visit comicshoplocator.com. For more information or to order direct, visit darkhorse.com.